Th
Creative Power of Thought

Man's Greatest Discovery

A Compilation of the Best Teachings on
The Creative Power of Thought

Compiled and Edited by
David Allen

Printed in the United States of America

First Paperback Edition, March 2017

ISBN: 978-0-9972801-8-0

Metaphysical / Law of Attraction Books

David Allen - The Power of I AM (2014), The Power of I AM - Volume 2 (2015) , The Power of I AM - Volume 3 (2017)

David Allen - The Creative Power of Thought, Man's Greatest Discovery (2017)

David Allen - The Secrets, Mysteries & Powers of The Subconscious Mind (2017)

David Allen - The Money Bible - The Secrets of Attracting Prosperity (2017)

David Allen - Your Faith Is Your Fortune, Your Unlimited Power

The Neville Goddard Collection (All 10 of his books plus 2 Lecture series) (2016)

Neville Goddard - Assumptions Harden Into Facts: The Book (2016)

Neville Goddard - Imagination: The Redemptive Power in Man (2016)

Neville Goddard - The World is At Your Command - The Very Best of Neville Goddard (2017)

Neville Goddard - Imagining Creates Reality - 365 Mystical Daily Quotes (2017)

Neville Goddard's Interpretation of Scripture (2018)

The Definitive Christian D. Larson Collection (6 Volumes, 30 books) (2014)

Acknowledgements

Benjamin Johnson, Charles Carroll Everett, Charles H. Wolf, Charles Wesley Kyle, Christian Larson, Dr. R. Swineburne Clymer, Edward Walker, Elinor S. Moody, Ella Adelia Fletcher, Emmet Fox, Ernest Holmes, Eugene Del Mar, F. E. Gariner, F. L. Rawson, Fenwicke L. Holmes, Frank B. Whitney, Frank L. Hammer, Frank Waller Allen, Franklin Fillmore Farrington, Genevieve Behrend, Glen Clark, Grace M. Brown, Harriette Augusta Curtiss, Helen Wilmans, Henry Frank, Henry Harrison Brown, Henry Thomas Hamblin, James Allen, Joseph Murphy, Kathleen M. H. Besly, Leander Edmund Whipple, Mary C. Ferriter, May E. Stevenson, Mildred Mann, Mrs Evelyn Lowes Wicker, Mrs. C. L. Baum, Neville Goddard, Nona L. Brooks, Orison Swett Marden, Prentice Mulford, Ralph Waldo Trine, Theron Q. Dumont, Wallace Wattles, William Walker Atkinson

My deepest and sincerest gratitude that these great minds left the world with such incredible knowledge.

Introduction

METAPHYSICIANS are frequently asked by students and patients, "What is thought?" This apparently simple question is now, as it has been through all the ages, the unanswered enigma. The ablest minds, the strongest individuals, the most religious men and women of the different stages of the world's civilization and unfoldment, have grappled with the problem of thought, and tried in some way, through reasoning, thinking, inspiration, deduction, induction, and the various methods employed by man in striving to comprehend a proposition, to reach a satisfactory solution of this greatest of all questions; to satisfy, or in some way appease the longing of the individual (even though the explanation were not sufficient for the world in general) for a partial answer, at least, of "What is thought?"

From the earliest periods of human existence, successively down through the more and more enlightened stratas of human social and mental growth and formation, eddying through such brains as Aristotle, Plato, and the greatest philosophers of the Roman and Greek supremacy; swirling here and there in the current of human unfoldment and enlightenment; retarded for a time by the greatest minds of Germany and France, who tried to stem the tide of the ever-increasing momentum of that unanswered question which seemed to men, at all times and periods, to shield from the race the discovery of the Absolute, it has been transmitted to us. The adepts of ancient India have been struggling with this all-absorbing question for thousands of years, teaching their pupils that thought is the cause of all things.

Over some of the temples of Egypt, now in ruins or buried by the sands of centuries, have been found the inscription, "Know thyself," which was considered the ultimate of all existence. Those fortunate enough to possess the means could, for an exorbitant sum, purchase a little book from the scribes, which merely contained the information that a knowledge of self, obtained through introspection, was all important for the future blessedness of the soul, and should be attained at any cost.

The above words written by Charles H. Wolf in 1918 seemed very fitting for an introduction to this compilation on The Creative Power of Thought. I thoroughly hope this book enlightens, inspires, illumines and blesses all with a brand new consciousness of this power that resides within us all, our thought, giving way to be free from the struggle and strife of life that so many are seeking. The truth does indeed set us free.

David Allen

Mind is the Master power that molds and makes, And Man is Mind, and evermore he takes The tool of Thought, and, shaping what he wills, Brings forth a thousand joys, a thousand ills: . . He thinks in secret, and it comes to pass: Environment is but his looking-glass.

James Allen

There is no thought without form. Every work of man, building, machine or structure of any nature, first took form in his mind. Everything is a replica of a mental image. The earth, the plants, the birds, the animals and man are all projections of the mental concepts and formations held in the mind of God. All that is perceived by and conceived in the mind, is first formed in and of this immaterial substance. Man was made in the image of God; a replica of Him, which includes everything, potentially.

When man shall come to understand this truth he will, by the power of constructive thought, free his mind of doubt and fear, and become so at-one with the great powers of life that disease will vanish and the body become what it was intended to be, a perfect instrument for the expression of health and happiness and peace, and its every energy be devoted to usefulness.

Charles Wesley Kyle

The Universe is governed by Law . . one great Law. Its manifestations are multiform, but viewed from the Ultimate there is but one Law. We are familiar with some of its manifestations, but are almost totally ignorant of certain others. Still we are learning a little more every day . . the veil is being gradually lifted.

We speak learnedly of the Law of Gravitation, but ignore that equally wonderful manifestation, The Law of Attraction in the THOUGHT WORLD. We are familiar with that wonderful manifestation of Law which draws and holds together the atoms of which matter is composed . . we recognize the power of the law that attracts bodies to the earth, that holds the circling worlds in their places, but we close our eyes to the mighty law that draws to us the things we desire or fear, that makes or mars our lives.

When we come to see that Thought is a force . . a manifestation of energy . . having a magnet-like power of attraction, we will begin to understand the why and wherefore of many things that have heretofore seemed dark to us. There is no study that will so well repay the student for his time and trouble as the study of the workings of this mighty law of the world of Thought . . the Law of Attraction.

William Walker Atkinson

The metaphysician knows that "thoughts are things," and at this point we wish to turn to Webster . . that practical materialist . . and confirm what we believe, teach and know to be the fact. The Unabridged Dictionary makes the following statement: "Thought is a creation of the mind, having a distinct existence from the mind that created it." In other words, this great thinker recognizes that thought is not a passing shadow, to again be resolved into nothing as soon as created, but is a creation of the mind, "separate and apart" and entirely distinct from it; a thing, a tangible, comprehensible existing formation, capable of being used, utilized and disposed of as man sees fit. Man, therefore, is the dispenser of what he, in thought, creates. He is the creator or master of what he desires. He is his own source of supply and demand . . manufacturer, dealer and consumer. If thought is the fashioner of environment, and can man create whatsoever in thought he will, then the conclusion inevitably follows that man is the creator of his environment, or the ruler of his universe.

Knowing this, we also know that there are certain laws which must be complied with in the realm of thought. Students of mind know that the thought thus created is capable of being absorbed by the subconscious mind, and is then a part of the stored up resource of the mind which often acts unbidden. They have recognized, therefore, that it is of the utmost importance to keep the thoughts of the highest character . . thoughts which are constructive, upbuilding, uplifting and creative, instead of detrimental, vice inspiring, degenerating, and hence destructive. The habit of thinking rightly is therefore cultivated with all diligence, and when that is once established in the mind, the law of production keeps on producing constructive thoughts, and the subconscious is gradually cleansed of its darkness.

Taking thoughts as things, we at once come to the conclusion that there is a creative power behind them which is not so apparent to us. There is only the one Creative Power . . the All-pervading Mind . . God! It is, therefore, evident that right thinking is an inspiration, or direct communion with the Universal Mind of God, or, as it might be expressed, a desire in the soul of man to think rightly. This is the highest form of thought . . thinking God's thoughts after him. This might be termed appropriating a part of the everywhere-present Mind, and utilizing and comprehending it . . making it manifest to ourselves. This is accomplished when we have stilled the subconscious or mortal thought, and have gained such control over ourselves that we can sit in the absolute silence and desire the One Great Mind to think with us, through us and for us.

Charles H. Wolf

Each individual life, after it has reached a certain age or degree of intelligence, lives in the midst of the surroundings or environments of its own creation; and this by reason of that wonderful power, the drawing power of mind, which is continually operating in every life, whether it is conscious of it or not.

We are all living, so to speak, in a vast ocean of thought. The very atmosphere about us is charged with the thought-forces that are being continually sent out. When the thought-forces leave the brain, they go out upon the atmosphere, the subtle conducting ether, much the same as sound-waves go out. It is by virtue of this law that thought transference is possible, and has become an established scientific fact, by virtue of which a person can so direct his thought-forces that a person at a distance, and in a receptive attitude, can get the thought much the same as sound, for example, is conducted through the agency of a connecting medium. Even though the thoughts as they leave a particular person, are not consciously directed, they go out; and all may be influenced by them in a greater or less degree, each one in proportion as he or she is more or less sensitively organized, or in proportion as he or she is negative, and so open to forces and influences from without.

The law operating here is one with that great law of the universe, . . that like attracts like, so that one continually attracts to himself forces and influences most akin to those of his own life. And his own life is determined by the thoughts and emotions he habitually entertains, for each is building his world from within. As within, so without; cause, effect.

Thought is the great builder in human life: it is the determining factor. Continually think thoughts that are good, and your life will show forth in goodness, and your body in health and beauty. Continually think evil and your life will show forth in evil, and your body in weakness and repulsiveness. Think thoughts of love, and you will love and will be loved. Think thoughts of hatred, and you will hate and will be hated. Each follows its kind.

Ralph Waldo Trine

What we think most about is constantly weaving itself into the fabric of our career, becoming a part of ourselves, increasing the power of our mental magnet to attract those things we most ardently desire. When the architect looks at the plan of his building he does not see the plan merely. That only suggests the building. It is the invisible building, the creation of his mind he sees. What he takes in from the plan with his eyes is not the reality at all. He sees in all its details the building of his mental vision. If he did not see it in this way, it would never become a reality. If he could see only the mechanical plans he would not be an architect at all.

The framework of your life structure is invisible. It is on the mental plane. You are laying the foundation for your future, fixing its limits by the expectations you are visualizing. You cannot do anything bigger than you plan to do. The mental plans always come first. Your future building will merely be carrying out in detail what you are visualizing today. The future is simply an extension of the present. You are right now by your thought habit, by your prevailing mental attitude, making your place in life. You are locating yourself, settling what you are to be. In other words, you are right now making your future, deciding what your position in the world shall be. And it will be broad, ever growing, ever expanding, or it will become narrower, more pinched and rutty, according to your mental plan, according to the vision you see.

The only world you will ever know anything about, the only world that is true for you at this moment, is the one you create mentally . . the world you are conscious of. The environment you fashion out of your thoughts, your beliefs, your ideals, your philosophy is the only one you will ever live in.

Orison Swett Marden

Withdraw and abstract your attention now from appearances of things and from sense evidence. Even though your senses deny what you pray for, affirm it as true in your heart. Bring your mind back from its wandering after the false Gods of fear and doubt (thought) to rest in the Omnipotence of the Spiritual Power within you. In the silence and quietude of your own mind, dwell on the fact that there is only One Power and One Presence.

This Power and Presence is now responding to your thought as guidance, strength, peace, and nourishment for the soul. Give all your mental attention to recognizing the absolute sovereignty of the Spiritual Power knowing that the God-Power has the answer, and is now showing you the way. Trust It; believe in It, and walk the earth in the Light your prayer is already answered.

Joseph Murphy

Thought is power; thought is creative; thought materializes to my desire in flesh and blood. As God materializes his thoughts, so will his son's ideas take shape and form as worlds and plants take shape from the One Over-Soul. I have but to LET the God-in-me work as it works outside me, to carry out my will, and a world shall grow about me as under God's direct thought this one grew for me.

Henry Harrison Brown

What you are inwardly, what you think inwardly, what you visualize inwardly, is what your future life will be. Your outward life is modeled on your inward life . . it is an exact replica of the life within. Therefore your subliminal mind is not only the source of inspiration and intuition, it is creative also. Your life is in your own hands, you can make it what you will. Your future is yours entirely, you can build it up with mathematical precision into any form you please. You are free to make or to mar, to build up or destroy. You can climb to the highest heights or descend to the lowest depths. You can be weak or strong, filthy or pure, miserable or happy, unsuccessful or successful, poverty stricken or prosperous, ill or healthy, hated or loved: It is all a matter of Thought-control and Scientific Thinking.

Henry Thomas Hamblin

The first law, which we must observe in the study of the Mind, is that of mutual response or the reciprocity of environment. Each of us is clothed with an invisible aura composed of the mental emanations that float from our habitual thoughts and daily actions. He only succeeds who works with or against this influence, as it affects him for good or ill. Just as the swimmer betimes floats at ease upon the surface of the water and safely trusts the current to carry him toward the shore, so one who buffets the waves of life's sea may at times implicitly trust the current of some force that sweeps over him from the shores of other minds. If he has found them soothing, genial, exhilarating, he knows they are friendly and need not fear. But if by sudden contact their approach chills, unnerves, affrights and weakens, let him beware; the swifter he buffets the opposing waves and makes for the shore of personal safety the wiser he proves himself by discretion over valor.

Each mind is in some way attuned to every other. Either harmonious or inharmonious are the mutual chords. If they respond to peace, they are attuned to harmony and happiness. If to discord, they jangle out of tune, and their note resounds with warning and approaching hazard. Each may test this law for himself. He who chooses wisely walks safely.

Henry Frank

Thought is the coin of heaven. Money is its earthly symbol. Every moment must be invested, and our inner talking reveals whether we are spending or investing. Be more interested in what you are inwardly "saying now" than what you "have said" by choosing wisely what you think and what you feel now.

Any time we feel misunderstood, misused, neglected, suspicious, afraid, we are spending our thoughts and wasting our time. Whenever we assume the feeling of being what we want to be, we are investing. We cannot abandon the moment to negative inner talking and expect to retain command of life. Before us go the results of all that seemingly is behind. Not gone is the last moment . . but oncoming. My word shall not return unto Me void, but it shall accomplish that which I please, and it shall prosper in the thing whereto I sent it.

Neville Goddard

"I have found out that the real essentials of greatness in men are not written in books, nor can they be found in the schools, They are written into the inner consciousness of everyone who intensely searches for perfection in creative achievement and are understandable to such men only."

"Successful men of all the ages have learned to multiply themselves by gathering thought energy into a high potential and using it in the direction of the purpose intended. Every successful man or great genius has three particular qualities in common.

The most conspicuous of these is that their minds grow more brilliant as they grow older, instead of less brilliant. Great men's lives begin at forty, where the mediocre man's life ends.

The genius remains an ever-flowing fountain of creative achievement until the very last breath he draws. The geniuses have learned how to gather thought energy together to use for transforming their conceptions into material forms.

The thinking of creative and successful men is never exerted in any direction other than that intended. That is why great men produce a prodigious amount of work, seemingly without effort and without fatigue.

The amount of work such men leave to posterity is amazing. When one considers such men of our times as Edison, Henry Ford or Theodore Roosevelt, one will find the three characteristics I have mentioned common to every one of them."

Glen Clark

There is nothing unusual or mysterious in the idea of your pictured desire coming into material evidence. It is the working of a universal, natural Law. The world was projected by the self-contemplation of the Universal Mind, and this same action is taking place in its individualized branch which is the Mind of Man. Everything in the whole world, from the hat on your head to the boots on your feet, has its beginning in mind and comes into existence in exactly the same manner. All are projected thoughts, solidified.

Your personal advance in evolution depends on your right use of the power of visualizing, and your use of it depends on whether you recognize that you, yourself, are a particular center through and in which the Originating Spirit is finding ever new expression for potentialities already existing within Itself. This is evolution.

Genevieve Behrend

This room is not filled with air. It is filled with that thinking Substance and as you think into it and speak into it, it vibrates. As you cause it to vibrate, you bring it into form. No one else in the universe is responsible for my good or evil but myself, and instead of blaming fate for conditions, I should "treat" myself and analyze my consciousness. Then I shall discover that I have been thinking and speaking the thing which I have not desired in form. Every thought that goes from your brain is a vibration and brings its results negatively or positively. You cannot say one word without having it register in this universal thinking Substance which we call Mind.

Franklin Fillmore Farrington

Think how your life has been controlled either by your own thinking or by the suggestions that have been made upon your mind, either consciously or unconsciously. When you were a child you took your thought from your family. Your world was what you made it, but it was an unconscious acceptance of the thought and manners of your family. After a while you began to think independently and your world changed that much for you. You began to control consciously the conditions of your life.

As your understanding grew you thought more and more independently of your associates, therefore your life became that much different from theirs. Did you continue to accept the suggestions of your environment or did you begin to think independently? Either consciously or unconsciously you are now conditioning your life. I will now take conscious control of my life. I will think only the things I want to think. I will control whatever is to come into my life, by controlling my thought.

Fenwicke L. Holmes

Mind is the Electrical current or spark from the Divine Force or Creation which lodges in the soul, or is the creating Light or spark of the soul, and the religion of the Twentieth Century must be based on the common everyday thinking mind. The mind is the electrical center of the Soul. Every thought is a current of good or bad radiating from that center. It also draws to it every current in harmony with its own vibration, and makes or mars the destiny of man. It is through mind (thought) that the works of God are manifest. It is through mind that the invisible law and force predominates.

Mind creates and manifests daily every thought that is drawn into it, and he knows, who sees, reads with accuracy where the law is obeyed or broken.

F. E. Gariner and Dr. R. Swineburne Clymer

STATION L-O-V-E BROADCASTING

IF THERE is too much lurid music or static coming from your radio, just turn the dial. Presto! It is done! It is so easy to tune out the discord and to find harmony!

If there are too many discordant thoughts racing through your mind, learn the trick of tuning out discord. Harmony will take its place. Mental static can be tuned out easily when you know the secret of doing so. If there is static in the air, a simple adjustment of the machine will tune it out. If there are discordant thoughts in your mental life, just "turn the dial"

You may need to experiment for a while, just as the novice does in getting acquainted with his radio. While you are trying to make the adjustment you may get stations H-A-T-E, P-A-I-N, F-E-A-R, and some of the other stations that always have seemed to you to be on the air. But be patient! When you have tuned them out, you can get the station you want.

Possibly, you will have to listen very closely to get station L-O-V-E, but it is always broadcasting. Just bring your ear a little closer if at first it does not seem to come in clear and strong. Your inner ears will hear its voice at the very center of your being. At first, you may hear just a faint "L-O-V-E" but you will rejoice and will want to "set the dial" so that you can get L-O-V-E at any time.

Remember, L-O-V-E is a powerful station. You cannot get F-E-A-R or P-A-I-N if you have properly tuned in for L-O-V-E. There are those who keep the "dial" set at L-O-V-E all the time. L-O-V-E is always broadcasting for them. They in turn become broadcasters for L-O-V-E.

Now, L-O-V-E is on a chain and often one may pick up L-I-F-E, P-L-E-N-T-Y, or J-O-Y when L-O-V-E is broadcasting. It seems as if Station L-O-V-E knows just what its listeners want and need, and then broadcasts the right program at the right time. Only one thing is necessary: to keep the dial set for L-O-V-E; then one will get the right program.

You must have an aerial that pierces the very heights of heaven in order to get this station. To get the music of the spheres, your aerial must reach high into heaven, below into heaven, and to all sides into heaven. Your aerial must have countless little points extending into heaven, heaven everywhere. Some folks lack a good aerial and L-O-V-E for them does not have much force. Their aerial extends in the wrong direction.

Some folks let their receiving sets become fouled. They do not keep their contacts clean. L-O-V-E keeps broadcasting, nevertheless, and comes in as strong as possible over the instrument provided.

Sometimes, a set next door may be tuned in on N-0-I-S-E, but station N-O-I-S-E soon ceases when L-O-V-E is broadcasting. There may be a roomful of sets variously tuned in to P-A-I-N, loudly voicing its program; to E-A-S-E, shouting its false message; to L-A-C-K, trying hard to make itself heard. When L-O-V-E is broadcasting these other stations just quit in despair. They seem to say: "There is L-O-V-E on the wire. H-E-A-L-T-H, J-O-Y, and P-L-E-N-T-Y are linked up with it tonight, so we might as well sign off. It is too powerful a station for us. Its wave length is too much for us."

This little story about station L-O-V-E has a big lesson in it for all of us. It shows us how easily we can tune out noise, pain, fear, hate, and lack. We just turn the dial; reverse the thought. We discover that when pain and lack and fear would make themselves heard we need only to "turn the dial." We find that we can tune out "jazzy" noises and static by the simple process of reversing the thought. We find that when we are mentally attuned to love, no discordant thoughts can find place in us. We no longer vibrate to hate and fear when we are attuned to love.

If we go into a room where disease and fear are being voiced, where propaganda adverse to love is afloat, the situation soon changes if we broadcast love. We find that pain and disease, hate and fear, cannot be broadcast when we are broadcasting love. We find that health and joy and plenty radiate from us when we are attuned to love.

When we hear long and vivid tales of the power of adversity and evil, what a privilege it is just to say silently within ourselves "Station L-O-V-E broadcasting"! When hate makes its appearance we have only to say silently to it, "L-O-V-E." Hate and fear cannot exist in the field where Love exists.

If our aerial extends to heaven, if our thought pierces to heights of spiritual consciousness, we can always be assured that we are tuned in properly to have love broadcast in our lives. If our aerial extends in every direction, if we are universal in our conception of life, then love dawns upon us more clearly. If our contact with Spirit is not fouled by adverse beliefs we can always receive the broadcastings of love from the station L-O-V-E, eternal in the heavens. We need not fear that L-O-V-E will sign off, when we realize that the spirit of love within and about us is eternally at work broadcasting love and its blessings for us.

Realizing the power of love, we can neutralize the power of hate and of fear. These are "tuned out" of our lives when we broadcast love. They simply do not exist in the realm in which we live that realm wherein only the voice of heaven, the voice of Truth, is heard and felt.

God is love. We are creations of His love and He lives as love at the very center of our being. He continues to broadcast His love in and through us. He never ceases to love us and to cause us to turn from pain, disease, sin, fear, hate, and lack. He would have us turn from the noise and nothingness of all these. He would have us tune in to Him at all times.

Frank B. Whitney

"The things that are seen are not made of the things that do appear." The only possible operation of intelligence is Thought, or "The Word." So all things were made by the Word, and "Without the Word was not anything made that hath been made." How simple the process of creation when we understand it. The Spirit speaks . . and since there is nothing but the Spirit and it is All-Power, it has only to speak and it is done; "The Word was with God and the Word was God."

From the Word, then, comes forth all that appears. Each life, human or divine, each manifestation is a different kind of word coming into expression. The great fact to dwell upon is that Spirit needs nothing to help It; It is self-conscious and has all power and all ability to do whatever It wishes to accomplish. It operates simply by speaking.

It is hard to get a clear concept of this great Ceaseless Cause, this something from which all things come; at times we get into a maze of confusion when we attempt to realize what the Spirit means. It is then that we should think of It as the great reason behind everything. Being all-knowledge It must know Itself, and must know everything It creates; so It knows us and It knows everyone. Since It is All-Presence we can contact anywhere and will never have to go to some particular spot to find It. As It is All-Knowing and operates through the power of the Word, It knows everything we think. Just how It creates we cannot know and need not attempt to understand, for whatever this process of creation is, we find it is always an inner thought process.

Ernest Holmes

When humanity learns to think orderly, that means to have high thoughts, and recognize the love principle, power and ability to become what is desirable, then there will not be so much sickness, as humanity will draw to itself the finer magnetism belonging to such thoughts, and the mind will be peaceful, and that will make the body strong and healthy.

The sooner we find out that it is our thoughts which make our lives unhappy, the sooner we shall change them and make it as habitual to think high as it is to think low.

When we can see practically that it is not so much what we do as what we think, then we shall have courage and individuality, and it will become manifest through our being, and we will find success in everything we undertake.

We shall see that we cannot limit God, or the power of thought, which is his expression, but it is in all things, and by suggesting our every action consciously, we apply the higher power in the matter with which we deal, and we will know the outcome of our every effort.

May E. Stevenson

There is but one basic power in the world, that of thought. Taking it in its broadest definition, it includes that which is conscious and unconscious (subconscious and super-conscious), intellectual, emotional, and intuitional; embracing physical form, which is its outward show or activity, mental consciousness, and spiritual realization.

Thought is the one instrument of the Soul and mind of man. In his power of choice, in his ability to think what and as he pleases, man has at his command, and subject to his direction and control, the one universal power. In the realization of his Oneness with the Infinite he knows that he possesses this power and can wield it.

Eugene Del Mar

Your destiny depends entirely upon your own mental conduct. It is the thoughts that you allow yourself to dwell upon all day long that make your mentality what it is, and your circumstances are made by your mentality.

You may think that you know this already, but if you do not act upon it, it is certain that you do not really know it. As a matter of fact, most people would be amazed to discover how much negative thinking they do indulge in, in the course of a day. Thought is so swift, and habit is so strong that, unless you are very careful, you will constantly transgress. Even your conversation may be much more negative than you suspect.

In other words, you cannot involve your thought in any subject without bringing the natural consequences upon yourself. You can call this involving yourself in the karma of that situation, if you like, but whatever you choose to call it, the fact will remain. To interfere mentally in any situation involves you in the consequences just as much as would a physical interference. Of course, where it is your duty to concern yourself in any matter, you must do so . . constructively and spiritually . . and then the consequences to you can only be good.

Emmet Fox

Each and every person is surrounded by a thought atmosphere, extending some distance from him, in which is reproduced the general character of his mental states, and which atmosphere may be, and is, felt by others with whom he comes in contact. The degree of strength of the thought atmosphere depends upon the degree of strength of the mental states. The degree of receptivity of others to this thought atmosphere depends upon the particular temperamental receptivity of the other persons.

This thought atmosphere is composed of subtle vibrations of the ether, just as real and actual as the vibrations which are known to us as electricity, magnetism, heat and light.

Edward Walker/William Walker Atkinson

When we understand the laws of thought and think accordingly, we have begun what may properly be termed scientific thinking; that is, we have begun designed thinking; thinking with a purpose in view; thinking in accordance with exact scientific system; and thinking for results.

When we think in this manner we think according to those laws of thought that are required in order to produce the results we have in view; therefore all the forces of mind will be directed to produce those very results. In this connection we should remember that every mental process produces its own results in the human system; therefore we can secure any result desired when we place in action the necessary mental process.

Christian Larson

One of the things which greatly hinders us from demonstrating a greater degree of prosperity we may call race thought or race consciousness. This is the result of all that the race has thought or believed. We are immersed in it, and those who are receptive to it are controlled by it. All thought seeks expression along the lines of least resistance. When we become negative or fearful we attract that kind of thought and condition.

We must be sure of ourselves; we must be positive; we must not be aggressive, but absolutely sure and poised within. Negative people are always picking up negative conditions; they get into trouble easily: Persons who are positive draw positive things; they are always successful. Few people realize that the law of thought is the great reality; that thoughts produce things. When we come to understand this power of thought, we will carefully watch our thinking to see that no thought enters that we should not want made into a thing.

We can guard our minds by knowing that no negative thought can enter; we can daily practice by saying that no race thought of limitation can enter the mind; that Spirit forms itself around us and protects us from all fear and from all limitation. Let us clothe ourselves in the great realization that all power is ours and that nothing else can enter; let us fill the atmosphere of our homes, and places of business with streams of positive thought. Other people will feel this and will like to be near us and enter into the things that we enter into. In this way we shall be continually drawing only the best.

Ernest Holmes

Heaven and hell are not future states awaiting us at death. We make our own hell and our own heaven by the way in which we think; and we have to wake up as fast as we can and get out of hell, the hell of the wrong thoughts that attack us, into heaven, a perfect state of consciousness, the world of perfect thoughts, perfect ideas, the real world that is here round us, if we could only see it.

"Love . . .. builds a heaven in hell's despair" (W. Blake).

The only way to escape the suffering which is always the result of sin is to stop sinning; and the only way to do this is to stop entertaining wrong thoughts

F. L. Rawson

We make our own heaven and our own hell through the conscious or unconscious use of the Law. We do it by the thoughts we think and the attitude we assume. For the Great Law receives our mental impression and brings out into form the ideas of our mind. We are not, therefore, the creatures of some chance environment or circumstances. There is something in us that attracts us to them and them to us. If it were not so we would move out of them. Do not complain about the world you live in. It is a reflection of your own thought.

Do not blame others. Seek the cause in your own thinking. Ask, "What is it that brought me here? What was my thought of failure that produced this?" Then decide on the environment and circumstance you desire and mentally see yourself in your new surroundings. Then you are on the road to attainment, and your changes will begin to take place naturally from within. Your good does not come from without.

The sooner you learn that you cannot expect someone else to hand it to you the better off you will be. You cannot change the unpleasant to the pleasant by a mere change of place. We are all surrounded by the atmosphere that most corresponds to our mental mood. So soon as we change our mood, we shall find ourselves in better conditions. Every person and every place is surrounded by an impalpable atmosphere which people feel even when they don't know what it is that affects them.

Before the writer had learned these great truths, he spent a night with a physician in whose house many operations were performed for appendicitis. The atmosphere was so strong of this fear that he caught the contagion of thought, and later was operated on to have the thought cut out.

Unless our mind is very positive, we become susceptible to the atmospheres about us. We must be careful not to attract ourselves to negative mental atmospheres, and should we find ourselves at any time open to negative influence, we must assume at once a positive attitude and declare ourselves superior to it. Disease often comes by some impression from without which we harbor; after a while the thought develops like the seed and grows from within. It can never become a disease for us until we accept it, either consciously or by tacit agreement to the race suggestion, and allow it to grow from within.

Fenwicke L. Holmes

The battle cry of freedom has rung down through the ages and people are always looking for a liberator to free them. The people will never be free until they free themselves through the exercise of thought and their God-given prerogative to reason for themselves. Those who deny men this right are their enemies and exploiters. Why fear to think? Who can prevent it? Bodies can be liquidated, free speech suppressed, but no power on earth can invade the kingdom of mind. The most powerful army cannot take possession of a single idea. The most cruel autocrat cannot destroy a solitary thought. No despot can hinder a man from thinking anything under the sun he chooses, or prevent him from sending these thoughts to others all over the world.

And through the power of thought people can free themselves, for by uniting mentally they can effect any change they desire, accomplish any plan or project for the benefit of mankind. Thoughts are the tools man uses to bring invisible things into visible form.

Frank L. Hammer

A human being is the greatest magnet in 'the Universe, and from the brain radiates a force which you can send where you please, as soon as you really understand you have such a force at your command. By generating this thought force in love, and realizing that in every other man is this same power, this same love principle, you establish a magnetic chain between you, thus giving him what you have for him and receiving in like manner.

You have within yourself, then, magnetism sufficient to draw to yourself all that you need from out the Universe . .

all that you desire, and all that you demand, but there must be no unbelief; simply have perfect faith that your requirements will be fulfilled. Truth is infinite and can never be exhausted. What a glorious realization it is that we are coming into the Consciousness of our oneness not only with each other but with Universal Truth.

Grace M. Brown

A friend a thousand miles away is rooted in your consciousness through your fixed ideas of him. To think of him and represent him to yourself inwardly in the state you desire him to be, confident that this subjective image is as true as it were already objectified, awakens in him a corresponding state which he must objectify. The results will be as obvious as the cause was hidden. The subject will express the awakened state within him and remain unaware of the true cause of his action. Your illusion of free will is but ignorance of the causes which make you act. Prayers depend upon your attitude of mind for their success and not upon the attitude of the subject.

The subject has no power to resist your controlled subjective ideas of him unless the state affirmed by you to be true of him is a state he is incapable of wishing as true of another. In that case it returns to you, the sender, and will realize itself in you. Provided the idea is acceptable, success depends entirely on the operator not upon the subject who, like compass needles on their pivots, are quite indifferent as to what direction you choose to give them. If your fixed idea is not subjectively accepted by the one toward whom it is directed, it rebounds to you from whom it came. "Who is he that will harm you, if ye be followers of that which is good? I have been young, and now am old; yet have I not seen the righteous forsaken, nor his seed begging bread." "There shall no evil happen to the just." Nothing befalls us that is not of the nature of ourselves.

A person who directs a malicious thought to another will be injured by its rebound if he fails to get subconscious acceptance of the other. "As ye sow, so shall ye reap." Furthermore, what you can wish and believe of another can be wished and believed of you, and you have no power to reject it if the one who desires it for you accepts it as true of you. The only power to reject a subjective word is to be incapable of wishing a similar state of another, to give presupposes the ability to receive. The possibility to impress an idea upon another mind presupposes the ability of that mind to receive that impression. Fools exploit the world; the wise transfigure it. It is the highest wisdom to know that in the living universe there is no destiny other than that created out of imagination of man. There is no influence outside of the mind of man.

"Whatsoever things are lovely, whatsoever are of good report; if there be any virtue and if there be any praise, think on these things." Never accept as true of others what you would not want to be true of you. To awaken a state within another it must first be awake within you. The state you would transmit to another can only be transmitted if it is believed by you. Therefore to give is to receive. You cannot give what you do not have and you have only what you believe. So to believe a state as true of another not only awakens that state within the other but it makes it alive within you. You are what you believe.

"Give and ye shall receive, full measure, pressed down and running over." Giving is simply believing, for what you truly believe of others you will awaken within them. The vibratory state transmitted by your belief persists until it awakens its corresponding vibration in him of whom it is believed. But before it can be transmitted it must first be awake within the transmitter. Whatever is awake within your consciousness, you are. Whether the belief pertains to self or another does not matter, for the believer is defined by the sum total of his beliefs or subconscious assumptions.

"As a man thinketh in his heart" . . in the deep subconscious of himself . . "so is he."

Disregard appearances and subjectively affirm as true that which you wish to be true. This awakens in you the tone of the state affirmed which in turn realizes itself in you and in the one of whom it is affirmed. Give and ye shall receive. Beliefs invariably awaken what they affirm. The world is a mirror wherein everyone sees himself reflected. The objective world reflects the beliefs of the subjective mind.

Neville Goddard

The other great obstacle to health and success is hate. There can be no health or success in life for the one who hates. He who hates emits a force which rebounds back upon himself. Hate injures the one who hates far more than the one hated. Hate poisons the blood of the one who hates and tears down his nervous system. Hate is negative and destructive, love is positive and upbuilding. Hate affects adversely all the vital processes. It destroys health, wrecks happiness and turns the life into an inferno of trouble.

Have you ever noticed the lives of those who indulge in hate? They are a continual round of trouble. Before they finish one brawl they find themselves engaged in another. They are at loggerheads with nearly everybody, and misfortunes seem to dog their footsteps. Misfortunes and troubles are attracted to them as a direct result of their hate. Through indulging in negative thoughts and emotions, negative conditions are produced and attracted.

That is why people who hate are not always in trouble through other people's hatred, but they attract to themselves troubles and disasters which seem to have no connection with hate, but which are in reality a direct result of that condition of mind. Therefore, dear reader, if you have hatred, malice or resentment in your mind or life, pluck it out and cast it away, because you can never be successful, never be happy until you have done so.

The best way to cast out hate is to hold your mind continually in the attitude of good will to all men. If hate is to you a real difficulty, if you blaze with resentment whenever you think of a certain person who has deeply wronged you, if there wells up within you a fierce desire to get even with the object of your hatred, or at least to wish him harm, remember this, that you can never make any progress in mind and thought control you can never be successful and happy until you have forgiven your enemy.

Henry Thomas Hamblin

Until now, he has sought and used Power outside himself. Now, through his Greatest Discovery, Thought is Power! Love is Power! Life is Power! He realizes that the soul is only a CENTER OF POWER IN POWER. He has within himself all Power. Thus Man has, whenever he will take it,

Dominion over all other manifestations of Power. Man has just awakened to a knowledge of his place in Unity. He is entering his "kingdom." Where Law heretofore ruled him, he will now, as Conscious Law, rule Law, and thus BE Law. O, the grandeur, beauty, glory, and the Almightiness of this Discovery! Lift up your heads, ye eternal gates and the king of glory shall come in! Who is this king of glory? The Lord strong and mighty! But that Lord is Man, coming to consciousness of his Power.

Among the possibilities that lie within the Power of Thought are those already mentioned and others hinted at, in the excerpts that introduce this essay. Knowledge is but the recognition of Power. Classified knowledge is Science. Science applied is Art. There is as yet no Science of Thought, and but very little knowledge of it. The Art of Thinking is almost unknown. It is the glory of the new century that it starts with the glimmerings of the Light which will yet illumine all mankind.

Henry Harrison Brown

We make our own lives and create our own atmosphere. The spoken word, which is the thought expressed, is the creative power. If we really desire to live the true life, we must guard our words carefully and send them to create right conditions. It is both foolish and harmful to give expression to depressive thoughts, just as it is to refer to disease or fear because these unfortunate expressions create like conditions.

Kathleen M. H. Besly

The greatest thing in all the world is wisdom. If a man possessed wisdom, he would not need wealth, health, or peace of mind; he would have the know-how of accomplishment. Wisdom is greater than a healing because if you had wisdom, you would not need a healing. You have wisdom when you are aware of the Presence and Power of God (consciousness) within you, and your capacity to contact and release limitless treasures into your experience and conditions of life. You possess wisdom when you know that thoughts are things, that what you feel you attract, that what you contemplate you become, that what you imagine and feel you create

Joseph Murphy

If but two people were to meet at regular intervals and talk of health, strength and vigor of body and mind, at the same time opening their minds to receive of the Supreme the best idea as to the ways and means for securing these blessings, they would attract to them a thought current of such idea.

If these two people or more kept up these conversations on these subjects at a regular time and place, and found pleasure in such communings, and they were not forced or stilted; if they could carry them on without controversy, and enter into them without preconceived idea, and not allow any shade of tattle or tale-bearing, or censure of others to drift into their talk, they would be astonished at the year's end at the beneficial results to mind and body.

Because in so doing and coming together with a silent demand of the Supreme to get the best idea, they would attract to them a current of Life-giving force. Let two so commence rather than more. For even two persons in the proper agreement and accord to bring the desired results are not easy to find. The desire for such meetings must be spontaneous, and any other motive will bar out the highest thought current for good.

Prentice Mulford

Every thought produces an image, and the image is the "substance of things hoped for, the evidence of things not seen." Whenever you say "I AM," no matter what thought follows the words, you are transforming thought into suggestion and the subconscious mind obediently transmutes it into form. Thought, backed by feeling, forms an image in the objective mind and when that image is passed into the subjective mind and there sanctioned and sealed, the two minds have agreed, and "When two shall agree on earth as touching anything it shall be done to them in heaven."

When the two minds have agreed, under the immutable law the universal will carry out that agreement. The law is not mocked and it will not let you plant a thought of one kind and reap fruit of another. If, however, thought is sent out without feeling, it merely joins itself to cosmic energy at its own rate of vibration. In order to create, thought must be strong with feeling. As a man thinketh in his heart, so is he.

Mary C. Ferriter

John tells us, "In the beginning was the Word."

What is the Word? The Word is the idea, the thought. 'In the beginning was the Idea, and the Idea was with God and the Idea was God.' The Idea, being God's was the Perfect Thought, and so manifested its perfection. If the idea had been imperfect, it would have manifested an imperfect projection; like attracts like.

Whatever you think with conviction, whatever you really believe in with conviction, that you will demonstrate or experience in your life. There is no doubt of that. For instance, if you want to raise roses in your garden, and you plant carnation seeds, you are not going to get roses. You will get carnations. If you want carrots and plant lettuce seeds, you will not get carrots, but lettuce. And so it is on every plane of life. Like attracts like.

The key to freedom lies in your hands. Could there be a greater gift? I don't know of any. Yet how seldom we discover it, and even less seldom use it! One way of examining your own thoughts . . forerunners of the conditions you are bringing into your life . . is to realize that you can think only two types of thoughts; positive, constructive thoughts, or fearful, negative thoughts. Everything else stems from that. You know, some people are constantly afraid; they are suspicious, jealous, worried, critical. These are all fear thoughts.

So the thing you will learn to do is to get over to the positive side . . the constructive side of life, and stay there. It requires training. Not any more than it would to study a new language or to learn to play a musical instrument. But it does need training and practice. Always remember the type of thoughts you have been thinking not only manifest in your life as the sort of thing that happens to you, but they manifest in your personality and your physical body as well.

Mildred Mann

Thought is the eternal movement; the divine action everywhere. It is God moving upon the face of the waters; God thinking; and as God thinks, this activity goes forth continuously. Thought is the commonest power we have and it is given to all alike. It is a steady and continuous flow through us, and just as the woodland stream bestows its beneficence equally on all the forms of vegetation along its banks, so Thought passing through us, offers to all alike the power which will come from its recognition and use. Thought thus becomes a great individual power; something that cannot be taken away from us nor received from any other individual. It flows continuously and cannot be held, bound or limited; it is as universal as God, which is its source; as subtle and intangible as sunshine, yet just as real.

Thought is one of the divine spiritual forces which we have power to use as we will. Other forces of like nature are love, faith and strength. Let us consider strength for a moment in an effort to illustrate Thought and implant a right idea concerning it. Strength is universal. It is that great omnipotent force which upholds everything in the universe and which is within us whether we are conscious of it or not. As we come into consciousness of strength we find that it is a perfectly impersonal force. Having no personality of its own, it cannot direct its own use. It is for us to use in any way we desire. It is as freely at our service as is the air we breathe. We are constantly using or misusing strength. We may use it to bless or to destroy; we may exert it to lift a little child that has fallen or to strike an injurious blow. Used in love, strength blesses both giver and receiver, but when put to any base or selfish use its results are negative to all concerned.

From this illustration the analogy between Thought and strength should be apparent. Thought is an impersonal force, neither good nor bad, though it may be put to base uses. Through it we may send out a divine idea of love and harmony and thus bless our world; or a negative conception which will produce discord. It is like electricity, which of itself is merely a force; and cannot elect the use to which it shall be put, but is ready for various purposes; and when not in use it continues to flow ready for use when wanted. Thought is the vital force actuating the universe and sustaining the race in its life journey. It is not generated within, nor can it be held there any more than sunshine could be held and accumulated. So the expression, "holding a thought" is in reality a misnomer.

The better view is that Thought is a force that flows through us continuously, and as we meditate on any subject, our beliefs or ideas are carried out by the stream of Thought into the universe. Thus, while we do not create Thought, we have the power to color it with the positive or negative qualities of our own understanding, utilizing it for good or base purposes. A simple illustration will make the idea clearer. Just as light, passing through the beautiful stained glass windows of a great cathedral assumes various colors, so Thought passing through us is colored by our state of mentality. We see, then, how essential it is that our thought be joyous, happy and free, unclouded by any delusion or false belief; for if we are gloomy and depressed. Thought passing through us will take on that quality.

Whence comes Thought? Every good gift and every perfect gift is from above, and as Thought is a good and perfect gift we know that it has its origin in Divine Mind and that it permeates the universe. We have many evidences of the universality of Thought and of the power of the individual to color it with his mentality. Take for example, the many instances of telepathic and psychic experience. We "feel" the unannounced presence of a person; we instinctively become aware of the likes and dislikes of individuals; we suddenly get a thought from someone without the intervention of spoken or written words; two friends in close accord will often speak of the same thing at the same time; and letters of friends pass in the mails because the thought of one person for the other inspired each to write at the same time. Thus instances could be multiplied without end.

Thought thus becomes a universal language through which we may all understand each other when spoken words would be unintelligible. If this force were universally recognized and used we would live in a constant state of love, harmony and peace; knowing that we send to, and receive from each other, either consciously or unconsciously, a continuous message of Thought which is colored by the degree of consciousness.

Without Thought we can do nothing; with it all power in heaven and earth is ours. We, then, may be moved to ask, If the Divine Mind is always thinking, if the activity is perfect and the result perfect, whence come inharmony, sickness, sin and negative conditions generally? The answer is, through the misuse of Thought.

Man sometimes applies this force to ignoble ends; instead of using it in love and cooperation, to the ends of peace, harmony, health and happiness, he misuses it with the result that negative conditions appear. It is necessary to emphasize what has been stated before, viz., that Thought in itself is a perfect force, impersonal, but susceptible to the coloring influence of individual consciousness. Not knowing the power of this divine force, we have considered ourselves wholly as matter, born of earth, subject to sin, sickness and death; and because we have believed this and have used Thought in this way, we have become subject to the belief with its resulting negative conditions. The truth is that the substance of the body is Spirit, indestructible, immortal and perfect, and in unity with all that eternally is. To know this perfectly would be to lose all conception of negative conditions.

Thought is a free force, illimitable and inexhaustible. We may use it consciously as much and as often as we will. Through it we And our unity with our Source; through it we come into direct communication with the universal, with the Infinite. It raises us out of the material and personal to a fuller conception of the spiritual and divine, and establishes the truth of what we really are.

We have seen, now, that the individual is master of the force we call Thought. This brings us to a consideration of what is called mental atmosphere. We have all recognized this subtle and intangible condition in our friends and acquaintances. The presence of one person is a blessing, while the advent of another brings in the utmost confusion and discord. Now the mental atmosphere of individuals is a direct result of their use of Thought.

If a man color his Thought with positive ideas of love, joy, cheerfulness, peace, courage, confidence and power, his mental atmosphere will show those qualities and people will feel them when in his presence. On the other hand, if he color Thought with sadness, gloom, faith in evil, fear, weakness, worry, sin and other negative beliefs, he will project them into his mental atmosphere and they will be apparent to all his associates. In the same way, the atmosphere of a home or of a gathering of people is instinctively felt, and represents the state of consciousness in that home or gathering. Plainly, then, the point to be observed is, to keep the consciousness so harmonious that Thought passing through us and out into the universe will produce a mental atmosphere of unity and harmony with the Infinite and with all creation.

Mrs. C. L. Baum

When you assert yourself, assert the spiritual "I," the God image in you, not the physical "I," the flesh of you. This would be mere egotism, and it is not asserting your egotism that will benefit you. This will only hurt you. But asserting the reality, the divinity of yourself will do everything for you. Your divine or real self is your potential self, your creative self, and when you assert the reality of your being, not the outward or bodily personality, you are simply asserting divinity, you are asserting omnipotence, omniscience, and you are asserting a power that can do things.

If we could only realize the creative power of affirmation, of assuming that we are the real embodiment of the thing we long to be or to attain, not that we possess all the qualities of good, but that we are these qualities, . . with the constant affirming, "I myself am a part of the great creative, sustaining principle of the universe, because my real, divine self and my Father are one" . . what happiness it would bring to earth's children! Affirmation is a living, vital force. The Bible owes much of its strength to this force. It is a book of affirmations, of strong, positive statements. But for this fact it would long ago have lost its power.

There is no parleying, no arguing, no attempt by the sacred writers to prove the truth of what they say. They merely assert, affirm dogmatically that certain things happened, and that certain other things would happen. Had they attempted to prove the authenticity of what they wrote, endeavored to convince the reader that they were honest men making genuine statements, they would have aroused doubts. But there is no appeal to sympathy, no appeal to the readers' credulity, no appeal for confirmation, no posing for effect, only unrelenting positiveness, persistent affirmations. They simply state facts and affirm principles. Every line breathes dominance, superiority and confidence. In this lies their tremendous power. There is no sentimental imploring even in the Lord's Prayer. It demands. It is "give us," "lead us not," forgive us," etc.

In your talks with yourself, be like the Biblical writers. Don't wobble, or "think," or "hope." Say stoutly, "I AM," "I Can," "I Will," "It is." Constantly, everlastingly affirm that you will become what your ambitions indicate as fitting and possible. Do not say, "I shall be a success sometime"; say "I AM a success now. Success is my birthright." Do not say that you are going to be happy in the future, say to yourself, "I was intended for happiness, made for it, and I AM happy now." Say with Walt Whitman, "'I, myself, am good fortune.'" Assert your actual possession of the things you need; of the qualities you long to have. Force your mind toward your goal; hold it there steadily, persistently, for this is the mental state that creates. This is what causes the word to be made flesh. The negative mind, which doubts, wavers, fears, creates nothing. It cannot send forth a positive, confident assertion.

We are constantly letting loose mighty thought forces, emotion forces, word forces which are forever multiplying and expressing themselves in the universal energy, which are forever fashioning our conditions. We are rich or poor, healthy or unhealthy, successful or unsuccessful, happy or unhappy, noble or ignoble, according to our use of our thought and word forces. The outer registration in the flesh, in all material circumstances and things, corresponds with the inner thought and the decisive positive word.

Let the spirit of you, the real self, constantly affirm the "I AM," and the power you have through the All-Power. Make your affirmations quietly, but with great confidence and positiveness. Say "I AM united with Him. I AM able to do what He wills me to do. It is my duty to obey the inner urge of my being, that divine ambition to measure up to my highest possibilities, which ever bids me up and on. I will never again allow anything to interfere with the free and full exercise of my physical, mental and spiritual faculties. I will unfold all the possibilities that the Creator has in-folded in the ego, the I of me. There is no lost day in God's calendar, no allowance for waste, and henceforth I will make the most of the stuff that has been given me. I will play the part of a son of Omnipotence."

But remember it is the life, the driving power of the spirit that gives the word its power. If you don't mean what you say, if you don't live the meaning into your words, they are mere idle breath.

The same word, for instance, means a very different thing when spoken by people of different types of character. The same words spoken by one person will heal diseases, while spoken by another they will have no influence whatever upon the patient.

The difference in results is due to the difference in the life, in the character, of the speakers. Some healers are unsuccessful, even when they are letter perfect in the intellectual understanding of the healing principle, simply because they lack the spiritual side, simply because their life does not match their teachings.

In fact, it is the life, the spiritual life that does the healing through the words which the intellect suggests. Just as faith without good works is of no avail without the spirit, without the life behind them, words are cold and ineffectual.

Orison Swett Marden

Thought is the force underlying all. And what do we mean by this? Simply this: Your every act . . every conscious act . . is preceded by a thought. Your dominating thoughts determine your dominating actions. The acts repeated crystallize themselves into the habit. The aggregate of your habits is your character. Whatever, then, you would have your acts, you must look well to the character of the thought you entertain. Whatever act you would not do, . . habit you would not acquire you must look well to it that you do not entertain the type of thought that will give birth to this act, this habit . It is a simple psychological law that any type of thought, if entertained for a sufficient length of time, will, by and by, reach the motor tracks of the brain, and finally burst forth into action. Murder can be and many times is committed in this way, the same as all undesirable things are done. On the other hand, the greatest powers are grown, the most God-like characteristics are engendered, the most heroic acts are performed in the same way.

The thing clearly to understand is this: That the thought is always parent to the act. Now, we have it entirely in our own hands to determine exactly what thoughts we entertain. In the realm of our own minds we have absolute control, or we should have, and if at any time we have not, then there is a method by which we can gain control, and in the realm of the mind become thorough masters.

Here let us refer to that law of the mind which is the same as is the law in connection with the reflex nerve system of the body, the law which says that whenever one does a certain thing in a certain way it is easier to do the same thing in the same way the next time, and still easier the next, and the next, and the next, until in time it comes to pass that no effort is required, or no effort worth speaking of; but on the contrary, to do the opposite would require the effort. The mind carries with it the power that perpetuates its own type of thought, the same as the body carries with it through the reflex nerve system the power which perpetuates and makes continually easier its own particular acts. Thus a simple effort to control one's thoughts, a simple setting about it, even if at first failure is the result, and even if for a time failure seems to be about the only result, will in time, sooner or later, bring him to the point of easy, full, and complete control.

Each one, then, can grow the power of determining, controlling his thought, the power of determining what types of thought he shall and what types he shall not entertain. For let us never part in mind with this fact, that every earnest effort along any line makes the end aimed at just a little easier for each succeeding effort, even if, as has been said, apparent failure is the result of the earlier efforts. This is a case where even failure is success, for the failure is not in the effort, and every earnest effort adds an increment of power that will eventually accomplish the end aimed at.

Ralph Waldo Trine

Man is the keeper of his heart; the watcher of his mind; the solitary sentinel of his citadel of life. As such, he can be diligent or negligent. He can keep his heart more and more carefully; he can more strenuously watch and purify his mind; and he can guard himself against the thinking of unrighteous thoughts: this is the way of enlightenment and bliss. On the other hand, he can live loosely and carelessly, neglecting the supreme task of rightly ordering his life: this is the way of self-delusion and suffering.

Let a man realize that life in its totality proceeds from the mind, and lo, the way of blessedness is opened up to him! For he will then discover that he possesses the power to rule his mind, and to fashion it in accordance with his Ideal. So will be elect to strongly and steadfastly walk those pathways of thought and action which are altogether excellent; to him life will become beautiful and sacred; and, sooner or later, he will put to flight all evil, confusion and suffering; for it is impossible for a man to fall short of liberation, enlightenment, and peace, who guards with unwearying diligence the gateway of his heart.

James Allen

Thought is the only power which can produce tangible riches from the formless substance. The stuff from which all things are made is a substance which thinks, and a thought of form in this substance produces the form. Original substance moves according to its thoughts; every form and process you see in nature is the visible expression of a thought in original substance.

As the formless stuff thinks of a form, it takes that form; as it thinks of a motion, it makes that motion. That is the way all things were created. We live in a thought world, which is part of a thought universe. The thought of a moving universe extended throughout formless substance, and the thinking stuff . . moving according to that thought . . took the form of systems of planets, and maintains that form. Thinking substance takes the form of its thought, and moves according to the thought.

Wallace Wattles

That great writer on the power of the mind - Prentice Mulford, has summed up much of his philosophy in the statement: "Thoughts are Things." In these words he gave expression to a mighty truth, which, if fully apprehended by mankind, would revolutionize the world. Thought is not only a dynamic force, it is a real thing, just as is any other material object. Thought is merely a finer form of matter, or grosser form of spirit . . you may call it either with equal correctness. Matter is but a grosser form of mind, mind but a finer form of matter. There is but one substance in nature, but that substance has many forms, ranging from the most material (so-called) forms, to the highest form . . Spirit.

When we think, we send out vibrations of a fine ethereal substance, which is as real as the finer vapors or gasses, the liquids, the solids. We do not see thought . . neither do we see the finer vapors or gasses. We cannot smell or taste thought . . neither do we smell or taste the pure air. We can feel it however, as many can testify . . which is more than we can say of the powerful magnetic vibrations of a mighty magnet, which, whilst exerting a force sufficient to attract toward it a piece of steel weighing a hundred pounds, is absolutely without effect upon us. Its vibrations may pass through our bodies and exert its force on the steel, while we may be unaware of its existence. Light and heat send out vibrations of a lower intensity than those of thought, but the principle is the same. The evidence of the five senses is not absolutely necessary to establish the existence of a material substance or force.

William Walker Atkinson

Mental development is built on the same idea. If you would be a great thinker, a wonderful producer, an example of what thought can do, you must also be prepared to pay the price by exercising your mental faculties vigorously and systematically, limiting your diet of careless thinking and doing without some things so that you may have others. From every experience in life something can be learned that will be of benefit. What might seem disaster may be turned into positive victory, but to see this is to be able to look from within . . out; not from without . . in, as one usually does.

Benjamin Johnson

THE axiom, "As a man thinketh in his heart so is he," is the most startling truth ever uttered of man. What an amazing statement! Power! Self-mastery! A being of Life, Love, and Intelligence, possessed of the power to create and rule himself and his environment by the choice and mastership of thought! A realization of the meaning of the above aphorism awakens a power in man that transforms him into a new being.

The wonderful fascination of this saying lies in the all-embracing statement which it so directly makes. It covers every possible act of man and clearly states that he is capable of exercising unlimited powers. Look which way we will we cannot escape from the finality of this decree.

The beauty of this saying is that it is true, just as it is written.

Man is a world within himself, and he is master of himself, it matters not how well or ill he may exercise his powers of mastership. He is the unquestioned thinker of his own thoughts, which are the tools of his workmanship. He is the master workman of his own designs, and he builds constructively or destructively as he wills. He makes himself sick or well, rich or poor, strong or feeble, sorrowful or joyous by the character of the thoughts he thinks.

Charles Wesley Kyle

Let a man radically alter his thoughts, and he will be astonished at the rapid transformation it will effect in the material conditions of his life.

Men imagine that thought can be kept secret, but it cannot. It rapidly crystallizes into habit, and habit solidifies into habits of drunkenness and sensuality, which solidify into circumstances of destitution and disease. Impure thoughts of every kind crystallize into enervating and confusing habits, which solidify into distracting and adverse circumstances. Thoughts of fear, doubt, and indecision crystallize into weak, unmanly, and irresolute habits, which solidify into circumstances of failure, indigence, and slavish dependence.

Lazy thoughts crystallize into habits of uncleanliness and dishonesty, which solidify into circumstances of foulness and beggary. Hateful and condemnatory thoughts crystallize into habits of accusation and violence, which solidify into circumstances of injury and persecution. Selfish thoughts of all kinds crystallize into habits of self-seeking, which solidify into circumstances more of less distressing.

On the other hand, beautiful thoughts of all crystallize into habits of grace and kindliness, which solidify into genial and sunny circumstances. Pure thoughts crystallize into habits of temperance and self-control, which solidify into circumstances of repose and peace.

Thoughts of courage, self-reliance, and decision crystallize into manly habits, which solidify into circumstances of success, plenty, and freedom.

Energetic thoughts crystallize into habits of cleanliness and industry, which solidify into circumstances of pleasantness. Gentle and forgiving thoughts crystallize into habits of gentleness, which solidify into protective and preservative circumstances. Loving and unselfish thoughts crystallize into habits of self-forgetfulness for others, which solidify into circumstances of sure and abiding prosperity and true riches.

A particular train of thought persisted in, be it good or bad, cannot fail to produce its results on the character and circumstances. A man cannot directly choose his circumstances, but he can choose his thoughts, and so indirectly, yet surely, shape his circumstances.

Nature helps every man to the gratification of the thoughts which he most encourages, and opportunities are presented which will most speedily bring to the surface both the good and evil thoughts.

James Allen

Whatever you long for you are headed toward, and whatever thought dominates you, or motive is uppermost in your mind, is attracting its affinities. How quickly, for example, a youth who goes from his country home to the city to seek his fortune gravitates toward the things which are uppermost in his mind. He may not know a soul in the city he enters, but in a very short time we find him with his own people, those whose tastes, whose desires and propensities are like his own. He has attracted his affinities.

One boy's mind is fixed on pleasure, and he gravitates to the saloon, to the dance hall, to the vicious dives, to the gambling table. Another boy's great desire is self-improvement, and he gravitates to the Y. M. C. A., to some church. We find him in the night schools, in the libraries, or attending lectures, trying 'to improve his education, to make as broad visioned, as cultured and successful a man as it is possible to make of himself. The same thing is true of girls. They gravitate toward their desires, their ideals, toward the things on which they have set their hearts. Led by their weaknesses or their strength, they are pulled in the direction on which their thoughts are fixed, whether good or bad. If ten thousand strangers from other cities were landed in New

York today and left to their own devices, they would very quickly be attracted to their affinities.

The gambler would find other gamblers, the musician would gravitate to other musicians, the artist would be drawn to art circles; the pure minded, those of high ideals, would soon find others on the same plane, while the impure minded, those with vulgar, low flying ideals, would as quickly find companions like themselves. A mental magnet cannot attract opposite qualities. It can only attract things like itself, and it is our privilege to give the magnet its quality. We can inject hate into it, jealousy, envy, revenge; we can in a very short time demagnetize the magnet which was pulling good things so that it will attract bad things.

It is for us to decide the quality of the magnetic current that shall flow out from us, but the mind is always a magnet sending out and attracting something, and this something which flows back to us always corresponds to the mental outflow. If we charge it with love, sincerity, genuineness, helpfulness, great spiritual hunger for the good, the beautiful and the true, a longing for a larger and a fuller life, we shall make the mind a powerful magnet to attract the affinities of these qualities.

But in an inconceivably short time we can so completely change our mental magnet with thoughts of hatred, spite and bitterness that it will drive away all the good and attract the opposite, strengthening the hatred and bitterness in our souls. In short, whatever is in the mind at the moment is the thing you are inviting to come and live with you. Your suspicion attracts suspicion. Jealousy brings more jealousy, hate more hate, just as love brings love to meet it, as friendliness brings more friendliness, as sympathy and good will toward all draw the same to you from others and increase your popularity and magnetic power. We build as we think. Our lives follow our thoughts. As we think so we are. Your personality and your world are limited by the extension of your own thought. You cannot project yourself beyond these self-limitations.

Many people limit themselves to such an extent by their gloomy doubts and fears that they utterly dwarf their divine powers and possibilities. They do not believe that their own is coming to them. They are always complaining, visualizing their poverty-stricken conditions, their lack of friends, their lack of sympathy, their lack of love, of opportunity, of social life, of everything desirable. They do not realize that they are their own jailers, that they are holding themselves in the very conditions they despise. They have not learned how to make themselves magnets for the things they desire. They do not know that our own is seeking us and will come to us, whether it is property, friends, love, happiness, or any other legitimate desire, unless we drive it away by our antagonistic thought.

Orison Swett Marden

When energy is impressed with a predominant mental thought, not only does it permeate the body but it is radiated in the atmosphere around you. The aura which you hear spoken of often is the extension of the energies of the body. It is around you at all times. It expresses your character and your personality. The predominant thought of the subconscious mind is radiated in your aura. The aura has the power of attraction or repulsion. In your hours of reflection . . when you are thinking things over . . if you have charged your mind and directed your thought along uplifting, inspiring courageous lines, your aura becomes charged with that type of thought. If you have used the time in worrying or entertaining thoughts of jealousy, malice or destructive thoughts, your aura is charged with those thoughts, and you have lost the power of attracting good.

You attract your own kind. Whenever you draw in your circle someone who is not true to you, you must know that it is a result of your own thoughts. The law of attraction brings you your environment. You are creating your law of attraction and if it brings to you people that you do not like, look back and see when it was that you thought along the line expressed by the person who came into your environment. The law of attraction is one of the great laws of the universe.

Mrs. Evelyn Lowes Wicker

In a universe where everything is governed by law, it is to be expected that we might find certain rules of action for the government of our existence here. The law of cause and effect is operative everywhere and if we desire to secure certain effects in our lives we must follow lines of action which will produce the desired results. Whether or not we recognize and observe the law makes no difference; the results are inexorable and no excuse of ignorance or forgetfulness avails anything. How important, then, to know and follow rules of action which will result in a life of harmony, peace and love.

Let us consider a few simple rules which, if faithfully lived, will bring only the results we most desire. The first one of these is stated as follows: "Whoever will never give another pain, either by thought, word or deed, is exempt from pain forever." — Annie Rix Militz.

The truth of this statement should be apparent at once. That which we send forth is constantly coming back to us, and if we are in that state which will not countenance the giving of pain in any manner, we shall also be oblivious to pain of any sort. This fact is noticeable in other forms as well. For example, one who is constantly in a frame of mind that contemplates only the good may ultimately attain a state of consciousness to which negation of any sort cannot present itself. It is as if darkness were to present itself to the sun for recognition as an entity. It would be instantly dissolved and its unreality proved. Thus a person filled with a consciousness of love could never give another pain, nor be touched by any angry words.

A little thought will show that there are many careless ways of giving pain. Condemnation, criticism and fault-finding are apt mostly to be uncharitable and, therefore, to give pain; but they will certainly react on the one so unfortunate as to indulge in them toward others. If the statement given above is kept in mind it will be like a ray of light in its power to cleanse the thought of unkind habits.

Mrs. C. L. Baum

Watch your thoughts, your words and your actions. Stay kind, stay positive, stay cheerful. It will take a little time and little training, but so does everything in life that is worthwhile. As you begin to watch yourself, you suddenly find you are very conscious of your thoughts, and know instantly when you are going negative. Every time you are negative you tear up some of the positive thoughts you planted through your meditation. That is inevitable.

Remember always that you are dealing with a little child, and the only way to teach a child is by reiteration, kindliness, and most important of all patience. Another thing, you never start looking for immediate results. You may have them. Many people do, but sometimes it is not immediate. If you think to yourself "I wonder if anything is really happening," your subconscious immediately senses the doubt, and says "She (or he) doesn't believe it." Then you will surely have difficulty getting results, Do not doubt that the thing will come true. The more you progress in metaphysics, the more you will realize how subtle doubts are. But for the present you are only to realize when you have a positive thought and when you have a negative one.

Mildred Mann

We need to be careful of what we think and talk. Because thought runs in currents as real as those of air and water. Of what we think and talk we attract to us a like current of thought. This acts on mind or body for good or ill.

If thought was visible to the physical eye we should see its currents flowing to and from people. We should see that persons similar in temperament, character and motive are in the same literal current of thought. We should see that the person in a despondent and angry mood was in the same current with others despondent or angry, and that each one in such moods serves as an additional battery or generator of such thought and is strengthening that particular current. We should see these forces working in similar manner and connecting the hopeful, courageous and cheerful, with all others hopeful, courageous and cheerful.

When you are in low spirits or "blue" you have acting on you the thought current coming from all others in low spirits. You are in oneness with the despondent order of thought. The mind is then sick. It can be cured, but a permanent cure cannot always come immediately when one has long been in the habit of opening the mind to this current of thought.

In attracting to us the current of any kind of evil, we become for a time one with evil. In the thought current of the Supreme Power for good we may become more and more as one with that power, or in Biblical phrase "One with God." That is the desirable thought current for us to attract.

If a group of people talk of any form of disease or suffering, of death-bed scenes and dying agonies, if they cultivate this morbid taste for the unhealthy and ghastly, and it forms their staple topics of conversation, they bring in themselves a like current of thought full of images of sickness, suffering and things revolting to a healthy mind. This current will act on them, and eventually bring them disease and suffering in some form.

If we are talking much of sick people or are much among them and thinking of them, be our motive what it may, we shall draw on ourselves a current of sickly thought, and its ill results will in time materialize itself in our bodies. We have far more to do to save ourselves than is now realized.

When men talk business together they attract a business current of idea and suggestion. The better they agree the more of this thought current do they attract and the more do they receive of idea and suggestion for improving and extending their business. In this way does the conference or discussion among the leading members of the company or corporation create the force that carries their business ahead.

Travel in first-class style, put up at first-class hotels and dress in apparel "as costly as your purse can buy," without running into the extreme of foppishness. In these things you find aids to place you in a current of relative power and success. If your purse does not now warrant such expenditure, or you think it does not, you can commence so living in mind. This will make you take the first steps in this direction. Successful people in the domain of finance unconsciously live up to this law. Desire for show influences some to this course. But there is another force and factor which so impels them. That is a wisdom of which their material minds are scarcely conscious. It is the wisdom of the spirit telling them to get in the thought current of the successful, and by such current be borne to success.

Prentice Mulford

Your individual world, i.e., experiences, conditions, circumstances, environment, as well as your physical health, financial states, social life, etc., is made out of your own mental images and after your own likeness. Like attracts like. Your world is a mirror reflecting back to you your inner world of thought, feeling, beliefs, and inner conversation. If you begin to imagine evil powers working against you, or that there is a jinx following you, or that other forces and people are working against you, there will be a response of your deeper mind to correspond with these negative pictures and fears in your mind; therefore you will begin to say that everything is against you, or that the stars are opposed to you, or you will blame karma, your past lives, or some demon.

Truly the only sin is ignorance. Pain is not a punishment; it is the consequence of the misuse of your inner power. Come back to the one Truth, and realize that there is only One Spiritual Power, and It functions through the thoughts and images of your mind. The problems, vexations, and strife are due to the fact that man has actually wandered away after false Gods of fear and error. He must return to the center . . the God-Presence within. Affirm now the sovereignty and authority of this Spiritual Power within you . . the Principle of all life. Claim Divine guidance, strength, nourishment, and peace, and this Power will respond accordingly.

Joseph Murphy

Nothing is ever formed from one form of force alone. Thought enters into combination with other forms of force and builds body; then, through hands, it builds whatever it wills. It is silently building, in union with silent forces, still other things as yet unrecognized. Thus Life and Thought are no longer unknown forces. As we know electricity, we know them. We will learn to use thought in carrying out our desires, as we now use electricity and chemical force in telegraph and cannon to carry out our purposes in other fields of activity.

Thought is Love transformed. Like Thought and Life, Love is limitless. It is the emotion of the Ego. There is but one possible out-motion, therefore Love is the only possible emotion. As it is not Life and death, but more or less Life, so it is not Love and hate, but more or less Love. Love is the Master Passion. We are in the habit of so naming only those states of intense passion, but this is naming only a degree, and not the emotion. The one motion from the Soul is directed and controlled by different thoughts. It is the thought accompaniment that differs and is named, and not the emotion. There is only Love.

Wherever is the most perfect manifestation of the Indwelling God, there is, is the most perfect manifestation of Love. Conversely, where there is the most perfect manifestation of Love, there is the most perfect manifestation of Life. For Life and Love are one. Love is only Life in expression. Let Life manifest in Love, and there is health. People are sick and die because they do not love enough. The streets are filled with dead and dying persons, dying because they will not let Life flow through them into expression. Repression is death. Were it not for Love, there would be no reproduction of the species. But for Love, no daily reproduction of the body. Love is the measure of life.

Corrolary: To be in health and enjoy life, we must be loving. Whenever we give any lesser degree of Love than normal, then cells created by the larger degrees die. This decay causes poison and disease is the result. Cure: More Love.

Henry Harrison Brown

The subconscious mind acts only according to instruction and instinct. Thoughts and commands flow from the seat of the Will through the conscious mind down into the subconscious mind and are immediately acted upon.

The subconscious mind is a blind intelligence. It cannot reason . . it can remember, it can act . . but it cannot think, plan or reason.

Yet we have a mind within us that can inspire, create, and bring forth the most wonderful thoughts. A mind which can solve our most complicated problems, that can guide us through the most difficult situations if we will but trust it. This cannot be the subconscious mind because we have already seen that this is a blind intelligence acting only upon instruction, suggestion and animal instinct. Therefore, there must be a mind or minds other than the subconscious, and this I have termed, for the want of a better word, the subliminal.

The subconscious mind is a kind of a sleepy giant, or a slumbering volcano. It only requires arousing to cause it to manifest extraordinary power.

It is a vast and wonderful intelligence, so wonderful that our consciousness cannot form any conception of its wonders. All that we know is that this wonderful center of life and action is as far above our understanding as our own consciousness is beyond the comprehension of a beetle. Yet this subconscious mind of ours is subject to our will and guidance. Within us is this wondrous power . . the almost infinite intelligence; yet its use and control are in our own hands.

Henry Thomas Hamblin

To realize your desire, an action must start in your imagination, apart from the evidence of the senses, involving movement of self and implying fulfillment of your desire. Whenever it is the action which the outer self takes to appease desire, that desire will be realized.

The movement of every visible object is caused not by things outside the body, but by things within it, which operate from within outward. The journey is in yourself. You travel along the highways of the inner world. Without inner movement, it is impossible to bring forth anything. Inner action is introverted sensation. If you will construct mentally a drama which implies that you have realized your objective, then close your eyes and drop your thoughts inward, centering your imagination all the while in the predetermined action and partake in that action, you will become a self-determined being.

Inner action orders all things according to the nature of itself. Try it and see whether a desirable ideal once formulated is possible, for only by this process of experiment can you realize your potentialities.

It is thus that this creative principle is being realized. So the clue to purposive living is to center your imagination in the action and feeling of fulfilled desire with such awareness, such sensitiveness, that you initiate and experience movement upon the inner world.

Ideas only act if they are felt, if they awaken inner movement. Inner movement is conditioned by self-motivation, outer movement by compulsion.

Neville Goddard

The mind that yields to fear sharpens the weapon that slays the body. Thought shapes the mold in which the frame is cast. The nerves are the whips that lash the blood to action, and these whips are swayed by the mental overseer. With a sluggish or indifferent mind, the nerves become flaccid and of slow action. The blood then moves slowly and grows, as it were, stagnant, in whose bosom all toxic substances find free and fertile soil. But when the nerves are roused by intelligent mental action and intense will-energy, the white scavengers (the phagocytes) cleanse the body of its impurities, while the blood rushes keenly through the system, performing its magical labors.

Hence a good, honest conscience, plenty of work and rest and sleep, properly proportioned, with a good degree of exercise out-of-doors, accompanied with deep breathing of fresh air and a sufficient supply of pure water, are all the requisites of normal health. If one utilizes these with regularity and keeps his thoughts on things noble, lofty, and unselfish, in all probability he will never need the doctor or be taxed by the druggist.

Henry Frank

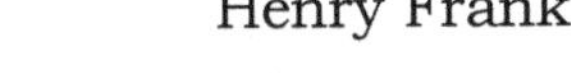

We will have the true learning when it is taught that man is mental: and that by controlling his thought man realizes life after the manner of his heart's desire.

The greatest discovery that man has ever made is that he is mind, his body but tributary to his thought: the greatest achievement of man is to change himself by changing his thought.

Ever we see things in the light of our own state of mind.

Ask the grouch. He knows that most everybody is sore about something all of the time, and sour about all things some of the time. That is his state of mind.

That grouch you had is not in the world, it is in you. The suspicion and doubt you find about you are really your own suspicion and doubt. The pruriency you seem to find about you is really your own rotten thought. Your distrust of the world is but your distrust of yourself.

Ask the prurient prier into other people's privacies, and he (she or it) will tell you that every little home has a scandal all its own. Of course it is his state of mind.

The libertine, overtly or imaginatively, knows beyond a doubt that virtue is an impossible ideal. Of course the only virtue he knows or understands is in his own mind.

The hypocrite is quite sure that everybody else is fundamentally insincere.

The liar doesn't expect anybody to tell the truth.

To the thief everybody is a crook.

To the shyster the good are those who have not been found out.

To the egotist a fool and his foot are soon in it.

To the man who has his price every man has his price.

Now ask the man in love with life: He knows that most everybody is glad about something all of the time, and happy about all things some of the time. . . . That, you see, is his state of mind.

Ask the people who are humble enough to know that they have their hands full attending to their own business, and they will tell you that the general run of folk are decent and as kind as the self-righteous meddler will allow them to be. As in a mirror they see in others the reflection of their own mental state.

Ask the really clean of mind . . for virtue is a state of mind . . and they will tell you that most people are genuinely pure of heart, that their follies are superficial, and that most of the filth is in the minds of the muck trucklers, whose perverse pleasure is in regulating others.

The sincere man knows that while there are many mistaken, and fooling one's self is about the easiest thing in the world, that the consciously insincere man is very rare. The high priests who accused Jesus were well-meaning. The promoters of the inquisition had good intentions.

The man of truth finds truth everywhere. He knows it to be omnipotent, omnipresent and omniscient.

Certainly that pleasant greeting with which people meet you is already in your own morning heart. That faith you have in your fellows is the reflection of your own faithfulness. Because you are normal and wholesome in your thoughts about men and women . . clean, poised, sane, gentle . . you are not bothered about the erotic, neurotic and the tommyrotic.

The honest man knows that unless confidence in honesty were the prevalent belief of men with reference to one another, the entire structure of modern commerce would not last thirty days. The business man knows that no matter what is his collateral, his biggest asset at the bank is his reputation for integrity.

Thought is the thing: thought is everything: action, conduct and personality is the externalization of the thought which has most definitely occupied our consciousness.

Life is mental: man is mental: control thought and you control yourself and master life.

In changing our old minds for the new mind, that mind which has been in all the great of characters from Jesus to Lincoln, we have but to understand that it is only the good and lovely in man that is representative of him.

My children, you will never see anything more lovely than yourselves. Then seek and see the loveliness within yourself.

Your world is your own consciousness: it is just as big and beautiful or as little and mean as your thought: your world takes its height and depth from your own heart.

Jesus, Judas and Caesar lived in as different worlds as if they had lived in different centuries on different planets.

You may make the world of your heart after the pattern of joy and usefulness if you but persist with patience in the work of making for yourself a new mind whose consciousness is filled with the expression of beauty, wisdom and goodwill.

How?

By "thinking on these things" until they are assimilated: by lining-up your conduct with your thought: by doing this with the same intelligence and patient application that was required to make you a merchant, lawyer, teacher, preacher, stenographer, writer, mechanic, coal digger or whatever may be your daily work.

Most men will admit that they can change the process of buying and bookkeeping in their business, or of teaching school or running a saw mill, yet they have but a hazy conception that a man may just as surely completely change his mind, and thereby change himself, by changing his thought processes.

Nothing is more true than that a man can change his personality and unfold his individuality just as completely as he can change and develop an art or a business. But it requires as much patience and work in changing his viewpoint . . his world . . as it does in introducing a new business method.

It is only by means of right thought, to which the conduct is patiently aligned, that men are made free: that loveliness is released: that beauty becomes a joy: that good-will becomes at once the strength and gentleness of life.

The thinker is the world's true pioneer. First the thought; then the thing.

The thinker is society's blazer of trails. First the dream; then the fact.

The thinker is humanity's teacher. First the seed; then the flower and the fruit.

To progress, the dangerous man is he who does not think.

To think, to think sympathy, justice and beauty, is to develop, to unfold, to live abundantly.

The thinker is the hope of the world. That is why Diogenes insisted, centuries ago, that education was the very foundation of the Greek state. That is the reason why education, training to think, is the hope of the race.

Not in dollars and dynasties is actual power and good to be found. Real dominion is in thought.

There is a new wisdom and it may be stated in five words:

Set your thought right first.

Nothing is more certain than that our personality is created in the image of that to which we give the most ardent thought. Likewise what is so of the individual is true of nations and the race.

The new wisdom is simple. Watch your thought that it be affirmative. This will not only bring you harmony and loveliness, but by just so much will you correct the thought of the world. It is the way to the beauty of the earth.

Frank Waller Allen

It becomes clear therefore that the thought of limitation is to be blamed on no one but ourselves. If we do not like our world and our environment, we must change it by our change of thought. Our environment is of our own making and we can move into the scenes and circumstances that fit our mental outlooks the moment we arrive at the consciousness that will draw us to our desired good. Heaven is a state of consciousness as possible on this plane as any other. Two people on the same street often live in worlds that are as wide apart as the spheres because in the case of one there is constant thought of ill with its physical correspondences, in the other there is the constant thought of good.

So we realize that the power to choose what he shall think and how he shall love constitutes the very vital spark of man's individuality. So too he can give or withhold his love from the Supreme Spirit. For God to have endowed him with less than choice would have been to make him a piece of mechanism. But he must pay for the freedom that he enjoys by the suffering that follows wrong thinking and failure to love. And his wrong thinking is due to his failure to love or establish harmony between himself and the Infinite Wisdom. For when he withholds his love he is out of harmony with wisdom and cannot be guided by those intuitive processes which keep him from making choices which plunge him into so much pain and unhappiness.

Fenwicke L. Holmes

GUARDING YOUR THOUGHTS

Are you disturbed by the thinking of adverse thoughts? Do you seem to be unable to discipline your mind and to rule out those thoughts that make for mental and physical inharmony? Then learn the very, very simple trick of guarding your thoughts. Learn how to discipline your thinking so that you will think just what you want to think.

Here is a woman who is thinking adverse thoughts about another woman. Seemingly without any self-control whatever, she falls into the habit of thinking thoughts of jealousy and envy about this other woman. She has prayed and concentrated and treated the situation; she has tried to send the woman love thoughts, but the adverse thoughts persist. What is the solution? How shall we instruct her to discipline her thinking and guard her thoughts of love and Truth from being overcome by evil ones?

In the first place, we must recognize that trying to win the cause through a battle of thoughts is almost futile. Trying to think good thoughts harder and faster than we think thoughts of evil is a process that involves mental tension. Such a battle cannot be won entirely by psychology. When adverse thoughts seem to obsess the mind, the will appears to be almost powerless.

What is the right process of guarding the thoughts? If mind power is not to be exercised, what power can we call into play? What is the power that will work the change without our driving our own mental energies at full speed? How will the power of Spirit be permitted to do its perfect work?

It is a very, very simple process. As a student of metaphysics and spiritual Truth, you have often witnessed the work of Spirit. It has operated in you and in your affairs as divine intelligence. It has revealed to you the uselessness of trying to work through personal consciousness. You have seen that trying to hate others or attempting to entertain thoughts of evil about them will do almost everything but reveal the heavenly way to you.

You have seen that working from the standpoint of mind alone cannot give you the things of Spirit peace, love, and happiness. Spirit has often shown you that you think thoughts of evil because you allow yourself to get into a state of mind in which evil thoughts exist.

During your instruction under the tutelage of Spirit, you have been shown that you must take the impersonal attitude in order to make personal demonstrations, those involving your relations with other persons. The impersonal attitude is the only antidote to the working of personal consciousness. You have been shown that personal situations do not involve other persons in your own demonstration, but indicate to you that you are in personal consciousness.

Regardless of how other persons appear to affect your own well-being or seem to stand in your light, as a student of Truth you must cease to blame persons or things or to think of them as involved in your own failure to overcome. You must recognize your demonstration as your demonstration, just as if there were no other person in the world but you and you were thinking evil, personal thoughts!

How will you guard your thoughts? Be not anxious about thoughts. Be more concerned about your loyalty to Spirit. Do you not accept as Truth the things of Truth that Spirit has revealed to you? Were Jesus Christ to appear before you and say to you, "Look to Spirit instead of to personality," would you not do so? Could the Spirit of truth in Jesus, in person, mean more to you than the Spirit of the impersonal Christ, of impersonal Truth?

Cease to look to persons and things as they appear. Cease to think of your seeming separation from Spirit as caused by the intervention of some personality. Cease to struggle with thoughts. Just give it all up and cast your burden upon the Lord (law). In the maze of personal consciousness you cannot find your way out through thinking personal thoughts. You just have to give up the whole thing and turn to Spirit, instead.

But what is the simple process of guarding your thoughts? The simplest thing in the world the business of doing nothing, of absolute personal detachment from the whole situation.

If you think that another dislikes you, cease to think about him for a while. The very situation shows that you are in personal consciousness. Do not try to think about him or to treat the situation while in this attitude of mind. Give it all up just as if he and the situation had never existed. Neither the personal man nor the personal situation ever existed in Spirit, Turn in thought to God (consciousness).

Live for a while in the realm where there are no thoughts of persons, personal limitations, and personal shortcomings. This experience will refresh your mind and guard it from the thoughts that you would avoid. You will have attained your purpose just by doing nothing about the very thing that has caused worry and tension. You will be resting in the presence of Spirit.

Out of this experience of giving up personal thoughts and just resting in the presence of God (consciousness) will come power, power to handle any situation, power to correct existing evils, power to overcome. From it you will see yourself, the world, and all your fellow beings in a new light. You will be free from the old worries, fears, hates, and feuds. No longer will they exist for you, since they do not exist in Spirit and in Truth.

The Spirit of truth will stand guard over your thoughts. You will not need to struggle and strain to deny evil and to grasp the good. You will exist in heaven, where there is only good. You will cease to live on the personal plane, where you must be busy sorting thoughts, killing out one kind and nourishing the other. This is the way of Spirit, the way of freedom, the way now open to you.

Frank B. Whitney

Spirit creates through law. The law is always mind in action. Mind cannot act unless intelligence sets it in motion. In the great universal mind man is a center of intelligence, and every time he 'thinks he sets mind into action. 'What is the activity of this mind in relation to man's thought? It has to be one of mental correspondence; that is, mind has to reflect whatever thought it casts into it. Wonderful as Universal Mind is, it has no choice but to create whatever thought is given it; if it could contradict that thought, it would not be a unit, since this would be recognizing something outside itself. This is a point in Truth which should not be overlooked.

The ONE MIND knows only its own ability to make whatever is given It; It sees no other power and never analyzes or dissects; It simply KNOWS, and the reason why people do not understand this is that they have not realized what mind is. The ordinary individual thinks of mind only from the limitation of his own environment. The concept he has of mind is the concept of his own thinking, which is very limited.

We are surrounded by an All Seeing, All Knowing Mind, which is One and runs through all. The belief in the dual mind has destroyed practically all philosophies and religions of the ages, and will continue to do so until the world comes to see that there is but One. Whatever name is given it there is but One. It is this One that creates for us, whatever we believe. Our thought operative through this One produces all our affairs. We are all centers in this Mind, centers of creative thought activity.

There is nothing which appears in the manifest Universe other than an objectified thought, whether it be a bump on your head, a growth on your foot or a planet. It could not be there were it not made out of Mind, for mind is all there is to make anything out of. Whatever is made is made out of it. Nothing exists or can exist without a source from which it springs.

Ernest Holmes

Thought seeks to embody itself in form; first in the body of the thinker, and then in his environment. Thought attracts to itself the material necessary for its embodiment, and then fashions it in its own image and likeness . . in its interpretation, in visibility of that which previously was invisible. It may fashion its interpretations after some visible form, or from the seeming void it may conjure up some new combination of primary factors. Inevitably thought takes on form, if only within the physical confines of the thinker. It fashions the mask that conceals the man; it builds the home in which he lives.

The home that each one fashions for himself is a mask to others because the latter also wear masks, and interpret those that surround them in the image and likeness of their own. Their vision is masked exactly as are their features and forms. Are their features masked in selfishness, greed, or cruelty, then their vision is directed along these channels of interpretation. To them other masks seem similarly distorted, for they bring to the surface of others the similitude of their own thoughts. Similarly, if their features are masked in altruism, generosity, or kindness.

A mirror reflects a true picture to the degree that its surface is clear, smooth, and unsullied, as it has behind it that which quickens its receptivity, as it is open, straightforward, and on the level. If it is curved, concavely or convexly, or crooked, or if its surface is distorted, or spotted, or marred in any way, the picture it reflects takes on the imperfections of the mirror. That which is pictured may be perfect in appearance, but the mirror reports it in its own language and interpretation.

The mask is Man's mirror. On a wave-tossed Soul the reflected pictures are blurred and indistinct. With emotions violent and uncontrolled, enthusiasm is misdirected, and energy lashes itself into a wild frenzy. With thought contradictory and chaotic, actions become inconsistent and erratic. Unless spiritually controlled, mind and body run amuck, and the mask pictures life as crippled and distorted.

The Soul seeks freedom of expression in form. The Soul uses the mind as its invisible medium, and the mind makes the body its visible counterpart. The Soul unfolds through the mind as the latter becomes receptive through its greater development, and the mind develops with the body's growth in refinement of texture. Each acts and reacts upon the others, and the Soul finds increasing freedom as the mind becomes receptive to it, and as it in turn finds freer circulation through its physical body. A mask serves to reveal to the degree that the Soul has found freedom, and it conceals to the extent that its Soul still remains enslaved.

The Soul that is free, though seemingly enmeshed, sees through or behind the masks of others; and freed Souls recognize each other despite the masks that effectually hide them from others. The freed Soul differentiates between masks and realities, and it looks beneath the surface-waves of the ocean of life to the calm depths below. The freed Soul may tear off the fetters that bind another, put aside the veil that obscures the other's vision, and enable the other's mind and body to bear the effulgence of the Soul that is awaiting its deliverance to freedom.

Eugene Del Mar

Thoughts are Things" . . many things, in fact. And one of the things that thought is, is a Magnet. Yes, a magnet . . an actual magnet, not merely a figure of speech magnet. This is one of the phases of the phenomena of thought "thingness" that possesses the most weird and magical interest to the investigator when he becomes aware of the truth of the proposition for the first time. Our thoughts constitute the elements of a great thought magnet that operates in the direction of drawing to us the persons, things, ideas, knowledge, and environment in harmony with our composite mental states and conducive to the expression of our static thought into dynamic action.

And, the reverse of this is true, for the same peculiar property of the thought magnet operates in the direction of repelling and repulsing persons, things, ideas, knowledge and environment of an opposite character and calculated to prevent the expression of our dominant thoughts.

All this may seem strange and fanciful to one who has never investigated the subject, but it is proven not only by investigation and experiment, but also by analogy. All through nature there is a manifestation of this law of attraction and repulsion. The atom attracts another in rhythmic harmony with itself, and repels and repulses one of opposing vibratory rhythm.

Chemical affinity, molecular attraction, cohesion . . physical laws, all of them . . as well as the phenomena of magnetism and electricity, all attest the universality of this law. The mineral may be dissolved in a liquid containing many other minerals or chemicals, and yet, when the opportunity for crystallization arises, we see the orderly formation of its special crystal, by gradual stages, the first granule attracting to itself the materials of its own kind, discarding and repelling atoms of different composition. The crystal acts almost as if it knew its own kind.

The seed planted in the earth draws to itself from the earth, and water, and light, precisely the kind of material it needs to build up its particular kind of plant. Take two tiny seeds, both practically alike so far as chemical analysis reveals, and plant them in the same earth, containing the same constituents . . plant them side by side if you will. And from that same earth, and from the same water that falls upon them, and from the same sunlight that invigorates them, each plant draws to itself exactly what is in rhythmic harmony with its inner nature . . and one develops into a deadly nightshade, and the other into a fragrant rose.

The honey of the bee, and the poison in its sting, are both extracted from the same nectar it sips from the flower. The milk of the cow, and the virus of the cobra are drawn from the same elementary substances. Why? There is no evidence of rational choice, as we use the term, in these things. There is but the operation of that universal principle . . the Law of Attraction. Birds of a feather flock together. Like attracts like.

Edward Walker/William Walker Atkinson

What man is, and what man does, determines in what conditions, circumstances and environments he shall be placed. And since man can change both himself and his actions, he can determine what his fate is to be.

To change himself, man must change his thought, because man is as he thinks; and to change his actions, he must change the purpose of his life, because every action is consciously or unconsciously inspired by the purpose held in view.

To change his thought, man must be able to determine what impressions are to form in his mind, because every thought is created in the likeness of a mental impression. To choose his own mental impressions, man must learn to govern the objective senses, and must acquire the art of original thought.

Everything that enters the mind through the physical senses will produce impressions upon the mind, unless prevented by original thought. These impressions will be direct reflections of the environment from whence they came; and since thoughts will be created in the exact likeness of these impressions, so long as man permits environment to impress the mind, his thoughts will be exactly like his environment: and since man becomes like the thoughts he thinks, he will also become like his environment.

But man, in this way, not only grows into the likeness of his environment, but is, in addition, controlled by his environment, because his thoughts, desires, motives and actions are suggested to him by the impressions that he willingly accepts from environment.

Therefore, one of the first essentials in the mastery of fate is to learn to govern the physical senses so thoroughly, that no impression can enter mind from without, unless it is consciously desired.

This is accomplished by holding the mind in a strong, firm, positive attitude at all times, but especially while surrounded by conditions that are inferior. This attitude will bring the senses under the supremacy of the subconscious will, and will finally produce a state of mind that never responds to impressions from without unless directed to do so.

To overcome the tendency of the physical senses to accept, indiscriminately, all sorts of impressions from without, mind should, at frequent intervals, employ the physical senses in trying to detect the superior possibilities that may be latent in the various surrounding conditions. And gradually, the senses themselves will become selective, and will instantaneously inform the mind whenever an undesirable impression demands admission. While the senses are being employed in the search of superior possibilities, the impressions thus received should be analyzed, and recombined in the constructive states of consciousness, and according to the mind's own original conception. This will promote original thinking, which will, in turn, counteract the tendency of the objective side of mind to receive suggestions from without.

Every original thought that mind may create, will to a degree, change man and remake him according to what he inwardly desires to be; because every original thought is patterned after man's conception of himself when he is at his best.

Thoughts inspired by environment are inferior or superior, according to what the environment may be; but an original thought is always superior, because it is inspired by man himself while the superior elements of his being are predominant.

When every thought that mind creates is an original thought, man will constantly grow in greatness, superiority and worth; and when all these original thoughts are created with the same purpose in view, man will become exactly what is indicated by that purpose.

Therefore, since man can base thinking upon any purpose that he may desire, he can, through original thinking, become whatever he may choose to become.

Fate is the result of man's being and doing; a direct effect of the life and the works of the individual; a natural creation of man; and the creation is always the image and likeness of the creator.

Therefore, when man, through original thinking, acquires the power to become what he chooses to become, his fate will of itself change as man changes; and through this law he can create for himself any fate desired.

Christian Larson

Ultimately all is Spirit, and Spirit which is the beginning is also the end of all manifestation. "I AM the Alpha and the Omega." Our life, then, is to be governed by Spirit. We need look no further. It will do for us all that we will ever ask, provided we believe. Why, then, has it not done so? The answer is that it has already done so, but we have not received it. The Spirit may offer, but we must accept the gift before it can be made. "Behold, I stand at the door and knock." We must understand that this receiving is a mental process; it is one of mentally taking.

The way, then, that we are using mind through our thought is the way that we are treating ourselves for prosperity. So simple, and yet we have not understood it! If a man says, "I have not." he will not receive; if he says, "I have," he will receive. "To those who have shall be given, and to those who have not shall be taken away even that which they have." This is a veiled statement of the law of cause and effect.

When you send out into mind the thought that you have not, it accepts the idea and takes away from you even that which you have. Reverse the process and say, "I have," and it will at once set to work to create for you even more than you now possess. You will readily see then that you are not dealing with two powers but with one, and that it operates through your own thought, doing unto all even as they believe.

Ernest Holmes

The Will and the Conscious Mind stand as sentinels at the door of the subconscious mind. To them is given the important task of deciding what shall, or what shall not, enter. Every kind of thought and suggestion, inimical to our welfare, meet us and strike us on every hand. Harmful thoughts seek to enter our minds at every turn. Books, magazines, race thought, the mental outlook of friends and acquaintances are all against our mental development.

The attitude of mind of the average person, of the common ruck, is not inspiring. It does not suggest "success," it expresses at best, only a passive acceptance of life. It takes like as it is, things as they come. It is not often that you meet a man who is conscious that he is "Master of his fate, the Captain of his soul."

Henry Thomas Hamblin

Power has been developed; Power has been controlled; Power has been discovered; Power has been harnessed. Through the mastery and application of Power, man has conquered all the Without. He has used external Power. Is there other Power? What is the Power that has thus found, developed, and harnessed, this external Power? Where does it dwell? It is the Power IN man. It is the Power of Ideas. This is recognized. Ideas rule the world. But that they are any kin to these external forces has scarcely been conceived, much less believed, until the last century. The greatest gift that the nineteenth century gave the twentieth was the demonstration that Thought is a Form of Energy.

This is the greatest gift of all the centuries. It is Man's Greatest Discovery and marks the beginning of the Psychic

Era: the Dawn of the Millennium. Today it is known, among thinkers and investigators, that Thought is Power. It is THE Power that controls all other Power. THOUGHT is POWER! THOUGHT IS POWER! This is the greatest discovery.

Henry Harrison Brown

And saith unto him, Every man at the beginning doth set forth good wine; *and when men have well drunk, then that which is worse: but thou hast kept the good wine until now.* (Book of John:10)

This is true of every man when he enters into truth. He sets out with high spirits and ambitions. He is the new broom that sweeps clean and he is full of good intentions. Oftentimes he forgets the Source of his power and becomes drunk with power, so to speak. In other words, he misuses the law and selfishly takes advantage of his fellow man. We find that many times men in high places become conceited, opinionated, and arrogant. This is all due to ignorance of the law. The law is that power, security, and riches are not to be obtained externally. They must come from the treasure-house of consciousness. If you remain in tune with the Infinite, you discover that you are always drinking of the wine of life, love, joy, and happiness. To the spiritually-minded man, God (consciousness) is the Eternal Now and his good is present at every moment of time and point of space.

Many people are drunk in the Biblical sense when they are full of fear, grief, and other discordant states. That is being drunk emotionally. The wonderful news is that God (consciousness) is the Eternal Now. You can change your thought this moment, and you change your destiny. At any moment of the day you can gather your mental garments together and go on a great psychological feast of joy and happiness. Enter on the high watch by realizing the ever-availability of the God-Presence and its immediate response to your thought. All our good is in the Greater Now. We have to leave the present now (our limitation) and imagine the reality of our desire in the meditative state. What you have seen and felt in the Greater Now, your consciousness, you shall see objectified as you walk through time and space. We will see our beliefs expressed. Man is belief expressed. (Quimby).

Joseph Murphy

Our thoughts must be concentrated to be efficacious. We must think clearly and specifically of that which we wish to demonstrate. All else must be excluded. As Divine Spirit is all pure, holy, good, so we must think only pure, holy and good thoughts if we would bring forth right conditions. We never reach positive results by dwelling upon the negative side. That is why we, who believe in the power of thought, must not allow our thoughts to concentrate upon evil, sin and disease. Depressing thoughts breed disease. Let the sunshine flood your mentality.

Do not say that you are stupid or dull or unhappy. Realize that you are a part of the great Spirit, and not an insignificant personality. When you merge that personality into the great and holy Spirit, the creative power, gloom is dispersed and life made beautiful. Love and truth, joy and happiness, are beautiful because they are the expression of Deity. Therefore, words are concrete thoughts. As thoughts are of value so the words will be of value. Prayers are thoughts, and all of our thoughts should be prayers. We may pray without ceasing only when every thought, every breath is a prayer.

Kathleen M. H. Besly

Surgeons report that after a great victory, for instance, the wounds of the soldiers, as has been noticed in many similar instances, heal much more rapidly than the wounds of the soldiers in the defeated army, showing that the mental exhilaration, which accompanies the consciousness of victory, is a stimulant, a tonic, while conversely the despondency, which accompanies defeat, is also a physical depressant.

The cells are practically an extension of the brain. Each is a substation connected with the central station of the brain. Anger, hatred, jealousy or malice in the brain means anger, hatred, jealousy or malice in every cell in the body. Trouble in the brain means trouble everywhere. Happiness in the brain means happiness everywhere. When the mind is full of hope, bright prospects, the body is full of hope, alert, efficient, eager to work. When there is discouragement in the mind there is discouragement, despondency everywhere in the body. Ambition is paralyzed, enthusiasm blighted, efficiency strangled.

For a long time surgeons have known that certain kinds of cancer are produced by mental influences; that not only cancerous tendencies latent in the system are thus aroused and their development encouraged, but that some kinds of cancers, even when there is no previous hereditary tendency or taint may be absolutely originated in this way. This scientific conclusion has been tremendously emphasized by the great increase in the development of cancer in those who have been hard hit by the war, especially those who have lost relatives or dear friends, or whose loved ones have been frightfully mangled, maimed for life. Their peculiar mental suffering, the mingled worry, grief and anxiety of these people has aggravated cancerous tendencies and originated many new cases of cancer where no previous tendencies to that dread disease existed.

A great Paris specialist, Dr. Theodore Truffler, cites a case where a patient who showed no predisposition whatever to cancer developed it after much mourning for the loss of his two sons in battle. This grief had simulated into a real cancer eruption which before had been apparently unimportant.

Not only do worry, fear, and anxiety and great grief induce cancer, but hatred, grudges, chronic jealousy, also originate several different kinds of cancer, and even materially hasten the development of cancerous tendencies which they do not originate. Many kinds of skin disease, kidney trouble, dyspepsia, liver trouble, brain and heart trouble, are now known to result from mental causes, such as chronic hatred and jealousy. These keep the blood and other secretions in a state of chronic poisoning, which devitalizes the whole body and encourages the development of latent disease tendencies or of disease germs.

Every physician knows that discouragement is a depressant, that melancholia will greatly increase the activity and hasten the development of physical diseases. We little realize what we are doing when we are constantly sending messages of discouragement, of fear, of worry through all the billions of cells in the body. We little realize what it means when we talk discouragement, when we give up to the "blues," when we lose courage, faith, hope, and confidence in ourselves. It really means panic, disorganization, all through the cell life of the body. Mental depression is felt in every remotest cell. It unnerves every organ, and reduces the entire organism to a state of weakness and inefficiency, if not to utter collapse.

This is the reason why people sometimes fall in a faint from the shock of bad news, when sudden death or a frightful accident comes to those dear to them. The painful sensation it causes is not all in the head; it is not all in the brain. The effect of the shock visits every cell in the body. They are depressed all over. The whole cell life feels the shock. Every bit of bad, discouraging news, depression, fear, worry, anxiety, jealousy, hatred, . . these send their disintegrating messages through all the cell colonies, all the dependencies in the body.

On the other hand, good news, the expectation of better things, the renewal of hope, confidence, the upbuilding of faith in glorious things that are coming in the near future . . these act like a tonic on those who are "down and out." They refresh and renew the entire being.

Orison Swett Marden

Thought is at the bottom of all progress or retrogression, of all success or failure, of all that is desirable or undesirable in human life. The type of thought we entertain both creates and draws conditions that crystallize about it, conditions exactly the same in nature as is the thought that gives them form. Thoughts are forces, and each creates of its kind, whether we realize it or not.

The great law of the drawing power of the mind, which says that like creates like, and that like attracts like, is continually working in every human life, for it is one of the great immutable laws of the universe. For one to take time to see clearly the things he would attain to, and then to hold that ideal steadily and continually before his mind, never allowing faith . . his positive thought-forces . . to give way to or to be neutralized by doubts and fears, and then to set about doing each day what his hands find to do, never complaining, but spending the time that he would otherwise spend in complaint in focusing his thought-forces upon the ideal that his mind has built, will sooner or later bring about the full materialization of that for which he sets out.

There are those who, when they begin to grasp the fact that there is what we may term a "science of thought," who, when they begin to realize that through the instrumentality of our interior, spiritual, thought-forces we have the power of gradually molding the everyday conditions of life as we would have them, in their early enthusiasm are not able to see results as quickly as they expect and are apt to think, therefore, that after all there is not very much in that which has but newly come to their knowledge.

They must remember, however, that in endeavoring to overcome an old habit or to grow a new habit, everything cannot be done all at once. In the degree that we attempt to use the thought-forces do we continually become able to use them more effectively. Progress is slow at first, more rapid as we proceed. Power grows by using, or, in other words, using brings a continually increasing power. This is governed by law the same as are all things in our lives, and all things in the universe about us.

Ralph Waldo Trine

Sickly thoughts about oneself, about one's body and food, should be abolished by all who are called by the name of man. The man who imagines that the wholesome food he is eating is going to injure him, needs to come to bodily vigor by the way of mental strength. To regard one's bodily health and safety as being dependent on a particular kind of food which is absent from nearly every household, is to court petty disorders. The vegetarian who says he dare not eat potatoes, that fruit produces indigestion, that apples give him acidity, that pulses are poison, that he is afraid of green vegetables and so on, is demoralizing the noble cause which he professes to have espoused, is making it look ridiculous in the eyes of those robust meat eaters who live above such sickly fears and morbid self-scrutinies.

To imagine that the fruits of the earth, eaten when one is hungry and in need of food, are destructive of health and life is to totally misunderstand the nature and office of food. The office of food is to sustain and preserve the body, not to undermine and destroy it. It is a strange delusion . . and one that must react deleteriously upon the body . . that possesses so many who are seeking health by the way of diet, the delusion that certain of the simplest, most natural, and purest of viands are bad of themselves, that they have in them the elements of death, and not of life. One of these food-reformers once told me that he believed his ailment (as well as the ailments of thousands of others) was caused by eating bread; not by an excess of bread, but by the bread itself; and yet this man's bread food consisted of nutty, home-made, whole meal loaves. Let us get rid of our sins, our sickly thoughts, our self-indulgences and foolish excesses before attributing our diseases to such innocent causes.

James Allen

It may seem almost incredible to you, but it is a fact, that all successful men owe their greatness to their earnest, forceful, concentrated thought vibrations. They fixed their mind upon a certain line of thought; brought the aid of Will . . the recognition of the I AM . . to bear on that line of thought; allowed that line of thought to mold their characters; went straight to the mark at which they and aimed in the beginning. Others had aimed for the same mark, but failed because they failed to hold the thought, and had allowed themselves to become discouraged, intimidated, tempted or coaxed away from their ideal.

The requisites for the successful follow-up of a thought ideal to the end, are, first, an overpowering Desire (not a mere wish); second, a strong belief in your ability to accomplish your desire (not a mere half-hearted faith); and, third, an invincible Determination to win (not a mere back boneless . . "I'll try to").

It is a strange thing and difficult to explain (without leading you into metaphysical depths), but the measure of success by this plan seems to depend materially upon your belief in the force. A half-hearted belief will bring only half-way results, whilst an earnest, firm, confident belief that "your win will come to you" will accomplish results little short of marvelous. Cultivate that sort of belief, and accompany it with a firm mental demand for what you want, and you will succeed. "Ask and you shall receive, knock and it shall be opened unto you," but accompany the asking and knocking with the firm belief and expectation of Success. Helen Wilman says: "He who dares assert the I May calmly wait While hurry fate Meets his demand with sure supply."

But the words "calmly wait" refer only to the state of mind . . and indicates that calm, confident expectation of a "sure thing." It does not mean that a man shall sit down and fold his hands and do nothing more than "calmly wait" for "hurrying fat" to drop his reward in his lap. Oh, no. Helen Wilmans never meant that . . she is not built that way. The man, who is possessed of the dominating desire, and concentrated thought impulses, does not sit down and merely wait . . he couldn't do that without sacrificing his keen desire and earnest pursuit. "Thought manifests itself in Action" . . the firmer the thought, the stronger the action. You may want a thing in the worst way, and be fully confident of your ability to secure it, but you are going after that thing the best way you know how, and are "going to get it." You will agree with Garfield, who said, "Do not wait for a thing to turn up . . go out and turn something up," with all your might and main, but carrying with you the calm demand that that thing will be "turned up as the result of your going out and turning." And you will feel all the time the confident expectation of the "thing" obeying your command.

I wish that my space would allow me to tell you of the wonderful results of this plan of thinking and acting, but I can merely touch upon it and call your attention to the workings of the Law. But, after all, one must learn a thing by experience before they will appreciate its truth. The I AM is not satisfied in any other way. You will have to accept what I say on faith, at first, but you will soon begin to demonstrate its correctness by personal experience, and then you will know it to be true, and will push forward toward Success. Anything is yours, if you only want it hard enough. Just think of it. ANYTHING. Try it. Try it in earnest and you will succeed. It is the operation of a mighty Law.

William Walker Atkinson

The day that starts wrong can often be made right by a single effort of the will and the resolution not to be upset by trifles. A simple and effective method for overcoming an inharmonious condition, brought about by immediate proximity with someone who is forcefully sending out destructive thoughts, or by your own carelessness in allowing these thoughts to remain in your mind, is to get away from everyone for a few moments, sit down, relax, breathe deeply and rhythmically for a few moments and insist that you are in harmony with the universe.

The constant repetition of the words, "I AM harmony, I AM harmony, I AM harmony," has such a soothing effect that it is strange it is not often used. Yet, because we take it for granted that people must indulge in destructive thoughts, no one is at all surprised when a relative or friend rushes wildly into a room, prances about, and exclaims, "I AM so mad I can hardly stand it!" If the same person came in quietly, declaring "I AM harmonious!" nearly everyone would look up in surprise.

Benjamin Johnson

Our conscious and subconscious mind are always interacting and from their union come forth all our experiences, conditions, and circumstances whether positive or negative. The harmonious and peaceful interrelationship of these two phases of our mind produce health, success, and joyous living. The male element in you may be considered as your thought, idea, plan, image, or purpose; the female in you is emotion, feeling, enthusiasm, faith, and receptivity. The male and female principle exists in all of us, and this is the reason you are creative and have the power to bring forth out of the depth of yourself that which you emotionalize and feel as true within yourself. When your idea and feeling unite and become one, that one is God in action, for your Divine Creative Power is now made manifest as guidance, healing, or true place in life.

There is one Creative Power in all the world, and that Creative Power is God. When you discover the power of your thought and feeling, you have discovered the Power of God in yourself. All the trials, tribulations, sufferings, and misery of our neurotic age are due to the inharmonious interaction between the conscious and the subconscious of men and women everywhere. When you enthrone the proper concepts and ideas in the conscious mind, these will generate the right feeling; then the mind and the heart or the male and female principle are working together in concord and unity.

If our thoughts are negative, our feelings will also be negative because emotions follow thought. If your thoughts are fearful, vicious, or destructive, powerful negative emotions are generated and lodged in the inner recesses of your subconscious mind. These negative emotions get snarled up and form complexes, and inasmuch as emotions must have an outlet, it is obvious that such emotions will erupt in disease and destructive mental aberrations of all kinds.

Joseph Murphy

Mankind is divided into two types, positive and negative. Let me try and describe each to you.

Positive man is magnetic, attractive, courageous, happy, cheerful, healthy, energetic, is full of vitality, power and ability to succeed. He never doubts his ability to win, he never worries when things go wrong; he does not complain when things are not smooth. If he meets with a temporary set-back he becomes the more determined to succeed. He does not lay upon other people the blame of his own mistakes, but instead learns a lesson from his temporary failure which shall be a guide and beacon in all future undertakings. The positive man can always find people to believe in him and to finance his operations. He never lacks friends, for just the type of people he wants are always anxious to be his friends. Consequently men, and with them, opportunities, are always coming his way. He is an optimist, but is not foolish or blind in his optimism. He is above being petty or mean, or selfish or cruel; neither does he let hate or anger sway him or influence his life or business. He inspires confidence, compels attention, is a leader rather than a follower, and literally exudes an atmosphere of success.

A negative man is, of course, the antithesis of this type. He is fearful, given to worry, apt to look on the dark side of things. Is afraid to act too much on his own responsibility and seeks the help and advice of other people. Has difficulty in making up his mind, and when he has made it up he often changes it. He lets others pass him in the race of life and then worries because he fails to get on. He is never much of a success in life, no matter what he achieves he might have done very much better. He seldom realizes that his failures are due to his own failings but, instead, lays the blame upon other people's shoulders or ascribes his troubles to chance or ill fortune. His company is not cheerful and is not sought by other people, except one or two as miserable as himself.

All his thought and conversation are tinged with pessimism and his face, in course of time, becomes lugubrious and miserable, an accurate index of the state of mind within. He has no belief in himself. He believes in fate and the influence of outside circumstances. He is, so he says, as God made him and as environment has shaped him. If he is a failure it is, he thinks, not his fault, and if his character is not all that it might be it is due to heredity and environment. There are, of course, infinite degrees of positiveness and also of negativeness.

Therefore one may be said to be more positive or less positive according to one's stage of development, or one can be more negative or less negative according to the degree of helplessness and misery in which one may be steeped; but the essential difference is this, that whereas the positive man looks within for his power to achieve, and looks forward with confidence to the future, the negative person, on the contrary, having no confidence in himself, looks to others and outside sources for help and assistance and fears what fate may bring him. The positive man believes in himself completely and absolutely, the negative person does not; that is the great difference.

It is hardly necessary to point out that all successful people are of the positive type and all the failures belong to the negative class. If you were able to make an examination of the minds of numbers of successful men ranging from such as Lord Northcliffe, Lord Haig and Lloyd George down to the successful tradesman in your own village or suburb, you would find them to be all of this positive type. If you could examine the minds of the leaders of the professions, the surgeons, physicians, lawyers, counsel, artists, journalists and poets, you would find them all of the positive type. On the other hand, if you get into conversation with a failure it does not matter what station in life he may belong to or what his education may have been . . he may be a discredited politician, or a tramp on the road . . you will find that his mind is of the negative type. It is obvious then that he who desires to succeed must belong to the positive type. If he belongs to the wrong class how can it be remedied?

We are what we are as a result of past thinking. Our mental attitude is built up by the thoughts we habitually harbor or cultivate. Thus if we entertain positive thoughts only, and deny negative thoughts, replacing them by their opposites whenever they intrude, we gradually build up a positive attitude of mind, which means that we become positive men or women, and as such cannot fail to be successful in life. Therefore it all comes back to the old question of thought control. "For one to govern his thinking, then, is to determine his life."

Thoughts are positive if they dwell upon the following: Success, achievement, accomplishment, overcoming, conquering, mastering, prosperity, power, courage, calmness, dignity, perseverance, purposefulness, patience, wisdom, faithfulness, confidence, faith, hope, cheerfulness, love, joy, peace, health and happiness.

Thoughts are negative if they dwell upon the following: Failure, difficulty, bad luck, hard lines, I can't, fear, dread, grief, worry, care, anxiety, loss, fate unfaithfulness, grievances, criticizing others, imputing bad motives to others, hate, envy, covetousness, brooding, lust, impurity immorality, selfishness, sensuality, misery, unhappiness, disease, ill-health and death. The former build up character of mind and health of body; they create serenity and peace. The latter break down the nervous system, produce ill health and disease, rob the life of nearly all its joys and destroy all hopes of success.

If you concentrate your thoughts upon the former for a few minutes and let the imagination play round each word, and call up in the mind just what it means, a sense of power, unlimited and all comprehensive will pervades one's being. This is the infinite powers of the subliminal mind being aroused. All these positive qualities which these words represent are within you, otherwise you could not arouse this sense of power. If, by concentrating your thoughts for a few minutes upon Success, a sense of unlimited powers of accomplishment stir within you, then you have actually within you unlimited powers of accomplishment. If, by thinking only of Joy for a few minutes, a sense of intense Joy pervades the mind, then you have simply called into activity an inexhaustible reservoir of Joy that already existed within you. You cannot call into activity that which does not exist. In the same way if you concentrate your thoughts upon a negative quality, such as misery, you will after a few minutes become gloomy and depressed, or if your mind dwells on fear, you will soon become full of dread and apprehension.

Therefore your success, health and happiness all depend upon the type of thought that you entertain. If your mind dwells upon positive thoughts only, then you become positive and by sustained action, successful. If, however, you think negative thoughts you become negative and consequently a failure.

How then shall you so control your thinking that only positive thoughts are allowed? The answer is, by eternal vigilance, constant watch and guard, and by incessant denials and affirmations. Whenever a weak or vile or unworthy thought attempts to enter your mind, deny its existence in your perfect Mental World, and affirm in its place a thought the exact opposite of the one which you have denied. For instance, the thought may come to you that you will fail at the examination for which you have shortly to sit or that a certain important interview will end disastrously for you, or that you will not be able to pay the rent next quarter day. Whatever the thought may be, if it is negative, deny it from the mind. Raise yourself into your perfect World of Mind and say "There is and can be no failure, man is a perfect mental creature, potentially all the powers of the Infinite are his, therefore he can never fail."

Henry Thomas Hamblin

The whole universe is alive with cosmic intelligence; it is Infinite Creative Mind at work. As we have already seen, mind gives birth to thought and then uses its thought as the model of its creation, just as the artist conceives the idea of his picture and then uses the ingenuity of his brain and hand to picture forth its beauties in form and color.

The mind, therefore, whether of the Universal or the Individual, has but *one* way to act at the beginning of any series; it must act by thought. And thought, in turn, always expresses in words. We always think in concrete terms or words.

So we are told by John, "In the beginning was the Word, and the Word was with God and the Word was God. All things were made by Him and without Him there was not anything made that was made." And we are told in another place in Scripture, "By the word of the Lord were the heavens made, and all the host of them by the breath of His mouth."

Fenwicke L. Holmes

Did you ever sit down alone within the silence and meditate carefully upon your actions, words and thoughts of the day?

If you have not, then you should do so. Interview yourself. Parade yourself AS YOU ARE before your own mind, and carefully weigh every view you get of yourself, and find out where you belong. We are but planting the seeds that shall be fruit of future lives. It will spring up into the grain we sow. We cannot harm one creature without harming ourselves more than anything else, and when we realize the Truths of this statement we may be able to keep ourselves on stronger ground.

True Mental Science is based upon the ground of Truth and Good Will to ALL men.

Godliness gives power, and power of godliness is greater than all power. When you can truthfully say that you think only good, sincere, uplifting thoughts toward all humanity you have accomplished the first and the hardest lesson of science . . True Soul Science. If you wish to develop your powers properly, sit alone quietly for ten or fifteen minutes every day and meditate upon thoughts of purity, love and peace to ALL. Include your enemies in your good will also, and you will be able to utilize and draw towards you all the forces of the Christs who have learned the most beautiful, but perhaps the hardest lesson of all . . to forgive. Remember that a thought is a vibration as strong as a charge of electricity, and goes in unerring accuracy in the direction in which it is sent.

It bears fruit of its kind.

It reaps what it sows.

And if you wish the best, then send out the best you have. Your thoughts mingle with the thoughts of others which are just like yours, and all these thoughts harbor, mingle together, and sustain, and strengthen each other and produce effects. Good, bad, indifferent, it is all the same. They float in waves, in masses, in the atmosphere of all minds, and cause these minds to act in harmony with them, and are able to influence every mind they come in contact with.

Much good can be accomplished through silent forces by this development of pure Soul Science. It is the first stage of the development of the Soul, and is, therefore, Mind-Soul Science. The Soul is the REAL. It is the connecting link between God and man. It is the Soul that vibrates in currents throughout the body, building and making that body in conformity to its laws and forces. Therefore, be careful what manner of sprit you have, lest it be reflected on your body.

F. E. Gariner and Dr. R. Swineburne Clymer

Man lives in a mind that presses in upon him from all sides with infinite possibilities, with infinite creative power. The divine urge of infinite love crowds itself upon him, and awaits his recognition. Being the image of this Power, his thought also must be the Word or cause it the life.

At the center of his being is all the power that he will need on the path of his unfoldment; all the mind that man has is as much of this Infinite Mind as he allows to flow through him. We have often thought of God as far off, and of man as a being separate from the All Good; now we are coming to see that God and man are one, and that that One is simply awaiting man's recognition, that he may spring into being and become to man all that he could wish or want.

"As the father has inherent life in himself, so hath he given to the Son to have life within himself." It could not be otherwise; we are all in Mind and Mind is always creating for us as we think; and as we are thinking creatures, always thinking, our happiness depends upon our thought. Let us consider the law of our life.

Ernest Holmes

Broadly speaking, feelings, thoughts, and acts are either constructive or destructive; they either help or hinder; either encourage growth or decay; either make or mar; either assist or retard evolution; either express love or hate; either represent + or —. If one should put two causes in operation, one a plus and the other a minus, and each of the same magnitude, their combined karma will be 1–1=0; one will have neutralized the other, both will have been dissipated, and neither will take form.

Eugene Del Mar

You think, and your thoughts materialize as experience; and thus it is, all unknown to yourself as a rule, that you are actually weaving the pattern of your own destiny, here and now, by the way in which you allow yourself to think, day by day and all day long.

It is altogether in your own hands. Nobody but yourself can keep you down. Nobody else can involve you in difficulty or limitation. Neither parents, nor wives, nor husbands, nor employers, nor neighbors; nor poverty, nor ignorance, nor any power whatever can keep you out of your own when once you have learned how to think.

Emmet Fox

Whether the individual is to move forward or not depends upon what he thinks. His actions, his intentions, his motives, his plans, his tendencies, his efforts . . all of these play their part, but they are all the products of thinking, and therefore are invariably like the process of thinking from which they sprang. Every thought is a power in the life where it is created and will either promote or retard the purpose of that life. Every thought you think is either for you or against you. It will either push you forward or hold you down.

When your own thought is against you all your actions, efforts, tendencies, plans, intentions, and everything that is produced by thought or directed by thought will also be against you; and conversely everything that you do with muscle or brain will be for you when your thought is for you. This is a fact the importance of which is certainly great. And since it has been fully demonstrated to be a fact we cannot afford to give it less than our most profound attention.

Christian Larson

One reason why the lives of many of us are so narrow and pinched, small and commonplace, is because we are afraid to fling out our desires, our longings, afraid to visualize them. We become so accustomed to putting our confidence only in things that we see on the physical plane, in the material that is real to the senses, that it is very difficult for us to realize that the capital power, the force that does things, resides in the mind. Instead of believing in our possession of the things we desire, we believe in our limitations, in our restrictions.

We demagnetize ourselves by wrong thinking and lack of faith. We see only the obstacles in our path, and forget that man, working with God, is greater than any obstacle that can oppose itself to his will. Benjamin Disraeli knew this when he said, "Man is not the creature of circumstances. Circumstances are the creatures of man." He demonstrated its truth in his own life. Alien in race and creed, with other circumstances apparently dead against him at the start, the resolute young Jew overcame all obstacles, and reached the goal of his ideal. He became Prime Minister of England, and was made Earl of Beaconsfield by his sovereign, Queen Victoria. Lowell did not utter a mere airy, poetic idea when he said, The thing we long for, that we are For one transcendent moment. He spoke a simple truth.

The poet is always the prophet. He goes ahead of the scientist, and points the way that leads upward to the ideal. Like faith, the poet knows and sees far in advance of the senses. He knows that the vision of our exalted moments is the model given us to make real on the material plane.

Orison Swett Marden

No man is helplessly bound. The very law by which he has become a self-bound slave, will enable him to become a self-emancipated master. To know this, he has but to act upon it . . that is, to deliberately and strenuously abandon the old lines of thought and conduct, and diligently fashion new and better lines. That he may not accomplish this in a day, a week, a month, a year, or five years, should not dishearten and dismay him. Time is required for the new repetitions to become established, and the old ones to be broken up; but the law of habit is certain and infallible, and a line of effort patiently pursued and never abandoned, is sure to be crowned with success; for if a bad condition, a mere negation, can become fixed and firm, how much more surely can a good condition, a positive principle, become established and powerful! A man is only powerless to overcome the wrong and unhappy elements in himself so long as he regards himself as powerless.

If to the bad habit is added the thought "I cannot" the bad habit will remain. Nothing can be overcome till the thought of powerlessness is uprooted and abolished from the mind. The great stumbling-block is not the habit itself, it is the belief in the impossibility of overcoming it. How can a man overcome a bad habit so long as he is convinced that it is impossible? How can a man be prevented from overcoming it when he knows that he can, and is determined to do it? The dominant thought by which man has enslaved himself is the thought I cannot overcome my sins. Bring this thought out into the light, in all its nakedness, and it is seen to be a belief in the power of evil, with its other pole, disbelief in the power of good. For a man to say, or believe, that he cannot rise above wrong-thinking and wrong-doing, is to submit to evil, is to abandon and renounce good.

By such thoughts, such beliefs, man binds himself; by their opposite thoughts, opposite beliefs, he sets himself free.

A changed attitude of mind changes the character, the habits, the life. Man is his own deliverer. He has brought about his thralldom; he can bring about his emancipation. All through the ages he has looked, and is still looking, for an external deliverer, but he still remains bound. The Great Deliverer is within; He is the Spirit of Truth; and the Spirit of Truth is the Spirit of Good; and he is in the Spirit of Good who dwells habitually in good thoughts and their effects, good actions.

Man is not bound by any power outside his own wrong thoughts, and from these he can set himself free; and foremost, the enslaving thoughts from which he needs to be delivered are I cannot rise, I cannot break away from bad habits, I cannot alter my nature, I cannot control and conquer myself, I CANNOT CEASE FROM SIN. All these can not's have no existence in the things to which they submit; they exist only in thought.

Such negations are bad thought-habits which need to be eradicated, and in their place should be planted the positive 'I can' which should be tended and developed until it becomes a powerful tree of habit, bearing the good and life-giving fruit of right and happy living.

Habit binds us; habit sets us free. Habit is primarily in thought, secondarily in deed. Turn the thought from bad to good, and the deed will immediately follow. Persist in the bad, and it will bind you tighter and tighter; persist in the good, and it will take you into ever-widening spheres of freedom. He who loves his bondage, let him remain bound. He who thirsts for freedom, let him come and be set free.

James Allen

Nearly all people are controlled by outer suggestions, and not by inner realizations. Ordinarily man thinks only what he sees others do, and hears others say. We must all learn so to control the inner life that outside things do not make an impression upon our mentalities. As we are thinking beings, and cannot help thinking, we cannot avoid making things happen to us, and what we need to do is so to control our thought processes that our thinking will not depart from the realization of that which is perfect.

Man is governed by a mind which casts back to him every thought he thinks; he cannot escape from this and need not try; it would be useless. The laws of mind are simple and easy to understand. The trouble with us has been that we have laid down great obstructions, and then have tried to overcome them. Stop trying, stop struggling, begin to be calm, to trust in the higher laws of life, even though you do not see them; they are still there.

Ernest Holmes

Man has the power to cause any event to transpire that he may decide upon; though to accomplish this it is necessary to understand the law of action and reaction as applied both to the physical and metaphysical worlds.

When man begins to recreate himself, he will rise superior to his present position; and since new and better opportunities always appear when man proves himself superior to his present position, he can, by changing himself as he desires, call forth any opportunity that he may desire.

To have the privilege to take advantage of better opportunities, is the direct path to better conditions, better circumstances and better environments; and since man can create this privilege at will, he can create his own fate, his own future, his own destiny.

However, the secret of creating this privilege at will, lies in man's power to form only such impressions upon his mind as will originate constructive thought. Because when all the thought he thinks is constructive, every mental process will be a building process, and will constantly increase the ability, the capacity and the personal worth of man himself. This in turn makes man competent to accept the larger places that are waiting everywhere for minds with sufficient capability to fill them.

Every thought has creative power; and this power will express itself according to the desire that was in mind when the thought was created. Therefore, if every thought is to express its creative power in the building up of man, mind must constantly be filled with the spirit of that purpose. When the desire for growth and superior attainment does not predominate in mind, the greater part of the creative energy of thought will misdirect, and artificial mental conditions will form, only to act as obstacles to man's welfare and advancement.

The creative power of thought is the only power employed in the construction and reconstruction of man; and for this reason man is as he thinks.

Consequently, when man thinks what he desires to think, he will become what he desires to become. But to think what he desires to think, he must consciously govern the process through which impressions are formed upon mind.

To govern this process is to have the power to exclude any impression from without that is not desired, and to completely impress upon mind every original thought that may be formed; thus giving mind the power to think only what it consciously chooses to think.

Before man can govern this process, he must understand the difference between the two leading attitudes of mind . . the attitude of self-submission, and the attitude of self-supremacy; and must learn how to completely eliminate the former, and how to establish all life, all thought, and all action absolutely upon the latter.

When this is done, no impression can form upon mind without man's conscious permission; and complete control of the creative power of thought is permanently secured. To master the creative power of thought is to master the personal self; and to master the personal self is to master fate.

Christian Larson

To fear loss, to feel hurt, to mourn over that which is passing is to give reality to the negative side of life, and to draw greater evil in its train. By the law of attraction we draw outer things to correspond to our inner thought and feeling, and soon the thing we greatly feared has come upon us. Rather let us say, "What is that to me? I really don't care. Now I start forgetting." Then we are ready for positive thinking. Then we put up to the Creative Mind the image of the good we desire and the law of correspondences will bring it to us. We claim from the law anything we desire from friends to fortune, but we do not demand this particular friend or that identical fortune. That is hypnotism and dictation to the law as to how it shall work.

That might be to demand something that will bring us hurt. Rather must we hold up the perfect idea of the good we seek and let Divine Mind specialize it for us and manifest it in form. We must follow the command, "Follow thou me." We are to follow not after the negative, but after the positive; we are to seek first the kingdom of consciousness, the inner spirit and faith in life, and all things shall be added unto us.

Fenwicke L. Holmes

A prolific source of suffering arises from the violation of the mental laws. Few people have the slightest conception that their thinking has a corresponding effect upon themselves and the external world. Yet it is in his creative capacity that man most closely resembles his Creator. THOUGHT IS THE CREATIVE POWER! BEWARE HOW YOU USE IT! Harboring thoughts of hate, envy, malice, ill-will, jealousy and the rest of their breed is inviting certain disaster. It is the nature of thoughts to become objective and man then finds himself surrounded by his mental creations.

Frank L. Hammer

We send out a vibration or current, or thought, of good will, love, and peace to our fellowmen. That vibration is drawn to others similar to itself. It draws strength from them, and becomes more or stronger. A dozen thoughts sent out accumulate yet more. These thoughts respond to thought. The hand in an act of evil deeds will draw back and respond in unity to the repentant that controls it. In this way the body, the dwelling place of the soul, becomes illuminated . . a Light of Goodness and Truth.

F. E. Gariner and Dr. R. Swineburne Clymer

"As a man thinketh in his heart, so is he"; the Bible reiterates this statement telling us many times of the creative power of thought; Jesus taught nothing else; He said "the words which I speak unto you, they are Spirit and they are life."

The Centurion coming to Jesus recognized the power of the word spoken by the latter. He said, "I also am one in authority"; but his authority was on the physical plane, and he saw that Jesus had authority on a Spiritual plane, for he said, "Speak the word only."

The Bible also tells us that the word (thought) is not afar off but in our own mouth. It is neither here nor there; it is within every living soul. We must take the responsibility for our own lives. All must awake to the facts that they have absolute control over their lives, and that nothing can happen by chance. Then they will have a broader concept of God, a greater tolerance for their neighbor, and a greater realization of their own divine nature. What a relief from strenuous labor; no more struggle or strife. "Be still and know that I AM God, and beside me there is none other." The Spirit being all there is, we cannot conceive of anything that can hinder its working. When the Spirit has spoken (thought), the Word becomes Law, for before the Law is the Word; It precedes all else.

Ernest Holmes

If all of the poverty-stricken people in the world today would quit thinking of poverty, quit dwelling on it, worrying about it and fearing it; if they would wipe the poverty thought out of their minds, if they would cut off mentally all relations with poverty and substitute the opulent thought, the prosperity thought, the mental attitude that faces toward prosperity, they would soon begin to change conditions.

It is the dwelling on the thing, fearing it, the worrying about it, the anxiety about it, and the terror of it that attracts us to it and attracts it to us. We cut off our supply current and establish relations with want, with poverty-stricken conditions.

Many people who have become interested in the new philosophy are greatly disappointed that they are not making any appreciable demonstration over poverty, that they are not advancing their position in life, not improving their conditions as they had expected they would.

Now, my friend, the law of abundance, of opulence, is as definite as the law of gravitation, and works just as unerringly. If you are not demonstrating as you expected to, you are probably still held under the bond of mental limitation, for there is no lack in "Him in whom all fullness lies." There is no limitation in the all-supply. The trouble is you try to tap it with a miserable little half or quarter inch pipe instead of a great big one, and the supply cannot flow through and flood your life with abundance.

If you pinch your supply pipe with your doubts and fears, your anxiety, the terror of coming to want, if you do not believe you can demonstrate abundance, you will get but a meager, limited supply instead of the inexhaustible flow you might have. In other words, the supply pipe is pinched only by your own mental limitations. By your doubts and fears and worries and unbelief, you can cut off all the supply and starve or, by a great magnetizing faith, a superb confidence in the all-supply, you can flood your life with all good things.

The law of supply is scientific. It will not act unless all the necessary conditions are fulfilled. Simply believing in the new philosophy and still keeping your old life doubts and fear habits, living in your old thought habits of lack and poverty, inefficiency, will not bring success. If you don't believe you will prosper and you don't practice what you believe, you will get no results. If you would reap its fruits you must obey the law of supply, the law of abundance, the law of prosperity.

Prosperity never comes by merely wishing or longing for it. Keeping your mind fixed on it, simply thinking of prosperity will never bring it to you. This is only the first step. You must cling to your prosperity thought, your prosperity ideal, but you must also back it up with scientific methods, the practical common-sense methods which all successful men employ in their work. You might dream of abundance and prosperity all your life-time and die in the poorhouse, if you did not back up your dream with businesslike efficiency methods.

That is, you must be methodical, orderly, systematic, accurate, thorough, and industrious. You must do everything to a finish. You must fling your energy, your heart into your business, your profession, your work, whatever it is.

One of the worst things about poverty is that it induces the habit of expecting poverty and failure, the habit of being half reconciled to its necessity. No matter how poor you may be, if you have the right mental attitude you will not long remain poor. If you are determined to turn your back upon poverty and face toward prosperity, however your actual conditions may contradict this; if you really believe that you are a child of the Creator and Possessor of all things, that you were not intended for poverty, but that on the contrary the good things, the beautiful things of life are for you, the life glorious and not the pauper or the drudge life, you at once open your mind to the inflow of the prosperity current.

Orison Swett Marden

The body is the image of the mind, and in it are traced the visible features of hidden thoughts. The outer obeys the inner, and the enlightened scientist of the future may be able to trace every bodily disorder to its ethical cause in the mentality.

Mental harmony, or moral wholeness, makes for bodily health. I say makes for it, for it will not produce it magically, as it were . . as though one should swallow a bottle of medicine and then be whole and free . . but if the mentality is becoming more poised and restful, if the moral stature is increasing, then a sure foundation of bodily wholeness is being laid, the forces are being conserved and are receiving a better direction and adjustment; and even if perfect health is not gained, the bodily derangement, whatever it be, will have lost its power to undermine the strengthened and uplifted mind.

One who suffers in body will not necessarily at once be cured when he begins to fashion his mind on moral and harmonious principles; indeed, for a time, while the body is bringing to a crisis, and throwing off, the effects of former inhamonies, the morbid condition may appear to be intensified.

As a man does not gain perfect peace immediately he enters upon the path of righteousness, but must, except in rare instances, pass through a painful period of adjustment; neither does he, with the same rare exceptions, at once acquire perfect health. Time is required for bodily as well as mental readjustment, and even if health is not reached, it will be approached.

If the mind be made robust, the bodily condition will take a secondary and subordinate place, and will cease to have that primary importance which so many give to it. If a disorder is not cured, the mind can rise above it, and refuse to be subdued by it. One can be happy, strong, and useful in spite of it.

The statement so often made by health specialists that a useful and happy life is impossible without bodily health is disproved by the fact that numbers of men who have accomplished the greatest works . . men of genius and superior talent in all departments . . have been afflicted in their bodies, and today there are plenty of living witnesses to this fact. Sometimes the bodily affliction acts as a stimulus to mental activity, and aids rather than hinders its work. To make a useful and happy life dependent upon health, is to put matter before mind, is to subordinate spirit to body.

Men of robust minds do not dwell upon their bodily condition if it be in any way disordered . . they ignore it, and work on, live on, as though it were not. This ignoring of the body not only keeps the mind sane and strong, but it is the best resource for curing the body. If we cannot have a perfectly sound body, we can have a healthy mind, and healthy mind is the best route to a sound body.

James Allen

God is the Great Invisible Mind . . the pure, omnipresent, omniscient, omnipotent, invisible principle of the universe, pervading everything that is. When the mind of man tries to conceive of this Great Mind, the process is much like the passing of steam into the condenser . . the impulse or desire of the Great Mind, and which in turn gives an impulse or desire to the lesser mind of man, and we have a semi-liquidation, or thought, which thought, through association, suggestion, or what not, is the cause of a further "liquefaction," and we have that material form which is described by Webster as a "thing."

Hence, most of the thoughts we think are the result of a "double-distilled" thought process, the "waters over the face of the universe," the condensation of the divine essence of thought, or divine impulse, into a thought which causes the upheaval, the recurrence of thoughts which we have heretofore dropped into the subconscious . . not the result of a direct connection with divine thought essence, which we receive in all its purity only through going to the fountain head direct.

But man, when he goes into the silence, does not have to let the process go on into the second thought stage. He is entitled, through his divine heritage, to appropriate the original desire of the Infinite Mind, and identify himself with the great ocean of thought which never becomes contaminated by human feeling, thought, emotion, aspirations or ambitions, but which, through the centuries, motionless, unchangeable, lying in perfect poise in, behind and through everything that is, is yearning to be recognized and appropriated and trusted for guidance by its children. Thus man, in the silence, becomes, as it were, a spigot of the great cask of Divine Mind, from which he can appropriate, through a recognition of the all-supply, whatsoever he chooses. In the perfect silence he is a creator . . he desires that the Great Mind shall desire through him, and thus he identifies himself with the impulse which creates the thought of the Divine Mind, thereby making an at-one-ment with the source of all creation, not its effects.

This conscious identity with the source, through the silence, is a constant, living denial of the things which retard, hinder and obscure our perception of things divine, which cannot find expression because of the jumbled mass of human thoughts lodged in the subconscious mind. Through this divine affirmation, or recognition of the divine origin of all things, the subconscious and conscious minds are cleansed and purified, and filled with the thoughts which comply with the Divine Law.

This is a subconscious and conscious unity with Divine Mind, and the body reflects that which is within; it glows with the light of the inner man; it out-pictures health, happiness, joy, satisfaction in all things, and creates a yearning for the perfection which it knows it had in the beginning. It begins to understand and comprehend its inherent ability to live and express the spiritual nature which is within, and to live through all eternity, as is its right, because of its sonship with the Father of all.

When that relation with the Divine Mind is established, then will man receive first-hand the cause and not the recognition of its effect . . the desire of the Almighty, and not the creation of that desire. The unity will be so firm and close that the inspiration of the source will be the thought of the creation, with no intervening obstructions between divine thought and human action. Then will the body be filled with light, and be spiritualized. Then will every need be instantaneously supplied by a thought; then will man be lifted up, even as the "Son of Man" was glorified, and become one with the great Sea of Life, which throbs and thrills, and seeks expression through all that is.

Then, acting immediately and directly on the impulse or thought of the Great Mind, each son will perform his work unfalteringly and unwaivingly, and will know that the Great One has spoken to him. Then will be brought about the consummation of all human ideals . . the binding together of all humanity by one great tie of love, under the reign of eternal harmony and divine order. Conflicting human interests will be blended into one absorbing desire to serve the whole, and human passions and evil desires will melt away and be forever lost in a great universal holy brotherhood. Then shall man be restored to the Garden of Eden.

Charles H. Wolf

No matter how far your thought waves may travel, they retain a certain connection with you and exert an influence over you as well as others. You cannot easily get rid of the influence over you as well as others. You cannot easily get rid of the influence of these "children of your mind." If you have been sending out bad thoughts, you are subject to their influence, and your only hope is to neutralize and counteract them by sending out strong, new thought waves of the proper sort, or by asserting the I AM, and thereby creating a mental aura, or by both means.

The old saying "Like attracts like" and "Birds of a feather flock together," are both literally exemplified by the tendencies of thought waves. There is what is known as the "Adductive Quality of Thought," the word "adductive" being derived from the Latin word adductum, to bring to. The manifestation of this quality of thought is one of the most wonderful features in the realm of psychic phenomena.

Fear or worry thought will attract others of their own kind, and will combine with them, the result being that you will be afflicted not only by the product of your own mind, but also by those emanating from the minds of others, the whole forming a heavy burden. And the longer that you persist in that line of thought, the heavier will be your burden. On the other hand, if you think bright, cheerful and happy thoughts they will draw to themselves others of the same degree, and you will feel brighter, more cheerful and happier from their combined influence. This is absolutely true, but you are not asked to accept it on faith alone. Try it and be convinced. But, in the experiment, be sure to couple the thoughts with a feeling of confidence in the outcome, and you will obtain much better and quicker results. Half-hearted, doubting thoughts have only a small percentage of the force of confident, expectant ones.

If you think along the lines of discouragement, lack of confidence, "afraid to try," "know I can't" lines, you will attract to yourself the force of other murky thoughts of the same kind, and you will find that you really "can't," and moreover, everyone else will seem to entertain just the same opinion regarding your ability. But just brace up and send out earnest, confident, fearless, "I can and I WILL" thought waves, and you will attract to yourself the similar thought waves of others, which will still further stimulate and strengthen you, and help you to accomplish your aims.

If you send out jealous, envious thoughts, they will come home bringing their mates with them, and you will be wretched until the effect passes off. So will waves of hate return to harm you, having gained force and power on their journey. The old proverb "Curses like chickens come home to roost," is much nearer the real truth than is generally supposed. Anger thought arouses anger in the other man (unless he has rendered himself positive to them), and he sends back his return thought waves; besides which other anger waves mingle and help on the vicious work. You have heard people say, "A man always finds what he looks for." Of course he does, he cannot help it, for his thought attracts others of the same sort, and he sees a world of the same color as his mental spectacles.

Good thought attracts good . . evil thoughts, evil. If you hate a man and send him your hate thoughts, you will get hate in return, and will face a hating and hateful world. In the thought world, you get back what you send out . . with good interest. Send out kind thoughts and kind thoughts will return to you, with compound interest, and you will find yourself greeted by a kind, helping world, and will be much the gainer. If only from a selfish point of view, it pays to think the best thoughts. If you will practice thinking along these lines for, say, one month, you will find the greatest difference in things, the greatest change in yourself, and you will find that you look with aversions and disgust upon your old, mean, low, miserable way of thinking, and would not return to it under any consideration . . no, not for a fortune. Before the month will have passed you will be conscious of the helpful force of the responsive thought waves, and your life will seem entirely different to you. Try it. Try it now. You will never regret it.

There are two particularly bad thoughts, which you should root out, first of all, and you will find that, when you have rid yourself of the balance will die out of their own accord. I allude to Fear and Hate. These two following weeds are the parents of most of the others. Worry is the oldest child of Fear, and bears a close resemblance to its father. Envy, Malice, and Anger are some of the numerous broods claiming Hate as their parent. Destroy the "old ones" and you will not be troubled with their offspring.

William Walker Atkinson

One of the most eminent workers in this field of thought development states that he worked alone for five years before he saw the results he desired from his efforts, because he was associated during this time with strong-minded, sarcastic, critical and antagonistic people. However, he persevered until he overcame, and now he is teaching the rest of the world from his own experience.

You can make your wireless send out your messages of "Success" until your thought is recognized; or, if you so choose, you can spell "Failure." Some will receive your message and respond.

One little woman who has overcome much on her road to prosperity tells me she always thinks of her mind as a wireless station and she telegraphs "Success" "Love," "Harmony," and "Wealth" waves every day of her life. When things seem a little trying, she starts with "Harmony"; when everything is smooth, she works hardest on "Success," and her messages bring back the answers she desires in the way of better business, truer friends, and more desirable acquaintances.

"Like attracts like" is an infallible law in the thought world. If you desire "Harmony," be harmonious yourself.

Benjamin Johnson

All that a man achieves and all that he fails to achieve is the direct result of his own thoughts. In a justly ordered universe, where loss of equipoise would mean total destruction, individual responsibility must be absolute. A man's weakness and strength, purity and impurity, are his own, and not another man's. They are brought about by himself, and not by another; and they can only be altered by himself, never by another. His condition is also his own, and not another man's. His suffering and his happiness are evolved from within. As he thinks, so he is; as he continues to think, so he remains.

A strong man cannot help a weaker unless the weaker is willing to be helped, and even then the weak man must become strong of himself. He must, by his own efforts, develop the strength which he admires in another. None but himself can alter his condition.

It has been usual for men to think and to say, "Many men are slaves because one is an oppressor; let us hate the oppressor." Now, however, there is among an increasing few a tendency to reverse this judgment, and to say, "One man is an oppressor because many are slaves; let us despise the slaves." The truth is that oppressor and slave are cooperators in ignorance, and, while seeming to afflict each other, are in reality afflicting themselves. A perfect Knowledge perceives the action of law in the weakness of the oppressed and the misapplied power of the oppressor. A perfect Love, seeing the suffering which both states entail, condemns neither. A perfect Compassion embraces both oppressor and oppressed.

He who has conquered weakness, and has put away all selfish thoughts, belongs neither to oppressor nor oppressed. He is free.

A man can only rise, conquer, and achieve by lifting up his thoughts. He can only remain weak, and abject, and miserable by refusing to lift up his thoughts.

James Allen

"My words are spirit and they are truth; and they shall not return to me void; but shall accomplish that whereunto they were sent." How many of us grasp the real significance of this Biblical utterance? Or of this other: "And the word was made flesh and dwelt among us"? How many of us ever think that our own words, our uttered thoughts are living forces and are made flesh? Yet it is literally true that they are being out pictured in our body, are chiseling our physique, shaping our faces, molding our expression to their likeness.

What we think and say reappears not only in our expression, but also in our physical condition, in our health, good or bad, according to the nature of our thoughts and words. Every word we speak is an indestructible force, because it affirms a thought, a sentiment, an emotion, a motive, which never ceases to exert its power.

Jesus evidently recognized that words are real forces, for He said, "Heaven and earth shall pass away, but my word shall not pass away." Material things might pass away, but His word was a force which could never cease to exercise its power.

All through the Bible the power of the word is emphasized. "The 'Word was made flesh and dwelt among us," "The Word was with God, and the Word was God," "He sent His Word and healed them."

There is a mysterious power in the spoken word, in the vigorous affirmation of a thought, which registers a profound impression on the subconscious mind, and the silent forces within us proceed to make the word flesh, to make the thing we affirm a reality. There is a tremendous constructive power in registering your vow, in vigorous, determined affirmation, backed by a persistent, dogged endeavor to bring about the thing we desire.

Orison Swett Marden

Every thought in the universe seeks its own kind. There is a law of attraction which permeates the thought world. "Like attracts like." Every thought that we think, when sent out into the ether is immediately, through the force of its own law, drawn to its own kind. When we think a thought of anger it immediately joins the other thoughts of anger that have been sent out in the world and becomes a part of that thought-current. When we think a thought of impatience the same thing happens, only in a lighter degree.

When you think of faith immediately that thought joins the higher plane of thought and you become connected with the thought of faith. Every thought has its own thought-current. Every mental picture that you have has a corresponding mental current in the ether. By constantly concentrating upon one type of thought, you become connected with that thought-plane of the universe, and you become a channel for those thoughts to play through. Let us suppose that thought current be hate. You have been hating someone or something. You are constantly thinking upon this destructive thought. You make it a part of yourself; you work your emotions up to a high pitch over the affront, or whatever it is that has brought this thought of hate to you. The more you concentrate upon it the more you become connected with the hate thought of the universe, until you become a channel for that thought-current. Not only do you suffer for your own hate thought, but you suffer from the hate thought of the whole world. When you have carried this far enough it becomes an obsession, and when hate becomes an obsession there is murder in the heart. The murders of the world have oftentimes been committed because the murderer connected up with the murder-thought of the world, and he became obsessed with the thought of murder and nothing but the doing of the deed could satisfy the obsession.

Mrs. Evelyn Lowes Wicker

There is something that casts back at us every thought that we think. "Vengeance is mine, I will repay, saith the Lord," is a statement of eternal truth and correspondences against which nothing can stand, and whatever man sets in motion in mind will be returned to him, even as he has conceived within himself and brought forth into manifestation. If we wish to transcend old thoughts we must rise above them and think higher things: We are dealing with the law of cause and effect and it is absolute; it receives the slightest as well as the greatest thought and at once begins to act upon it.

And sometimes even when we know this we are surprised at the rapidity with which it works. If we have been misusing this law we need not fail; all that we have to do is to turn from the old way and begin in the new. We will soon work up out of the old law into the new which is being established for us. When we desire only the good the evil slips from us and returns no more.

Ernest Holmes

Each and every change in one's thought registers itself in the body, even though it does not always evidence itself at once on the surface. Each thought has either an affirmative and constructive tendency, or a negative and destructive one. The former represents Truth and is health giving, while the latter portrays falsity and is productive of disease. Health is normal and evidences itself in harmonious accord, while disease is abnormal and shows forth in discord and inharmony.

From the time when one becomes self-conscious and assumes responsibility for his own thinking, he takes his life in his own hands. Whether he knows it or not, he is influencing and determining both the interior and exterior conditions of his body, his health or disease, his relations to the world without and the God within, and he has become the arbiter of his own fate. The character analyst, from an examination of the exterior lines of one's body, can delineate very clearly the interior lines of thought that one has traversed, and the trend of their present direction.

Eugene Del Mar

Mind is the pattern by which the word creates, for before we speak into being the thing or condition which brings to us pleasure or pain, we have either consciously or unconsciously been fashioning that thing or condition in the mental workshop, have been impressing, as it were, this pattern on the creative substance within and all about us.

And it must come into sight, either in our acts or words, both of which express or objectify our thought children. In this way do our thoughts build themselves into our personalities, and so become what we appear to be.

Elinor S. Moody

Not only are we largely what we have thought ourselves into being, but we have around us largely those things that we have attracted to us by our thoughts. This may be objected to by some who say that they have reaped the things they feared, rather than the things they desired . . "the thing I feared has come upon me." But what of that? Is not a fear a mental state as much as is desire? Fear is the negative pole of the mental state of which the positive pole is desire. In both cases a strong mental picture is held, and the thought processes are set into operation to materialize it into objectivity.

The man who continually holds the mental picture of poverty in his mind, surely attracts those conditions to him. The man who holds the idea of prosperity before him attracts his own to himself. And right here, at this very place, we wish to give you the antidote and remedy for fear. It is this: If you dislike a thing, and therefore find yourself evincing a fear that it may materialize in your life . . stop right there and take mental stock of yourself. Then begin by steadily refusing to allow your mind to dwell upon the fear, but in its place build up the desire for, and the thought picture of, the very opposite thing . . the thing or condition which if realized will save you from the thing you are beginning to fear.

Then concentrate all your efforts upon the mental growth of this idea, desire, feeling, and hope for the thing you want . . and try to forget the thing you have feared, driving it out of your mind by will, and determination. You will find that by cultivating and dwelling upon the positives, you will neutralize and kill out the negatives. If you will but realize the value of this little bit of advice that we have just given you; and will begin to act upon it, you will ever look back upon this moment of the first reading of it, with feelings of joy and thankfulness. For it is the antidote for fear . . and fear is the deadly nightshade of the mind.

Each of use is a great thought-magnet, ever drawing to us things, persons, and environment . . circumstances even . . in harmony with our composite thoughts, and tending to enable those thoughts to express themselves. And at the same time we are ever repelling, driving away and repulsing the things of the opposite character. This being so, does it not become of the greatest importance for us to cultivate the right sort of thought-magnet, that we may draw to ourselves that which we would desire?

Does it not become our duty to drive out from our thought realm the thoughts that tend to attract to us the people and conditions calculated to pull us down in the quicksands of life?

Does it not become our duty to ourselves to drag up by the roots that deadly nightshade of the mind . . Fear? And with it its companion plants of Hate, Anger and jealousy, all of which tend to bring about undesirable conditions for us . . and all of which are negatives and not positives?

We are all thought-magnets whether we wish to be or not. And this being so is it not the height of folly to refuse to take advantage of the understanding of this law, and to cultivate the positive qualities of thought that will serve to draw to us the things that will aid us, and bring us greater happiness, health, and success? If asked to choose between the results of the positive qualities, and those of the negative qualities, no sane man or woman would hesitate a moment.

And yet many shiver on the brink of the great lake of life, unable to decide whether it is worthwhile to choose between the boat of Positivity which will take them safely across to the shore of Attainment, by the use of the oars of the will and the reason, on the one hand; or the rotten, heavy, flat-bottomed scow of Negativity, which has no oars, but just "drifts" along until it becomes waterlogged and sinks, on the other hand. It is a matter for your own choice. We have pointed out the way, and stated the rules . . you must do the rest. In the pattern of the day: "It is now up to you."

Edward Walker/William Walker Atkinson

Since it is natural to have definite aims in life, in fact absolutely necessary in order to be in harmony with the purpose of life, and since it is natural to move forward, it must be natural to have only such thoughts as are for you; thoughts that can push you forward and that will be instrumental in promoting the purpose you have in view. In other words, to comply with the laws of nature, physical and metaphysical, it is necessary to think in such a way that all mental action tends to produce growth, advancement and progress. In this connection we find that nature's laws do not conflict.

One law declares that the individual must move forward constantly if he would be in accord with nature, and another law declares that our thoughts will either promote or retard the forward movement. Therefore when our thinking retards our progress we violate natural law and will consequently produce conditions that are detrimental.

Christian Larson

When you have a real thing to do, keep it to yourself. Don't talk about it. Just know in your own mind what it is that you want and keep still about it. Often when we think that we will do some big thing we begin to talk about it and the first thing we know all the power seems to be gone.

This is what happens. We are all sending out into Mind a constant stream of thought; the clearer it is, the better will it manifest; if it becomes doubtful it will not have so clear a manifestation. If it is confused it will manifest only confusion. All this is according to the Law of Cause and Effect, and we cannot change that Law. Too often, when we tell our friends what we are going to do, they confuse our thought by laughing about it, or by doubting our capacity to do so large a thing. Of course this would not happen if we were always positive, but when we become the least bit negative it will react and we will lose that power of clearness which is absolutely necessary to good creative work.

When you want to do a big thing, get the mental pattern, make it perfect, know just what it means, enlarge your thought, keep it to yourself, pass it over to the creative power behind all things, wait and listen, and when the impression comes, follow it with assurance. Don't talk to anyone about it. Never listen to negative talk or pay any attention to it and you will succeed where all others fail.

Ernest Holmes

Our every word, thought and feeling thus finds expression in our body or personality. Each word or thought is a ruler, though it be king for but an instant; and the law is its servant. Our personality is the aggregate of our thinking expressed in form. The totality of our thinking makes us what we are. The aggregate of the thanking of a normal person is healthy. Therefore, he has health. The chronic invalid is one whose mind consciously or unconsciously dwells more on disease than health.

Some people appear always unlucky. They expect it; and the law works out their misfortune to its bitter conclusion. Others are proverbially "lucky." They expect luck and good fortune therefore smiles upon them. Our attitudes of mind therefore control our destiny. Men who succeed are found to be those who expect success and men who fail are those who most fear failure. Of course in any particular case it is not always possible to trace out the full working of the law of cause and effect, because so many elements work in. Often the habitually fearful have days of hope and the habitually hopeful have days of fear. What All of Us Need to Do, Therefore, Is to Bring up the Aggregate of Our Thinking for Health, Wealth, and Love So That It Shall Outbalance Any Possible Amount of Negative Thinking.

We all need to bring our thought up to the highest point of cheer that we possibly can so that we can counteract the currents of fear into which we may for a time allow ourselves to be swept.

And into these currents every one of us tends at times to be drawn through a false idea of sympathy. We allow ourselves to "feel sorry" about ourselves or someone else. The heart of great compassion naturally goes out in loving regard for those who are in the path of error, sorrow, or loss. This is right and natural. But many of us allow this sentiment to degenerate into pity, not for them, but for their misfortune. Instead of doing what we can to alleviate the suffering, we simply condole and "sympathize" with the error, thus allowing ourselves to feel the reality of "evil" or negation and so making ourselves at one with it. Pity of This Kind Is Evil. Do Not Indulge in It. Do Not Allow Yourself to Be Indulged in It. How easy it is for us to want others to sympathize with us, to pity us, to feel sorry about us! It is not only a great sign of weakness, it is also very selfish, and it opens us to all their negative thinking about us.

Fenwicke L. Holmes

This same power that brought universal substance into existence will bring your individual thought or mental picture into physical form. There is no difference in the power. The only difference is a difference of degree. The power and the substance themselves are the same. Only in working out your mental picture, it has transferred its creative energy from the Universal to the particular, and is working in the same unfailing manner from its specific center, your mind.

Genevieve Behrend

The thought that we encourage is the power that kills and makes alive. To fear is to fail; to dread is to despair. The action fits the word, and the word fits the thought. As we think, indeed, we are. Why not then entertain thoughts of happiness and hope, for we can conjure them if we wish, even when clouds hang low and life seems uninviting.

Henry Frank

The circumstances and conditions of life are out-pictured inner talking, solidified sound. Inner speech calls events into existence. In every event is the creative sound that is its life and being. All that a man believes and consents to as true reveals itself in his inner speech. It is his Word, his life.

Try to notice what you are saying in yourself at this moment, to what thoughts and feelings you are consenting. They will be perfectly woven into your tapestry of life. To change your life, you must change your inner talking, for "life", said Hermes, "is the union of Word and Mind". When imagination matches your inner speech to fulfilled desire, there will then be a straight path in yourself from within out, and the without will instantly reflect the within for you, and you will know reality is only actualized inner talking, your thoughts.

Neville Goddard

It cannot be emphasized too much that success is not a something to be won, instead it is rather a mental state, an attitude of the mind. The mind itself has unlimited power, and mental power or thought is the power or force that is greater than all power or forces, therefore the power to accomplish all things is within us. This potent power however, cannot find expression in the life if the attitude of the mind is wrong. When the mind is naturally of the success type or is made so by training, then its intense powers become focused into one powerful beam, which shapes and molds the outward life, on the form of the inward pattern.

There is nothing of "magic" about this, it is capable of the simplest explanation. When your mind is of this type, the impulses sent to the subconscious mind can only result in successful actions. As we have already seen, the subconscious mind is the seat of all action and contains unlimited power and energy. This power and energy only needs directing into the right channel to accomplish anything that we may desire to accomplish. When, therefore, the mind is cast in the "Success" mold, then only "success" thoughts and suggestions can go to the subconscious mind, and these in turn must of necessity be translated into successful actions.

The only difference between a successful type of man and an unsuccessful type, provided they are of equal energy, is one of mind . . of thought. The successful man's attitude of mind is such that he generates the right kind of thought, which passing to his subconscious mind, is transmuted into the right type of action. The unsuccessful man, on the other hand, through his mind being of a negative type, generates the wrong kind of thought and this in turn results in the wrong type of action. This is why it is impossible to keep the "success" type of man down for any length of time. You can bankrupt him, bereave him, maim him, cast him into the gutter and jump on him, and he will come to the top again. It is impossible to keep such a man down for long, simply because his mind will not allow it.

This also is why it is impossible to help a man of a negative type. The more one helps such a man the weaker and more hopeless he becomes, and the more helplessly he clings round one's neck for sustenance and support. Place him in affluent circumstances, find him work, prospects, influence, friends, place in his hands everything possible with which to aid him, and he will let it all slip through his fingers and come right down to want and penury. Therefore, success in life is the result of "success" actions, which are the result of "success" thoughts, which are the result of a "success" attitude of mind, and this is the result of the affirmation "I AM success."

As the attitude of the mind alters from negative to positive there is developed what is called personal magnetism; one radiates an influence which attracts people. It is impossible to estimate the difference which this alone makes to one's prospects of success. If a man is in business for himself, what an enormous difference the drawing influence of a well-ordered mind will make to that business. His clients or customers will increase a hundredfold in number, and a better type of client or customer will gradually be attracted.

Thus does success and prosperity crowd in upon the man or woman who cultivates the right type of mind. Once the right attitude of mind has been built up the trouble is not how to get business, but how to execute it. It comes crowding in so rapidly it is difficult to cope with.

Again, in all businesses difficulties appear from time to time, and although these may and do extinguish men of negative type, they cause only temporary trouble to one whose mind has been trained on "success" lines.

Henry Thomas Hamblin

Do you imagine evil of others? If you do, notice the emotion generated in your deeper self; it is negative and destructive to your health and prosperity. Circumstances can affect you only as you permit them. You can voluntarily and definitely change your attitude toward life and all things. You can become master of your fate, and captain of your soul (subconscious mind). Through disciplined, directed, and controlled imagination you can dominate and master your emotions and mental attitude in general.

If you imagine, for example, that the other is mean, dishonest, and jealous, notice the emotion you evoked within yourself. Now reverse the situation. Begin to imagine the same girl or boy is honest, sincere, loving, and kind; notice the reaction it calls forth in you. Are you not, therefore, master of your attitudes? In reality the truth of the whole matter is that it is your real concept of God (consciousness) which determines your Whole attitude toward life in general. Your dominant idea about God (consciousness) is your idea of life; for God (consciousness) is Life.

If you have the dominant idea or attitude that God (consciousness) is the Spiritual Power within you responsive to your thought, and that, therefore, since your habitual thinking is constructive and harmonious, this Power is guiding and prospering you in all ways; this dominant attitude will color everything. You will be looking at the world through the positive, affirmative attitude of mind. Your outlook will be positive, and you will have a joyous expectancy of the best.

Joseph Murphy

The thought consciously formed in the intelligent mind precedes the visible act, which then becomes a reproducing duplicate of the operation first planned in the mind. The thought therefore is the "cause" and the outward action becomes its natural "effect." The supreme fact that this is a matter of natural law, fundamental to all human and animal life, is rapidly assuming shape in the comprehension of thinking individuals everywhere. It has been too long overlooked by the majority. Its acceptance as a foundation fact of individual life opens up many channels of exceedingly interesting investigation.

Leander Edmund Whipple

Every thought travels in its own matter, that means, the magnetism which each thought attracts, for it must be remembered that it is a compounded variety, and as the thought is in quality, so will be the material which it sets in action. Mind never acts alone nor travels alone, but is clothed according to the law.

When we think of, and recognize evil, hatred, anger, jealousy, etc., we cannot attract to us good magnetism, but it will be in quality like the thoughts, and it is as certain to poison the blood into which the magnetism goes, as such thoughts are sure to inflict injury on the minds upon others. It will not be long until science finds out that all the incurable troubles of mind and body are caused by low thoughts, and we shall then find how easy it will be to cure.

When humanity learns to think orderly, that means to have high thoughts, and recognize the love principle, power and ability to become what is desirable, then there will not be so much sickness, as humanity will draw to itself the finer magnetism belonging to such thoughts, and the mind will be peaceful, and that will make the body strong and healthy.

The sooner we find out that it is our thoughts which make our lives unhappy, the sooner we shall change them and make it as habitual to think high as it is to think low.

When we can see practically that it is not so much what we do as what we think, then we shall have courage and individuality, and it will become manifest through our being, and we will find success in everything we undertake.

May E. Stevenson

The Omnipresence of good is in a positive state of harmony, health and perfection always. We show forth negative conditions because we think of them; we believe in them. They seem to be real to us. Consider for a moment the daily condition of your life. Do you have calmness and harmony in your home? If not, turn within and make a change there. We never. get anywhere by working with externals. We should bring out that which we know to be within. We must declare the truth of our divinity. We are declaring something all the time and our lives show what we are declaring. Whatever our declarations are, we may be sure they are going to bear fruit. Whatever we are sowing in thought, that will the harvest be. What we are really conscious of, we must manifest. From within, OUT is the law.

If we want to change all our old ways of thought and make God manifest, we begin by speaking words which we know to be the truth of our real being. We desert the old words of negation, and begin to practice the presence of God, the "I AM." We may not know it, but we have our own true name which God has given us from the beginning, and that name is "I AM." Whatever we declare in that name is made manifest to us, and we continually speak in that name. The Bible says: "Thou shalt not take the name of the Lord thy God in vain; for the Lord will not hold him guiltless that taketh His name in vain."

Whenever we declare a negative condition in the name of "I AM" we are bringing that condition into manifestation. When we hear people say, "I am sick!" we think within ourselves, how could "I AM" be sick. The "I AM" is never sick; is never weak; is never miserable; is never in poor health. The Spirit of God in us is always whole. We must get this impressed upon us so strongly that we will never again take the name of the Lord our God in vain. Never couple negative statements with "I AM." Our negative statements do not change the "I AM" but they make us feel sick, weak and uncomfortable.

We need to begin right at the beginning, right at the "I AM" to apply truth. We go back of effect to our real being. Change in thought produces corresponding change in the external. When we dwell in thought upon the Truth we necessarily express our divine nature. When we think only the thoughts of God after Him we shall have perfect harmony in our lives; then we will so know the truth that we cannot help but manifest it. Ail the ills of life arise from false thinking and false speaking and they must vanish as we think and speak the Truth.

Mrs. C. L. Baum

This is a marvelous revelation to man, the significance of which most of us have not grasped. Only here and there is there one who utilizes it in his daily living. But science is recognizing it. Edison says all scientists feel that "about and through everything there is the play of an Eternal Mind." They are recognizing that this is the first great Cause. It is difficult to realize that every instant, under the impulse of Eternal Mind, miracles are leaping out from the cosmic ocean of energy into objectivity to meet our wants, to supply all our needs. Most of us are not able to grasp the idea that there is wealth and beauty and unthinkable luxuries waiting here for God's children. And because of this we do not materialize the things we desire.

It is one of the most marvelous things, in this wonderful plan of creation, that we actually live, move and have our being in this invisible ocean of limitless creative material, and that all we have to do to attract what we want is to hold the right mental attitude toward it and do our best on the physical plane to match it with its reality. Noah might have lighted the Ark had he known enough. The force was there just as today. When we once get it firmly fixed in our minds that in this invisible world of possibilities is everything which matches every legitimate desire and ambition, and that our own will come to us if we visualize it intensely enough, persistently enough, and do our best to make it real, we will no longer live in poverty and misery.

If you want to get away from poverty, if you wish to demonstrate abundance, prosperity, you must form the habit of mentally living in abundance; live in the ideal of what you want; that is, you must live the prosperity thought, you must hold the thought of abundance. Saturate yourself with it. Then the poverty thought cannot touch you. It will be neutralized because you cannot hold in your mind two opposite thoughts at the same time, and whatever thought you hold is a real creative force.

The great majority of poor people are poor thinkers, poor planners, and poor executives. They do not think prosperity, they do not obey the law of opulence, and so they stay poor in the midst of abundance.

You can no more attain opulence while holding the opposite thought than a youth could become a great lawyer by concentrating upon something else, thinking of other things all the time. The specialist makes his mind a magnet to attract the thing he is trying to attain. He dwells upon it, thinks of it, bends all his energies toward it, dreams it, lives it; and eventually draws it to him. In the same way, opulence, prosperity, obeys the law of attraction.

The idea of opulence must be implanted firmly in the subconscious mind, just as everything else which we desire to bring about, to draw out of the universal supply, must be impressed upon the subconscious mind by registering our vow, our determination there until it has become a fixed motive or actuating principle. Then it becomes an active influence in the life, an ever-increasing mental magnet that attracts the thing desired. Whatever we wish to bring about in the actual, we must first establish in the subconscious mind by a constant, positive, affirmative attitude toward that thing.

Orison Swett Marden

Habit is repetition. Man repeats the same thoughts, the same actions, the same experiences over and over again until they are incorporated with his being, until they are built into his character as part of himself. Faculty is fixed habit. Evolution is mental accumulation. Man, today, is the result of millions of repetitious thoughts and acts. He is not ready made, he becomes, and is still becoming. His character is predetermined by his own choice. The thought, the act, which he chooses, that, by habit, he becomes.

Thus each man is an accumulation of thoughts and deeds. The characteristics which he manifests instinctively and without effort are lines of thought and action become, by long repetition, automatic; for it is the nature of habit to become, at last, unconscious, to repeat, as it were, itself without any apparent choice or effort on the part of its possessor; and in due time it takes such complete possession of the individual as to appear to render his will powerless to counteract it. This is the case with all habits, whether good or bad; when bad, the man is spoken of as being the "victim" of a bad habit or a vicious mind; when good, he is referred to as having, by nature, a "good disposition".

All men are, and will continue to be, subject to their own habits, whether they be good or bad . . that is, subject to their own reiterated and accumulated thoughts and deeds. Knowing this, the wise man chooses to subject himself to good habits, for such service is joy, bliss, and freedom; while to become subject to bad habits is misery, wretchedness, slavery. This law of habit is beneficent, for while it enables a man to bind himself to the chains of slavish practices, it enables him to become so fixed in good courses as to do them unconsciously, to instinctively do that which is right, without restraint or exertion, and in perfect happiness and freedom. Observing this automatism in life, men have denied the existence of will or freedom on man's part. They speak of him as being "born" good or bad, and regard him as the helpless instrument of blind forces.

It is true that man is the instrument of mental forces or, to be more accurate, he is those forces but they are not blind, and he can direct them, and redirect them into new channels. In a word, he can take himself in hand and reconstruct his habits; for though it is also true that he is born with a given character, that character is the product of numberless lives during which it has been slowly built up by choice and effort, and in this life it will be considerably modified by new experiences.

James Allen

The man or woman in search of success must make of that desired thing his ruling passion . . he must keep his mind on the main chance. Success is jealous . . that's why we speak of her as feminine. She demands a man's whole affection, and if he begins flirting with other fair charmers, she soon turns her back upon him. If a man allows his strong interest in the main chance to be sidetracked, he will be the loser. Mental Force operates best when it is concentrated. You must give to the desired thing your best and most earnest thought. Just as the man who is thoroughly in love will think out plans and schemes whereby he may please the fair one, so will the man who is in love with his work or business give it his best thought, and the result will be that a hundred and one plans will come into his field of consciousness, many of which are very important.

The mind works on the subconscious plane, remember, and almost always along the lines of the ruling passion or desire. It will fix up things, and patch together plans and schemes, and when you need them the most it will pop them into your consciousness, and you will feel like hurrahing, just as if you had received some valuable aid from outside.

But if you scatter your thought-force, the subconscious mind will not know just how to please you, and the result is that you are apt to be put off from this source of aid and assistance. Beside this, you will miss the powerful result of concentrated thought in the conscious working out of the details of your plans. And then again the man whose mind is full of a dozen interests fails to exert the attracting power that is manifested by the man of the one ruling passion, and he fails to draw to him persons, things, and results that will aid in the working out of his plans, and will also fail to place himself in the current of attraction whereby he is brought into contact with those who will be glad to help him because of harmonious interests.

I have noticed, in my own affairs, that when I would allow myself to be side-tracked by anything outside of my regular line of work, it would be only a short time before my receipts dropped off, and my business showed signs of a lack of vitality. Now, many may say that this was because I left undone some things that I would have done if my mind had been centered on the business. This is true; but I have noticed like results in cases where there was nothing to be done . . cases in which the seed was sown, and the crop was awaited. And in just such cases, as soon as I directed my thought to the matter the seed began to sprout. I do not mean that I had to send out great mental waves with the idea of affecting people . . not a bit of it.

I simply began to realize what a good thing I had, and how much people wanted it, and how glad they would be to know of it and all that sort of thing, and lo! My thought seemed to vitalize the work, and the seed began to sprout. This is no mere fancy, for I have experienced it on several occasions; I have spoken to many others on the subject, and I find that our experiences tally perfectly. So don't get into the habit of permitting these mental leaks. Keep your Desire fresh and active, and let it get in its work without interference from conflicting desires. Keep in love with the thing you wish to attain . . feed your fancy with it . . see it as accomplished already, but don't lose your interest. Keep your eye on the main chance, and keep your one ruling passion strong and vigorous. Don't be a mental polygamist . . one mental love is all that a man needs . . that is, one at a time.

William Walker Atkinson

The man who thinks, knows that his body is but the instrument of his thought, and that he can cleanse it of disease by thought as certainly as he cleans the pen with which he writes.

Charles Wesley Kyle

You can develop the right, mental attitude when you realize that nothing externally can upset you or hurt you without your mental consent. You are the only thinker in your world; consequently nothing can move you to anger, grief, or sorrow without your mental consent. The suggestions that come to you from the outside have no power whatsoever, except you permit them to move you in thought negatively.

Realize you are master of your thought-world. Emotions follow thought; hence you are supreme in your own orbit. Do you permit others to influence you? Do you allow the headlines in the newspapers, or the gossip, or criticism of others to upset you, or bring about mental depression? If you do, you must admit you are the cause of your own mood; you created your emotional reaction. Your attitude is wrong.

Joseph Murphy

All the phenomena of the various religions of the world, of the mystics and psychics, of ancient and modern Spiritualism, all the strange and mysterious in life, are made clear when it is seen that Thought is Power; that the Universe is One; that Life is One. Mind acts upon mind, therefore there is no separation. All we have to do is to learn to talk in thought and not in oral speech; to listen to thoughts, and not with the external ear to the slower vibrations called sound.

All the intelligences that ever lived are then with us and we with them. As all fishes in the sea, or all birds in the air, are in one common vibratory medium, and can at will converse, so are we in Thought in the ALL. But greater than this: THOUGHT is ALL THE POWER, for all is Mind. Matter never had existence. All is Mind. All is Vibration. All man's power is the Power of Mind. This Power is directed by Conscious thought. It can be directed to do anything. It can literally "move mountains."

Henry Harrison Brown

The Objective or conscious mind is the mind of the senses. It learns from books, persons, experience and experiments. It reasons on things learnt, and on thoughts received from a variety of sources,: and having passed judgment, rejects some things as error, and accepts others as truth. Things considered to be truth are passed down into the subconscious mind to add to its existing store of memory and experiences.

Whatever is passed to the subconscious mind becomes translated into action. Thus if immoral or impure thoughts are entertained, then immediately physical changes take place in the body, which are simply these thoughts being translated into action by the subconscious mind. Thus if one repeatedly imbibes this class of thought, a time arrives when one is compelled by the subconscious mind to indulge in immoral practices. This is why many people who have been all their lives apparently quite moral, and well behaved, suddenly break out into flagrant immorality. It is a great surprise and causes great distress to relations and friends.

They think that it is a sudden transformation, or that it is due to a certain temptation, or to the evil influence of a certain wicked person. It is instead none of these things. It is simply the result of evil thinking. Evil thoughts produce evil actions. Evil thoughts also attract other thoughts just as evil as themselves. In the same way a person who indulges in evil thinking, attracts other people of similar character.

There is a law running through the Universe which is that "like attracts like," and the operation of this law is unalterable.

Henry Thomas Hamblin

Since all is mind, and it is done unto us as we mentally think, all life is simply a law of thought . . activity of consciousness. In our life the power flows through us. If we provide a big receptivity, it will do a big thing; if, on the other hand, we only believe in a small way, the activity must be a small one. The Spirit can do for us only what it can do through us. Unless we are able to provide the consciousness, it cannot make the gift. Few people have a great consciousness, and this explains why so few excel.

The power behind all things of itself is without limit; it is all-power; in us it has to become what we make it. We carry within our own soul the key to all expression, but few enter in. The door is not seen with the physical eye, and as yet but few have gained the ability to see; the majority merely look.

Realizing, then, that while the power is limitless it must become operative through our own thought, we shall see that what we need is not some greater power, but that what we really need is a greater consciousness, a deeper realization of life, a grander concept of being. We must unify ourselves with the great whole.

The man who dares to fling his thought out into universal intelligence with the positive assurance of one who knows and dares to claim all there is will find that it will be done. God will honor his request. On the other hand, the one who fears to speak lest God will smite will find himself smitten of the law, not because God is angry, but because it is done as he believes.

We have a right to have and should expect to have in this world all that will make for the comfort and for the luxuries of life. What matter how much we have, if we rob no other soul to get it? Shall not the Power that so lavishly spreads Itself out into nature give to us Its highest expression, all that we can ask? We dishonor God when we claim less than all. Until we can expand our thought so that we shall be able to say also, "I AM," we need not expect to get great results.

Ernest Holmes

Thoughtless people sometimes say that our affirmations and meditations are foolish because we state what is not so. "To claim that my body is well or being healed when it is not, is only to tell a lie," said one distinguished man some years ago.

This is to misunderstand the whole principle. We affirm the harmony that we seek in order to provide the subconscious with a blue print of the work to be done. When you decide to build a house, you purchase a vacant piece of ground and then your architect prepares drawings of a complete house. Actually, of course, there is no such house on the lot today, but you would not think of saying that the architect was drawing a lie. He is drawing what is to be, in order that it may be. So, we build in thought the conditions that will later come into manifestation on the physical plane.

To wait like Mr. Micawber for things to "turn up" is foolish, because you will probably die before they do so. What is your intelligence for if not to be used in building the kind of life that you want? Very primitive men in prehistoric times rejoiced when they found food growing anywhere, and then they waited, perhaps for years, until they happened to find another crop. Today we use our intelligence, and plant in good time the actual crops that we want, and the amount that we consider necessary. We do not sit about hoping that wheat or barley may fortunately come up somewhere. If we did that, civilization would collapse.

The time has come when intelligent men and women must understand the laws of Mind, and plant consciously the crops that they desire; and just as carefully pull up the weeds that they do not want.

Emmet Fox

The power of concentrated thought is the greatest power in the world, and until we decide to acquire the habit of individual thinking, we shall be only about one-third efficient in making use of the opportunities that come to us daily.

Elinor S. Moody

Love is the ultimate law of Life: the consciousness of harmony through affirmative, positive, and constructive thoughts. The higher ideal does not destroy or reject the lower, but appropriates and includes it. It disposes of a negative, not by denying it, but by expression of the more inclusive affirmative. It is neither necessary nor advisable to prohibit prohibition or inhibit inhibition.

Simply install the new in place of the old, the constructive in place of the destructive, the affirmative in place of the negative, and the greater good in the place of the lesser good.

The darkness of the lesser will fade away in the light of the greater.

Eugene Del Mar

Make a choice now! Begin to think constructively and harmoniously. To think is to speak. Your thought is your word. Let your words be as a honeycomb, sweet to the ear, and pleasant to the bones." Let your words be "like apples of Gold in pictures of silver." The future is the present grown up; it is your invisible word or thought made visible. Are your words sweet to the ear? What is your inner speech like at this moment? No one heard you; it is your own silent thought. Perhaps you are saying to yourself, "I can't; it is impossible." "I'm too old now." "What chance have I?" "Mary can, but I can't. I have no money. I can't afford this or that. I've tried; it's no use." You can see your words are not as a honeycomb; they are not sweet to your ear; they do not lift you up or inspire you.

Ouspensky was always stressing the importance of inner speech, inner conversation, or inner talking. It is really the way you feel inside; for the inside mirrors the outside. Is your inner speech pleasant to the bones? Does it exalt you, thrill you, and make you happy?

Joseph Murphy

The more you get into the thought current coming from the Infinite Mind, making yourself more and more a part of that mind (exactly as you may become a part of any vein of low, morbid, unhealthy mind in opening yourself to that current), the quicker are you freshened, and renewed physically and mentally. You become continually a newer being. Changes for the better come quicker and quicker. Your power increases to bring results. You lose gradually all fear as it is proven more and more to you that when you are in the thought current of Infinite good there is nothing to fear.

You realize more and more clearly that there is a great power and force which cares for you. You are wonderstruck at the fact that when your mind is set in the right direction all material things come to you with very little physical or external effort. You wonder then at man's toiling and striving, fagging himself literally to death, when through such excess of effort he actually drives from him the rounded-out good of health, happiness and material prosperity all combined.

Prentice Mulford

Have you, who are beating against the iron bars of poverty, ever stopped to think what marvelous things the Creator has everywhere provided for us His children? Just imagine the entire universe, the great cosmic ocean of creative intelligence, packed with all the riches, all the glorious things, the magnificent possibilities the human mind can conceive, and then try to picture what it would mean to you and to all who are complaining of lack and want if by some magic they could call out of this universal supply of creative intelligence anything which would match their desires, their heart longings. Imagine this vast universe, this ocean of creative energy, packed with possibilities from which human beings could draw everything which the wildest imagination could conceive, everything they desire in life, everything they need for comfort and convenience, even luxuries, . . also cities, railroads, telegraphs and all sorts of wonderful inventions and discoveries.

You will say, doubtless, that such a thing is too silly to contemplate for a moment. Yet, haven't human beings been doing this very thing since the dawn of civilization, all up through the ages?

Every discovery, every invention, every improvement, every facility, every home, every building, every city, every railroad, every ship, everything that man has created for our use and benefit he has fashioned out of this vast invisible cosmic ocean of intelligence by thought force. Everything we use, everything we have, every achievement of man is preceded by a mental vision, a plan. Everything man has accomplished on this earth is a result of a desire, has been preceded by a mental picture of it. Everything he has produced on this plane of existence has been drawn out of this invisible ocean of divine intelligence by his thought force.

His imagination first pictured the thing he wanted to do; he kept visualizing this mental conception, never stopped thinking, creating, until his efforts to match his visions with their realities drew to him the thing he had concentrated on.

We all imagine that we actually, of ourselves, create these things. We do not. We simply work in unison with the Creator, and draw them out of the vast invisible cosmic ocean of supply. But we must do our part or there will be no realization for us. Just as the first step in an architect's building is his plan, so must we first make a plan or picture of the thing we desire. The architect first sees in all its details in his mind's eye the building to be erected even before he draws his plan on paper. He mentally sees the real building long before there are any materials on the spot for its construction. His plan has come out of the invisible, out of the fathomless ocean of possibilities which surrounds us. All of our wants and desires can find their fulfillment in this unlimited supply.

Orison Swett Marden

The Bible is the "textbook of the soul", and gives us examples of everything that could happen to any human being. It states exactly what happens, and how people learn to get out of it. To translate the Bible's message in 20th century English, we might say that this is a mental and spiritual world we live in; a mental and spiritual universe, where "thoughts are things", as William James told us.

By Divine endowment, we are creators. We can think things into existence, and by the same token we can think them out of existence.

There isn't a thing in the world that has ever been done, there is not a thing in the world that ever will be done, that first is not a thought or an idea. If an architect builds a skyscraper, he must first have the idea of the type of building, then draw the blueprint, before it can be constructed, But he had to have the idea, .and the idea is what comes into effect. The thing that is so marvelous for all of us, and so simple, is the fact that you can always choose your ideas. What kind of life would you have? Tell me your life, and I'll tell you what you have been thinking. That applies to each and every one of us.

You can always choose your own thought, your blueprint of the life you are building for yourself. Nobody else can choose it for you. That very simple fact . . that you have free choice of thought . . is really dynamite. It is the answer to your regeneration or degeneration. Nobody else can make your choice for you. Nobody can change your thinking for you. You can listen to me, you can listen to every metaphysical teacher in the world, read every book on the subject, but you have to do it for yourself. I could invite you to my home for dinner, cook you a wonderful meal, serve it to you most beautifully . . but I couldn't eat or digest it for you!

We come to the realization that thought is the clue to the whole secret. In the beginning we start by deliberately changing our thoughts to change our lives in certain degrees and in certain things, and in the end we use our thought as a purely transcendent possession; not only to change our lives, but to create for ourselves and others the good that is spiritually our divine heritage.

Mildred Mann

As you cannot have a sweet and wholesome abode unless you admit the air and sunshine freely into your rooms, so a strong body and a bright, happy, or serene countenance can only result from the free admittance into the mind of thoughts of joy and good will and serenity.

On the faces of the aged there are wrinkles made by sympathy, others by strong and pure thought, others are carved by passion. Who cannot distinguish them? With those who have lived righteously, age is calm, peaceful, and softly mellowed, like the setting sun. I have recently seen a philosopher on his deathbed. He was not old except in years. He died as sweetly and peacefully as he had lived.

There is no physician like cheerful thought for dissipating the ills of the body; there is no comforter to compare with good will for dispersing the shadows of grief and sorrow. To live continually in thoughts of ill will, cynicism, suspicion, and envy, is to be confined in a self-made prison hole. But to think well of all, to be cheerful with all, to patiently learn to find the good in all . . such unselfish thoughts are the very portals of heaven; and to dwell day to day in thoughts of peace toward every creature will bring abounding peace to their possessor.

James Allen

Thought itself is a free force that percolates the fibers of the brain, conditioned only in its expression by the limitations of the physical organs. Thought is manifestly an energy superior to the instrument through which it is expressed. If it were not, then there would be no expanse, no growth of thought.

The fact that thought evolves and expands in the individual, parallel with the higher complexity of the brain development, does not necessarily indicate that the thought exudes from the cell-formation, but rather that the thought seeks to express itself through more highly developed organs, and waits till such organs have been unfolded. " The only tenable supposition is, that mental and physical proceed together, as undivided twins. When, therefore, we speak of a mental cause, a mental agency, we have always a two-sided cause; the effect produced is not the effect of mind alone, but of mind in company with body."

Henry Frank

If antagonistic thoughts are set against you, meet them with love, for love is fire, and fire consumes EVERYTHING. The stronger the love forces, the easier it is to counterbalance hate, envy and malice. There is more heat in love than in hate. There is more strength in affirmation and goodness than in denial. Good overcomes if genuine and strong.

Keep your mind clean and free from all poisonous thoughts, and you can only send out or transfer vibrations that build up and restore lost health, Mentally or Morally. Concentrate forcibly on whatever you desire. Concentration accumulates all vibrations in tune or harmony with the mind. Concentration draws to you what you desire.

F. E. Gariner and Dr. R. Swineburne Clymer

Knowing that Mind is, we have a principle that is absolute; it is exact; it is going to correspond to our thinking about it. The first great necessity is to believe this; without belief we can do nothing. This is the reason Jesus said "It is done unto you even as you have believed." Always it is done unto people as they believe, and there is Something that does it which never fails.

We must believe that our word is formed upon and around by this creative Mind; for instance, we wish to create activity in our business; we believe that our word is law about that thing, and there is something that takes our thought and executes it for us. If we have accepted the fact that all is mind and that the thought is the thing, we shall see at once that our word is the power behind the thing, and that it depends upon the word or thought that we are sending out.

So plastic is mind, so receptive, that the slightest thought makes an impression upon it. People who think many kinds of thought must expect to receive a confused manifestation in their lives. If a gardener plants a thousand kinds of seeds, he will get a thousand kinds of plants; it is the same in mind.

Ernest Holmes

No matter what problem you may have to face today, there is a solution, because you have nothing to deal with but your own thoughts. As you know, you have the power to select and control your thoughts, difficult though it may be at times to do so. As long as you think that your destiny is in the hands of other people, the situation is hopeless. People say: "It is useless for me to struggle because of such and such a reason. If only I had a profession. If only I had married someone else. If only I had not bought this business.

If only I had gone abroad when I had the chance" . . and so on.

But this is a vital mistake, because you have nothing to deal with but your own thoughts.

Remind yourself of this fact constantly. Repeat it to yourself a hundred times a day until you really do begin to grasp all that it means to you. Write it down where you will see it often. Have it on your desk, or wherever you work. Hang it in your bedroom where you will easily see it. Write it in your pocketbook. Write it on your soul, by constantly dwelling upon it. It will transform your life. It will lead you out of the land of Egypt and out of the House of Bondage.

Emmet Fox

It is of the greatest importance that we keep our thoughts under control, and we must not make any suggestions of things which we do not want, nor have gloomy suggestions before we retire, as our souls will then travel in the lower magnetism while we sleep and wear out our bodies, because we open the door for unconscious souls who will come around us when we cannot protect ourselves and draw our magnetic forces away and exhaust our nerves.

May E. Stevenson

Our study of applied metaphysics is designed to make clear these facts: In the beginning there is only Mind or Spirit. Whatever is made, therefore, must be made out of Mind. Mind can act only by thinking; therefore it is thought that takes the substance called mind and molds it into form. God makes a world out of himself. As everything in the cosmos starts in thought and manifests in form, creation is the process by which the activity takes place. We may call it evolution or we may call it law.

By law we mean the method Spirit follows in making things. This is the law of cause and effect whether it be in the making of a planet or a man; the thought is the cause and the manifestation is the effect. Even the so-called laws of the physical universe are simply the activity of this one law in some form.

Fenwicke L. Holmes

Man creates himself, or call it evolution, if you like . . the word is nothing, and the instrument he uses in creating himself is the mind, for the mind's action, which is thought, is the dominant force of his life . . and he creates himself and his conditions by the quality of his thought.

Seemingly, in a degree, we are creatures of circumstances, but in reality we create our own lives, for there are no circumstances that cannot be overcome by conforming to the law in thought, word, and deed, and using common sense and reason in so doing. When I speak of the law, I always mean the law of harmony and love . . the law that expresses the Christ principle and is nature's law. The word is greater than the deed, and the thought is greater than the word, because the thought must come before, and must control the word and the deed. There is no phase of charity so great as thinking charity, because, if you think kindly and lovingly of everyone, the word and the deed must follow.

Grace M. Brown

By thinking and controlling thoughts and feelings through eliminating on the one hand what is a death-thought and realizing on the other hand the Life-Power, we become just the thing which we will to be and have in our experience. I have said that a man does not attract to himself what he wants. He attracts to himself what he is.

If I want something that I am not, I cannot get it, no matter how much I struggle; but if I become that thing, I will be it and have it. If I want Wisdom, then I ally myself with Wisdom within. If I want Life, I ally myself with the Life principle. I have taught you how to begin. If I want Love, I ally myself with the Love principle. That builds me up in the terms of being and wholeness.

Frank Waller Allen

The more enthusiasm and faith you are able to put into your picture, the more quickly it will come into visible form, and your enthusiasm is increased by keeping your desire secret. The moment you speak it to any living soul, that moment your power is weakened. Your power, your magnet of attraction is not that strong, and consequently cannot reach so far.

The more perfectly a secret between your mind and your outer self is guarded, the more vitality you give your power of attraction. One tells one's troubles to weaken them, to get them off one's mind, and when a thought is given out, its power is dissipated. Talk it over with yourself, and even write it down, then destroy the paper.

Genevieve Behrend

The thoughtless, the ignorant, and the indolent, seeing only the apparent effects of things and not the things themselves, talk of luck, of fortune, and chance. See a man grow rich, they say, "How lucky he is!" Observing another become intellectual, they exclaim, "How highly favored he is!" And noting the saintly character and wide influence of another, the remark, "How chance aids him at every turn!"

They do not see the trials and failures and struggles which these men have voluntarily encountered in order to gain their experience. They have no knowledge of the sacrifices they have made, of the undaunted efforts they have put forth, of the faith they have exercised, that they might overcome the apparently insurmountable, and realize the Vision of their heart.

They do not know the darkness and the heartaches; they only see the light and joy, and call it "luck"; do not see the long and arduous journey, but only behold the pleasant goal, and call it "good fortune"; do not understand the process, but only perceive the result, and call it "chance."

In all human affairs there are efforts, and there are results, and the strength of the effort is the measure of the result. Chance is not. "Gifts," powers, material, intellectual, and spiritual possessions are the fruits of effort. They are thoughts completed, objects accomplished, visions realized.

The vision that you glorify in your mind, the Ideal that you enthrone in your heart . . this you will build your life by, this you will become.

James Allen

Mind finds expression of itself in thought and word. Mind is the Creator; thought and word Its creation. Every word and thought is in Mind before coming forth. Creation is in the Creator before it appears in the visible. Creation, or the visible, is the thought and word of the Infinite Mind and Intelligence. The visible form is the expression of Infinite Spirit.

Nona L. Brooks

Every word we speak, even uttered thought, is power for good or ill, and we must remember that it is what we put into the word that gives it its meaning, and determines its quality and its force. Words themselves are the clothes for our thoughts. We can take a word and think love into it, think service into it, think friendliness into it, and it will create a corresponding feeling in the one it is addressed to. Or we can take the same word and think hatred into it, think jealousy into it, think envy into it, and hurl it out and arouse antagonism, jealousy, hatred or envy in another mind. We know that we can do the same thing with a dog, and he will feel the thought . . the love or the hate, the anger or the contempt . . which we put into the word.

We can fling out hatred and bitterness, sarcasm, malice, in words; we can arouse the anger which kills, or we can call out love, admiration, sympathy, friendship. Everything depends upon the thought behind the word. It is the mental attitude that gives the word its real meaning. And your words are messengers of life or death to yourself and to others.

Words have put civilization where it is today. The word wedded to the thought has built everything that man has achieved. He speaks and it is done, just as God spoke and the earth was created, man and every living thing was created. Everything is made out of God's thoughts, out of God's ideas, and He speaks through man.

There is a force in spoken words which is not stirred by going over the same words mentally. When vocalized they make a more lasting impression upon the mind. You know how much more powerfully you are impressed and inspired by listening to a great lecture or sermon than you would be if you read the same thing in print. We remember the spoken word when we forget the cold type which carries thought to the brain. It makes a deeper impression on the inner self.

We can talk to our inner or other self, just as we would talk to a child; and we know from experience that it will listen to and act on our suggestions. We are constantly sending suggestions or commands to this inner self. We may not do so audibly, but we do so silently, mentally. Unconsciously we advise, we suggest, we try to influence it in certain directions.

By consciously, audibly addressing it, in heart-to-heart talks with ourselves, we find that we can even materially influence our habits, our motives, our methods of living. In fact, the possibilities of influencing the character and the life by this means are practically limitless.

Many people have killed character enemies, peace and happiness enemies, have doubled and quadrupled their self-confidence, have strengthened tremendously their initiative, their executive ability; have literally made themselves over, by heart-to-heart talks with themselves.

Orison Swett Marden

The primal cause of activity is Mind, yet we do not seem willing to say that Mind is the only power working in our lives and bodies. Yet in truth Mind is the only power working in our lives today. If our environment is filled with love, peace and harmony, we may know that it is because in our silent thought and outer words we are conforming to the principle of peace, love, and harmony that is the reality of the universe.

If, however, our environment is inharmonious, we may know that the change must come through an inner change of thought. Fear contracts and love expands, so as we change in our thought we find love expanding where before fear was contracting. That is why it is so necessary to keep our thoughts in peace and harmony, in order that love may show forth in our environment.

Mrs. C. L. Baum

"Ether is the subtle, universal, magnetic, fluidic medium in which all things are embedded." That is the opinion of the scientific world. The ether is the God Substance, and "in Him we live and move and have our being." That was the teaching of Christ. In this universal substance, which is the consciousness or essence of mind, we exist; it permeates our body; we swim in the great sea of ether, or Divine Mind, if you prefer to call it that. And in the silence we consciously direct our thoughts into the ethers, believing that we have received; and that is the attitude which assures us that we are one . . we feel it.

That is the secret of the silence and what it brings to us. Think love to a friend; your love will go to him precisely as you think it, and with no greater or less intensity than you feel it. When we go into the silence we shut out all the senses, and merge them into feeling. Lose the sense of sight first; second the sense of sound and then the sense of motion . . and you are still. Then lose the sense of color, and all becomes the Great White Light.

The ether, or the Universal Mind, is the great storehouse of God, in which is everything conceivable by the mind of man. The subconscious mind is the universal storehouse. Did you ever stand by a river and watch a vortex whirling round and round, drawing into itself everything which came floating down the current? Each of us is a vortex in the great sea of God consciousness and we draw into ourselves according to the energy of thought and feeling; and we draw, according to our attitude of mind, the thing we feel is Truth. According to your faith (feeling) be it done unto you; for the thing that we feel, is the thing in which we have faith.

The universal ethers are no respecters of persons. They yield to you and connect you with any of their parts. The ether does not retard or impair any force you send into it, but brings back to you precisely what you send forth with faith. It will back you to your own success or to your own destruction. Consciously direct your thought into the ether and it will reach the person to whom you direct it. The thought makes a little pathway to that person, and the path acts as the wire over which your message is sent. The action of the thought is exactly comparable to wireless telegraphy, even down to the wave lengths.

Mary C. Ferriter

In the first chapter of Genesis is recorded, "And God said let there be light and there was light." The record of each act of creation is prefaced by the words, "And God said." The creative force is thus expressed by the word. A word is merely the expression of thought. Thought is the power.

Kathleen M. H. Besly

There is a designer, an architect, and a weaver within you; it takes the fabric of your mind, your thoughts, feelings, and beliefs, and molds them into a pattern of life which brings you peace or discord, health or sickness. You can imagine a life which will take you up to the third heaven where you will see unspeakable and unutterable things of God, or through the distorted, morbid use of your imagination you can sink to the depths of degradation. Man is the tabernacle of God, and no matter how low a man has sunk, the Healing Presence is there waiting to minister to him. It is within us waiting for us to call upon It.

Joseph Murphy

This is the Prophecy: Thought will in the future become subject to conscious control. We shall yet intelligently do all that the Hindus are now credited with doing. Life is subject to will. Thought is a manifestation of Infinite Life. Thought is Infinite. We know it is Power. It is one with all other forms of power. Its source is limitless. It will flow through us in any required amount. We can direct it to any desired end. This is demonstrated by telepathy; by bodily renovation; by the building of body to will.

Thought will be used to control all the lesser forms of force; to direct fire, water, wind, wave, light, electricity and gravity. The fire will cease to burn at command. "The wind and the wave obey him." Plant and animal life will come at his thought to him willing servants. Dream! Illusion! Rhapsody! all this may be called. It is only the calm reasoning from present scientific knowledge. Let it stand for future generations to verify.

The time is now for us to begin this dominion of Mind over Nature. Beginning with our own body, we will progress until even the largest of our environments is subject to our will.

Henry Harrison Brown

It will be helpful for you to think of your subliminal Mind as another person, one who is always listening, listening, listening. He hears all that you say, and ACTS UPON all the thoughts that you let pass the threshold of the inner mind.

"Hush! he is listening," should be the watch-word of your life. Let no thought of evil, of impurity, of weakness, of ill-health, of failure, of hate, of anger, of fear, enter your Subliminal Mind, for he will receive them as orders which he will obey, and being all-powerful, great and terrible will be the results. Therefore let only thoughts of good, purity, strength, health, success, love, self-control, courage and determination enter this greater mind of vast intelligence and power. Do this, and your Subliminal Mind will take these thoughts as orders, and will shape your life and health accordingly. Thus in a general way your Subliminal Mind will be led to develop your life on healthful and successful, noble and harmonious lines.

Henry Thomas Hamblin

When people come together and in any way talk out their ill-will towards others they are drawing to themselves with ten-fold power an injurious thought current. Because the more minds united on any purpose the more power do they attract to effect that purpose.

The thought current so attracted by those chronic complainers, grumblers and scandal mongers, will injure their bodies. Because whatever thought is most held in mind is most materialized in the body. If we are always thinking and talking of people's imperfections we are drawing to us ever of that thought current, and thereby incorporating into ourselves those very imperfections.

Prentice Mulford

We are apt to think of the body as a collection of different organs and that these organs are in a way separate, of different material or construction. But we are simply one enormous mass of tiny cells closely related to one another. Because the bones, for example, are harder than the brain, we think there can be little affinity between them, but, as a matter of fact, all the twelve different tissues of the body are made up of cells of varying consistency, all of which have come from one primordial cell . . and what affects one cell anywhere in the body affects all. Each cell is an entity or little self, and we are made up of these billions of our little selves or cells.

These tiny selves are like members of a great orchestra which instantly respond to the keynote given them by their leader. Whatever tune our mentality plays they play. They become like our thought. Every suggestion, every motive that moves the individual, is reflected in these cells. Every cell in the body vibrates in unison with every thought, every emotion, every passion that sways us, and the result on the cell life corresponds with the character of the thought, the emotion or passion.

The ego is the master spirit, the leader of all the little self or cell communities. All the cells of the body will do its bidding. The ego can think health into the cells or it can think disease. It can think discord or harmony into them. It can think efficiency or inefficiency into them. It can send a success thrill or a failure thrill through all of the cells, a thrill of masterfulness or of weakness. It can send through them a vibration of fear or of courage, of selfishness or of generosity. It can send vibrating through all the cells of the body a thrill of hope or of despair, a thrill of love or of hate; a triumphant vibration or a vibration of defeat, of failure, of disgrace.

In short, whatever thought the ego, or I, sends out will stamp itself on every cell in the body, will make it like itself.

Orison Swett Marden

Man can reign over his own mind, his own thoughts; can be lord over himself. Until he does so reign, his life is unsatisfactory and imperfect. His spiritual dominion is the empire of the mental forces of which his nature is composed. The body has no causative power. The ruling of the body . . that is, of appetite and passion is the discipline of mental forces. The subduing, modifying, redirecting and transmuting of the antagonizing spiritual elements within, is the wonderful and mighty work which all men must, sooner or later, undertake.

For a long time man regards himself as the slave of external forces, but there comes a day when his spiritual eyes open, and he sees that he has been a slave this long time to none and nothing but his own ungoverned, unpurified self. In that day, he rises up and, ascending his spiritual throne, he no longer obeys his desires, appetites, and passions, as their slave, but henceforth rules them as his subjects. The mental kingdom through which he has been wont to wander as a puling beggar and a whipped serf, he now discovers is his by right of lordly self control . . his to set in order, to organize and harmonize, to abolish its dissensions and painful contradictions, and bring it to a state of peace.

Thus rising up and exercising his rightful spiritual authority, he enters the company of those kingly ones who in all ages have conquered and attained, who have overcome ignorance, darkness, and mental suffering, and have ascended into Truth.

James Allen

They who have even a slight understanding of the power of mind can speak the healing word for another, and every word spoken for health and love and prosperity for your neighbor opens the channel within yourself, that you may be filled again. When the word of power goes out, the vacuum created is filled with the SUBSTANCE which that word contains; and whatever we put into the universal substance in thought or spoken word, we take out in form. As ye sow so shall ye reap. When Jesus healed he did so by conscious use of the cosmic forces. He knew the law of mind and understood it so perfectly that it had become his servant.

Stimulation is the law of the conscious mind, and it works through desire and imagination. Suggestion is the law of the subconscious mind, and it works through will and obedience. Through the conscious mind, ever open to stimulation from without, we image the thing which, through its suggestion to the subconscious mind, will later take form in our lives. When the mental images are such that they work out in us as disease or lack they are mental devils; and you cast out the devils by reversing your thought. Change your thought images and all trouble vanishes. You may use your imagination constructively or destructively, as you will. And when you have allowed undesirable images to enter your mind, and even after you have stamped them into your flesh, you can destroy them and cast out the devils.

Don't be afraid of the destructive power; only be sure that you know what you are doing when you use it. You can destroy fair flesh as well as the diseased. Always keep your powers under the direction of the mind. The law is all within yourself, all within your mind, and when the objective and subjective minds work in harmony together you will never have to call in a healer. Nor can any healer ever set in motion for you a law outside yourself. The truth which sets your law in motion, however, is always given as a suggestion, or affirmation; it must be strong enough to reverse your own thought and to destroy the mental images you have created. You can learn to do this for yourself and for others. The world needs teachers to go out with the new message, which is the old message given in a new way.

Mary C. Ferriter

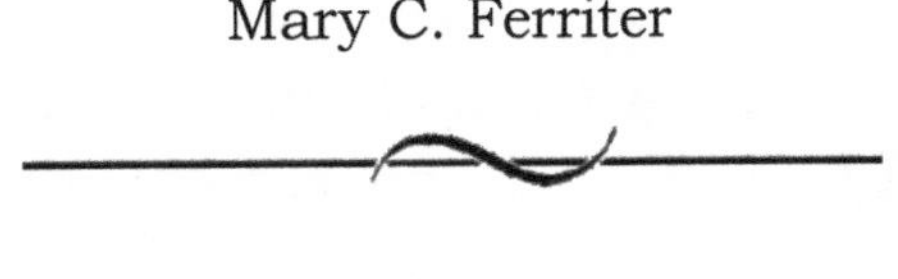

Thought and Love work together. Love goes, but it must carry the Thought wave to produce the conscious and the chosen effect. Love alone would never cure without a thought of health accompanying it. It would intensify the activity of the soul in the way it was going. Love is help in the way of power, but it is not directive. Thought, the will of the conscious man, must come in to give direction. Suggestion must be that the chosen activity can be. Otherwise there will be activity, without self-direction. The Force that directs individual expression is Thought. The Force that is directed is Love.

The time will come when, through the demonstrations of Telepathy and the study of Suggestion, man will study Thought and Love, as he now studies light and sound. He will formulate his knowledge of these into science and develop an Art of Thinking and Loving. The promise and the prophecy of this is herein the present schools of Mental Science, and in the fast developing Art of Suggestion. Thus do the phenomena of Telepathy contain within them more for the good of the race, contain more promise for the future of man than all the previous facts he has gathered. Thus is it that when man demonstrated Thought to be a form of Force, to be a mode of motion, he made his Greatest Discovery.

All that we know of Vibration is true of Thought and Love as forms of Vibration. As other forms of motion have been studied, so can these two, which we now throw into the category of force, studied. As all lesser forces are less only when compared with some other forms of lower pitch, and as all lesser forms are subject to the greater, it follows logically and scientifically that all other forms of force are subject to the greatest form, Thought. They will obey human will.

Thus is Thought master of all the other forms of the One Universal Energy. Love and Thought being ONE in Man, it follows that Love is the only manifestation of the Absolute. Thought is the Individual expression; Love, the Absolute expression. The design of evolution being to bring the Individual into supremacy, to bring Man into "the Kingdom," it follows that Love, which is the highest mode of motion in the ONE, should thus be subject to the only form of individual, self-directed motion, Thought.

Love must be thought-directed. In his Thought, each man differs from all other men. His individual stamp is placed upon his perception of Absolute Truth. But Love is in each individual, one and the same. Thus does Individuality consist only in the pitch, or in the octave of thought in which each individual moves. As these octaves are limitless and as there is no limit to the possible range of pitch, it follows that there is no limit to the variety of Human Life. ONE in origin, ONE in substance, ONE in possibility, ONE in the Absolute Truth, we are Individuals only in the sphere of Thought.

Only to the degree that a person thinks for himself does he attain Individuality. To Think is to be an Individual. To Love is to Live. Love is the primal energy; Thought is the Human. Thought can raise or lower the pitch of life. Love can keep life in the animal scale, or octave, where man started, or it can raise it daily in pitch toward the Ideal Man, as typified in Jesus and other seers.

Henry Harrison Brown

"Thoughts," said Prentice Mulford, "are things." "Thoughts," says T. Sharper Knowlson, "so far from being mere brain flashes, are, judging solely from their effects, real entities, apparently composed of spiritual substance, the nature of which is outside the range of discovery of our present faculties." "Thought," says Levy, "is not an event which dies in a world ethereal, super-sensible, imperceptible; it has continually its likeness and repercussion in our organism." "Thought is not," says Ralph Waldo Trine, "as is many times supposed, a mere indefinite abstraction, or something of a like nature. It is, on the contrary, a vital, living force, the most vital, subtle and irresistible force in the Universe."

In our very laboratory experiments we are demonstrating the great fact that thoughts are forces. They have form, and quality, and substance, and power, and we are beginning to find that there is what we may term a science of thought.

We are beginning to find also that through the instrumentality of our thought forces we have creative power in reality. Many more authorities could be quoted, but these will suffice to show that thoughts are just as much "things" as town halls or mountains are "things." It is a great mistake to imagine that because you can see a thing with your physical eyes, feel it with your hands, or hit it with a hammer, that it is for that reason more real than something you can neither see nor feel. On the contrary the "Unseen" is vastly more powerful, lasting and forceful than anything you can see with your physical eyes. What you see with your eyes is only the effect of greater causes which are invisible.

"Everything exists in the unseen before it is manifested in the seen, and in this sense it is true that the unseen things are real, while the things that are seen are the unreal. The unseen things are cause; the seen things are effect. The unseen things are eternal; the seen things are the changing, the transient."

Thoughts then are "entities," are things," are "forces," are vital subtle "powers." They, like everything else, and every other force in the universe, are subject to law. This law is the Law of Attraction.

Whatever thoughts you think will attract to you thoughts of a similar nature. According as you create good or bad thoughts, so do you determine whether your life shall be blessed or cursed. If you think a good thought and dwell upon it, and, as it were, nourish it with your meditations, it will not only bless and enrich your life, but will attract hosts of other thoughts of equal power and beauty, which will hasten to minister to you. Thus, if you think "Success" thoughts, and affirm them, and cling to them in the face of apparent defeat and failure, you will attract to yourself such a wave of powerful, upbuilding and inspiring thoughts that you will be lifted right over your difficulty and carried, as by invisible forces, along the path of accomplishment.

On the other hand, it is equally true that if you think a weak thought, a low thought, a vile thought, or a thought of failure, there will be attracted to you a host of thoughts of like character, which by their nature will curse you and drag you down. "Unto him that hath shall be given, and from him that hath not shall be taken away that which he hath" is simply the working of the Law of Attraction. Think "Success" and thousands of invisible forces will fly to your aid. Think "failure" and innumerable forces will help to make your failure even more complete.

If thought is the "greatest power of all powers," "the most vital, subtle and irresistible force in the universe," and if your thoughts have the power to attract other thoughts of a like character, then the choice of your thoughts is the most important act of your life.

By choosing your thoughts you choose either success or failure, happiness or misery, health or disease, hope or despair.

Henry Thomas Hamblin

All is mind and we are mental, we are in mind and can only get from it what we first think into it. We must not only think but we must know. We have to provide within ourselves a mental and spiritual likeness for the thing desired. The reason why so few succeed, then, must be because they have not mentally really believed to the exclusion of all that would deny the thing which they believe in. And the reason why others do succeed must also be because they have absolutely believed and allowed real power to flow through and out into expression.

They must have a real concept of life. Hold an object in front of a mirror and it will image in the mirror the exact size of the object. Hold a thought in mind and it will image in matter the exact likeness of the thought. Let us take this image which we hold before a mirror and change it ever so slightly and there will be a corresponding change in the reflection. It is just the same in the mental world; whatever is imaged is brought forth from mind into manifestation.

We must not deny that which we affirm. We must reason only from that cause which is spiritual and mental and weed out all thought that would deny its power in our lives. There seems to be something in the race thought that says man is poor; man is limited; that there is a lack of opportunity; that times are hard; that prices are high; that nobody wants what

I have to offer. No person succeeds who speaks these ideas. When we express ourselves in this way we are using a destructive power. All such thoughts must go, and we must all realize that we are an active center in the only power there is.

We must get the perfect vision, the perfect conception; we must enlarge our thought until it realizes all good, and then we must swing right out and use this Almighty Power for definite purposes. We should daily feel a deeper union with Life, a greater sense of that indwelling God, the God of the everywhere, within us. When we speak into this Mind we have sown the seed of thought in the Absolute and may rest in peace. We do not have to make haste, because it is done unto all as they believe. "In that day that they shall call upon me I will answer."

Ernest Holmes

To a much greater extent than most of us realize, our thoughts are the architects of our fortunes, for it is in the mental realm that we first formulate our decrees; from thence, speaking the creative word into the substance all about us, which is to create for us the condition or thing that will do its part in making or marring, to a greater or less degree, a portion of our lives.

Elinor S. Moody

We have known of many cases where present failure was simply the prelude to a greater success. Sometimes the accumulated thoughts of failure and sorrow or in harmony have been swept away by flood or fire or bankruptcy only to sweep the mind clean for higher attainment. Thousands have thus begun at the bottom only to climb still higher in the new work. To fear failure will not help. Have faith. This is the one great essential. Have faith in yourself. Have faith in others. Have faith in the future. Have faith in God. Courage and faith are half the battle. Determination, will, and work are the other half.

You can if you think you can. I know I can succeed and I will succeed. I AM success. I AM courage. I AM faith. I AM the victory. Faith is the victory that overcomes the world, and I have all the faith there is. Then concentrate your thought for a moment on the positive thing you want. Make up your mind that you will have the best and the best only. If you do not know now just what course to follow, there is a Mind in you that does. Depend on it. Resolve to be lead by the Divine Wisdom that speaks through you. Step out in faith on the new venture for health, wealth, or love and expect great things. The spirit in you will soon lead you into the best.

Fenwicke L. Holmes

It is true that we are whelmed and moved by forces that flow into us. We think the thoughts that are thought into us. We do not originate thought, but thought awakens our thinking. The infinite is replete with multifarious ideas or mental impulses that have floated down the centuries, since the primal fancies of primitive man were conjured by passing wind and boisterous elements.

We are born into this sea of thoughts. As a fish thrives only in its native watery element, so the mind of man thrives only in a sea of mental phantasms. What we are and become is the result of what mental currents we meet in the vast ocean of being and the effect they have upon us.

But because we are thus environed by an invisible ocean of mental forces, is not to conclude that these forces become the absolute molders of our being and makers of our destiny. While we are surrounded and invaded, we must remember that within ourselves there is aggregated a vast number of individualized forces which constitute our personality. These are the opposing powers we may bring to play on sinister and obnoxious forces that would o'ermaster us. There is no authority in the stars, whatever possible truth there may be in astrology, to command our destiny, be we but opposing and obstreperous enough to parry with it and assert our independence and confident assurance.

The stream of influences which has swept down the centuries and entered the channels of our blood, is not sufficient of itself to shape our character or complexion our wills, be we but conscious of the resident forces we may conjure, to drive away the pernicious intruders. When we shall learn so to adjust ourselves to the forces that play upon us, that we shall compel them to be our benefactors and not our foes, we shall have learned the secret of life's success.

Henry Frank

This Universe is the reason, first of an Infinite Intelligence which speaks or thinks, and as this thought becomes active within itself, it creates from itself, at the power of its own word, the visible Universe. We are living in a Universal activity of mental law, we are surrounded by a Mind which receives every impression of our thought and returns to us just what we think.

Every man, then, is living in a world made for him from the activity of his thought. It is a self-evident proposition that Mind must create out of Itself; and this Self being Limitless, it follows that its creative power is without limit.

Ernest Holmes

Man, claim your divinity. Know thyself; and know that all that is, and ever will be, is dormant within you, ready and willing to be awakened by your magic touch. With thought definite and exalted, emotion controlled and refined, and energy conserved and responsive to command, man is prepared to meet and to overcome, assimilate, or harmonize with whatever may meet him on the path of life. He has been furnished with the equipment of a conqueror!

Man is divine! He is living in eternity now. Whatever he shall ever manifest, he now is. Whatever he dares to do, he already is. It is through the alchemy of thought alone that his being may be expressed and manifested; and, in the full realization of his inheritance as a Child of God, he shall rule as master over his illimitable kingdom of thought!

Eugene Del Mar

We see, therefore, that the Creative Principle is the Word. "By the Word of the Lord were the heavens made." OUR CREATIVE WORD. We do not need to go further to draw the inference as to our own creative word. If we share the nature of God, if our thought acts on Original Substance, that is, in the Divine Mind; then every word we speak, whether we are shallow or deep, is a creative word. That is why we are told, "By thy words thou shalt be justified and by thy words thou shalt be condemned." Such is the fateful activity of the word we send forth into the universe.

Fenwicke L. Holmes

If people only knew the possibilities which center in the highest development of their visualizing powers it would revolutionize their lives. Until comparatively recent times most of the country between Omaha and the Rocky Mountains was a vast barren desert, and it looked as though it would always be absolutely worthless. Many intelligent men wondered why the Creator ever made such a dreary waste as these millions of acres presented, and when it was suggested in Congress that the Government assist in building a railroad across this desert from the Missouri River to the Pacific Slope, even men like Webster laughed at the idea.

Webster said that such an undertaking would be a wicked waste of public money, and he suggested the importation of camels for the purpose of carrying the United States mail across the Western desert. He believed this was the only use that could be made of those waste lands. But the vision seen by the men who conceived the Union Pacific Railroad was no idle dream; it was a foreshadowing of the reality. Before a rail had been laid, these men saw great thriving cities, vast populations and millions of fertile farms springing up like magic where the men without a vision of its possibilities saw nothing but alkali plains, sage brush and coyotes.

It was the men who were not limited by appearances, by what the senses told them, who transformed the desert into a thing of beauty and untold wealth. Human beings are like this arid desert, packed with marvelous possibilities which are just waiting for that which will arouse their latent forces and make the germs of those wonderful possibilities blossom into beauty and power. What we need is a firm belief in the vision of ourselves which we see in the moment of our highest inspiration. As soon as we feel the touch of the awakening, arousing, energizing power of an unalterable faith in our own divinity, in our ability to be "the thing we long for," our lives will blossom into beauty and grandeur.

The realization of our power to create ideals and to make these live in reality is destined to revolutionize the world, because we build life through our ideals. This power to build mentally is the pathway of achievement, the way which will lead to the millennium. 'We cannot accomplish anything, do anything, create anything except through an ideal, a vision. "The vision that you glorify in your mind," says James Allen, "the ideal that you enthrone in your heart . . this you will build your life by, this you will become.

Orison Swett Marden

Let a man cease from his sinful thoughts, and all the world will soften toward him, and be ready to help him. Let him put away his weakly and sickly thoughts, and lo! opportunities will spring up on every hand to aid his strong resolves. Let him encourage good thoughts, and no hard fate shall bind him down to wretchedness and shame. The world is your kaleidoscope, and the varying combinations of colors which at every succeeding moment it presents to you. The body is the servant of the mind. It obeys the operations of the mind, whether they be deliberately chosen or automatically expressed. At the bidding of unlawful thoughts the body sinks rapidly into disease and decay; at the command of glad and beautiful thoughts it becomes clothed with youthfulness and beauty.

Disease and health, like circumstances, are rooted in thought. Sickly thoughts will express themselves through a sickly body. Thoughts of fear have been known to kill a man as speedily as a bullet, and they are continually killing thousands of people just as surely though less rapidly. The people who live in fear of disease are the people who get it. Anxiety quickly demoralizes the whole body, and lays it open to the entrance of disease; while impure thoughts, even if not physically indulged, will soon shatter the nervous system.

Strong, pure, and happy thoughts build up the body in vigor and grace. The body is a delicate and plastic instrument, which responds readily to the thoughts by which it is impressed, and habits of thought will produce their own effects, good or bad, upon it.

Men will continue to have impure and poisoned blood so long as they propagate unclean thoughts. Out of a clean heart comes a clean life and a clean body. Out of a defiled mind proceeds a defiled life and corrupt body. Thought is the fountain of action, life and manifestation; make the fountain pure, and all will be pure.

Change of diet will not help a man who will not change his thoughts. When a man makes his thoughts pure, he no longer desires impure food.

If you would perfect your body, guard your mind. If you would renew your body, beautify your mind. Thoughts of malice, envy, disappointment, despondency, rob the body of its health and grace. A sour face does not come by chance; it is made by sour thoughts. Wrinkles that mar are drawn by folly, passion, pride.re the exquisitely adjusted pictures of your ever-moving thoughts.

James Allen

There is but one Word that man is responsible for and that is the inner Word of his own consciousness. He has it in his own power to unfold that consciousness as steadfastly as he pleases, and he will find that according as he works within, he will manifest externally. If the consciousness is one of peace, joy and harmony, the environment will be the same and that individual will enjoy heaven here and now. On the other hand, if the mentality is mixed, life will have some discord, sickness and unrest in it. Heaven and hell are but mental experiences. The man who is filled with the ideas of love, peace and trust, is in heaven, just as the one who is filled with the beliefs of injustice, selfishness and hatred, is in hell.

The silent word within you speaks itself forth into manifestation. Whatever you are thinking will come forth and you cannot experience the abundance of supply in any form if you are holding the thought of lack. You cannot be well or happy if you are holding the thought of hatred or jealousy.

The Word of God which is the divine Spirit within you can manifest nothing which is not a likeness of itself. That we have not known this truth of our Perfection and have not progressed in the spiritual life argues nothing against our being just what the Divine Presence is. We have hitherto manifested nothing higher than our consciousness of the Truth, which perhaps was not very great, but now we perceive the enlargement of consciousness which we are to experience. How shall we accomplish this change? According to the simple rule that "Truth embodied displaces or disembodies error." Wherefore, if you are thinking error, or are not thinking positively and earnestly on the side of Truth, change your methods and displace the error in your thought which you are manifesting in your body and life, with Truth, which you will just as certainly express. This will be the Word of God healing and changing all that is external to you by first being realized in your thought.

Mrs. C. L. Baum

No matter what theory of mind we entertain, we must admit that the brain is the organ and instrument of the mind, in our present state of existence, at least, and that the brain must be considered in this matter. The brain is like a wonderful musical instrument, having millions of keys, upon which we may play innumerable combinations of sounds.

We come into the world with certain tendencies, temperaments, and predispositions, We may account for these tendencies by heredity, or we may account for them upon theories of preexistence, but the facts remain the same. Certain keys seem to respond to our touch more easily than others. Certain notes seem to sound forth as the current of circumstances sweeps over the strings. And certain other notes are less easily vibrated.

But we find that if we but make an effort of the will to restrain the utterance of some of these easily sounded strings, they will grow more difficult to sound, and less liable to be stirred by the passing breeze. And if we will pay attention to some of the other strings that have not been giving forth a clear tone, we will soon get them in good working order; their notes will chime forth clear and vibrant, and will drown the less pleasant sounds. This is the Power of Thought.

William Walker Atkinson

As long as man recognizes only external Power, what Emerson calls "Material force," he will have faith in that alone and will use that alone. When he shall recognize interior, "Spiritual," Power, then he will have faith in that form and will learn to use it. He once was used by the "material" forms of force which he now controls. He is now used as a leaf in the Mississippi of Spiritual Thought-Power. He will learn to use it, and then be the Master of Fate. When he thinks of himself as Power, he will use himself as Power and will be Power. Then will all other forms be obedient to him or be useless. Thought is Power. It is the highest form of Power that man, the director of the Omnipotence in himself, can use. He is Thought. He is Power conscious of itself. Jesus said: "The kingdom of God is within you! " "Kingdom" means, if it means anything, Power. That Power is God. God is Omnipotent and Ever-present. Then it follows that where God is, or where God's kingdom is, there is Omnipotence. He is daily manifesting the Universal Power within himself. He IS Omnipotence.

Can Omnipotence be limited? Not by Itself. Man only can limit himself. Self-Limitation is then the only possible limitation to the power of man. This limitation is a thought man places over himself. This thought is born in ignorance. When he knows himself as he is, he will not be limited. The power to limit is equal to the power limited. Man, therefore, as an individual, balances the Absolute. He is the equal in Power to all that is not himself. The Me and the Non-Me are equal. The Universe is ONE. The ultimate seat of power, so long sought, is found. It is in man. The Ultimate Power so long sought is MAN. As far as Man is concerned, he is all power, and has only to use that which he himself IS. Any power outside himself has influence upon him only so far as he, by recognition of it, has given it power.

Henry Harrison Brown

The deeper mind is responsive to your thought. The subconscious . . sometimes called "subjective or deeper mind" . . sets in operation its unconscious intelligence which attracts to the individual the conditions necessary for his success. Man should make it a special point to do the thing he loves to do. When you are happy in your endeavor, you are a success.

Accept the fact that you have an inner Creative Power. Let this be a positive conviction. This Infinite Power is responsive and reactive to your thought. To know, understand, and apply this principle causes doubt, fear, and worry to gradually disappear.

If a man dwells on the thought, for example, of failure, the thought of failure attracts failure. The subconscious takes the thought of failure as his request, and proceeds to make it manifest in his experience, because he indulges in the mental practice of conceiving failure. The subconscious mind is impersonal and nonselective.

Joseph Murphy

Remember the three great Laws: (1) The Law of Love and Attraction. "Give love, and love to YOUR heart will flow, a strength in your utmost need." (2) The Law of Compensation. "Then give to the World the best you have, and the best will come back to you." (3) The Law of Absolute Justice. "For with what measure ye mete, it shall be measured to you again."

Therefore the ability to win the highest and truest success, to draw to yourself the greatest happiness, to create in your life the highest good, all depend upon giving. The mistaken idea of the animal mind that, to be happy and successful, one must seize and grab, is entirely false, and leads to bitter disappointment. The voice of Wisdom that is heard in the "Silence" tells us that only as we give do we receive. That if we give of our best . . our best thoughts, emotions, service, love . . then the best will come back to us in the exact proportion, no more, no less.

Henry Thomas Hamblin

"There shall no evil happen to the just."

Nothing befalls us that is not of the nature of ourselves.

A person who directs a malicious thought to another will be injured by its rebound if he fails to get subconscious acceptance of the other.

"As ye sow, so shall ye reap."

Neville Goddard

Words are sacred things though few there be who realize it. Words should be to thought what steam is to the engine; if directed to the cylinder and flywheel the engine does perfect work, but if the steam escapes through many tiny holes and cracks the power available for real work is diminished; and wasted steam, like idle words, is an indication of dissipated power.

Man alone has the power to formulate thought into words. A parrot can imitate the sounds of words, but only man has reached the point of development where he is capable of rightly using this gift. It is a great responsibility.

Every word we utter has not only its vibrations, but, together with the form, color and number of the letters composing it, possesses a potency that will never die, but go on and on through the ages until we, their creator, by the power of The Christ within, shall have redeemed them.

Be their power for good or ill it forms one of the very considerable forces that go to make up the Law of Karma. It is one of those crops the sowing of which we are told we shall surely reap. Learn to value words as an index of thought. Make them your obedient servants. Do not waste them. Make every one count for something, for "For every idle word must thou give an account." Do not consider them idle, however, even if apparently trifling and foolish, provided they bring cheer and comfort into the life of some other.

Harriette Augusta Curtiss

The Persian poet wrote: "There is no Heaven or Hell but that which man creates for himself" He might have added with equal truth that man creates himself, builds himself around the life which is his. He does it by his thought, just as he creates his conditions by his thought. So again let me impress upon you the importance of concentration; according to your thought are you created, for you are recreated, reincarnated daily. You change every hour, and the change is the result of the thought. So think thoughts of life, thoughts of reality, thoughts of vital love, and attract that understanding which is life everlasting.

Grace M. Brown

We should keep this in mind . . the Spirit makes all things out of Itself. Everything comes into being without effort, and when we exert ourselves we are not in accord with the Creative Spirit in the way in which It works. The impulse of the Spirit to move must be caused by a desire to express what It feels Itself to be . . Beauty, Form, Color, Life, Love and Power. All things else we find in the manifest universe are attributes of the Spirit, and are caused to spring into being through the Word, because the Spirit wants to enjoy Itself.

We find, then, that the Word, which is the inner activity of thought, comes first in the creative series, and all else comes from the effect of the Word operating upon a universal substance. If the Word precedes all else, then the Word is what we are looking for, and when we get it we shall have what the world has sought from time immemorial. We must, if we wish to prove the power of the Spirit in our lives, look not to outside things or effects, but to the Word alone. The human eye sees and the human hand touches only that which is an effect. Unseen law controls everything; but this Law also is an effect; Law did not make itself; the Law is not intelligence or causation.

Before there can be a Law there must be something that acts, and the Law is the way it acts; it is intelligence. "In the beginning was the Word." This Word or the activity of the Spirit, is the cause of the law, and the law in its place is the cause of the thing, and the thing is always an effect; that is, it did not make itself; it is a result. The Word always comes first in the creative series; "The Word was with God and the Word was God" and the Word still is God.

When we realize that man is like God (and he could not be otherwise, being made out of God), we will realize that his word also has power. If there is but One Mind then it follows that our word, our Thought is the activity of that One Mind in our consciousness; the power that holds the planets in their place is the same power that flows through man.

We must place the Word where it belongs, whether it is the word of God in the Universe or the word of man in the individual; it is always first, before all else, in the beginning. The real sequence is this: Cause, Spirit, Intelligence, God; the Word, the activity of Intelligence; the effect, or the visible thing, whether it is a planet or a peanut. All are made out of the same thing.

What we need to do is to learn how to use the word so that all will come to see that they are creative centers within themselves.

Ernest Holmes

Stop thinking trouble if you want to attract its opposite; stop thinking poverty if you wish to attract plenty. Refuse to have anything to do with the things you fear, the things you do not want. A piece of magnetized steel will attract only the products of iron ore. It has no affinity for wood, copper, rubber, or any other substance that has not iron in it. When you were a boy you found that your little steel magnet would pick up a needle but not a match or a toothpick. It would draw to itself only that like itself.

Men and women are human magnets. Just as a steel magnet drawn through a pile of rubbish will pull out only the things which have an affinity for it, so we are constantly drawing to us, establishing relations with, the things and the people that respond to our thoughts and ideals.

Our environment, our associates, our general condition are the result of our mental attraction. These things have come to us on the physical plane because we have concentrated upon them, have related ourselves to them mentally; they are our affinities, and will remain with us as long as the affinity for them continues to exist in our minds. Your thoughts, your viewpoints, your conception of what your status and position in life will be, your ideal of your future, will draw you exactly to that plane like a lodestone.

Focus your mind, your predictions, your expectations on poverty, failure and wretchedness; banish ambition, hope, expectation of good things, and give full sway in your mentality to fear, worry, doubt, anticipation of evil, and the ego magnet will draw you unerringly to squalid surroundings, to an inferior position, to association with persons of a lower order of mind on a meaner social plane.

Orison Swett Marden

The world of things is the other half of the world of thoughts. The inner informs the outer. The greater embraces the lesser. Matter is the counterpart of mind. Events are streams of thought. Circumstances are combinations of thought, and the outer conditions and actions of others in which each man is involved are intimately related to his own mental needs and development. Man is a part of his surroundings. He is not separate from his fellows, but is bound closely to them by the peculiar intimacy and interaction of deeds, and by those fundamental laws of thought which are the roots of human society.

One cannot alter external things to suit his passing whims and wishes, but he can set aside his whims and wishes; he can so alter his attitude of mind towards externals that they will assume a different aspect. He cannot mold the actions of others towards him, but he can rightly fashion his actions towards them. He cannot break down the wall of circumstance by which he is surrounded, but he can wisely adapt himself to it, or find the way out into enlarged circumstances by extending his mental horizon. Things follow thoughts. Alter your thoughts, and things will receive a new adjustment. To reflect truly the mirror must be true. A warped glass gives back an exaggerated image.

A disturbed mind gives a distorted reflection of the world. Subdue the mind, organize and tranquilize it, and a more beautiful image of the universe, a more prefect perception of the world-order will be the result.

James Allen

The character of the thought vibrations sent out by us depends upon the nature of the thought itself. If thought had color (and some say that they have), we should see our fear and worry thought as murky, heavy, clouds hanging close to the earth; our bright, cheerful and happy, confident, "I can and I will' thought as light, fleecy, vapory clouds hanging close to the earth; our bright, cheerful and happy, confident, "I can and I Will" thoughts as light, fleecy, vapory clouds, traveling swiftly and mingling with others of their kind, forming fleecy cloud banks, high above the level of the dense, mephitic, foul exhalations produced by fear and worry "I can't" thoughts.

William Walker Atkinson

It is the nature of thought to manifest itself. It is not lifeless like the stone; it is germinant. It cannot be repressed or hidden. Not merely does it develop itself according to the laws of its own nature, that is, as thought; like the sprouting seed, it shows itself above the soil in which it springs. Words and acts are its inevitable expression. Thought runs through all the framework of our outward life, as the nerves run through the body, forming a separate system, yet giving life to all.

Charles Carroll Everett

Faith is a way of thinking, an inner attitude, a feeling, or inner awareness. A man can have faith in failure, success, misfortune, and poverty, and he will express all these states in his life. This is faith in reverse. Faith is what you behold, agree with, and accept in your mind; actually it is a thought in your mind, and thoughts being creative, we create what we think for man is belief expressed. We create what we really believe in our mind and heart. It is what you really believe deep down in your heart that is important, not that to which you merely give formal or intellectual assent.

Joseph Murphy

Light has broken through the vestments of mortality and Immortality has come to light in the discovery of Thought as Power. The Science of Thought has begun. The Art of Thinking is at hand. Man is learning How to think and What to think. When he thinks as he can and will think, there will be no sickness, disease, poverty, accident, suffering, or want. This is as scientific a prophecy as was ever made in a chemical laboratory. "When I know how to harness steam," said Watt. When any one knows how to harness thought to his desire, then will he not only master all environment, but he will fulfill the prophecy of Paul: "The last enemy to be destroyed is Death.' 'Bodies are Thought-built. They are Thought-destroyed.

What Thought does unconsciously under Law, Thought can do consciously under Law. Thought under Law builds diseased bodies. Thought under Conscious Law will build imperishable bodies. Thought under Law destroys bodies. Thought under Conscious Law will regenerate bodies, will purify them, will refine them, will lift them in their pitch until hands that feel only, and eyes that see only, on the plane of the senses, will also see and feel, at will, bodies that are still here but unseen. The bodies in which men live, when made under Conscious Law will be made and unmade at pleasure, as the possessor shall raise or lower them in pitch, just as the musician changes the pitch of his instrument.

Henry Harrison Brown

The great lesson for you, dear reader, to learn is this, that if the subconscious mind translates each thought into action, then thought control is the one great transcendental fact of life. If you possess the power to control your thoughts, you have at once the power to control your actions. If you can control your actions what a life of possibility opens before you!

One of the principal causes of failure in life is due to inability to control the thoughts. Wrong thoughts reach the subconscious mind, these are translated into wrong actions and these bring failure and disaster in their train.

When the thoughts are uncontrolled, then the subconscious mind will act upon any thought or suggestion that may "float" in.

Now thoughts and suggestions are born not only within the consciousness, they are also received from without. Like a wireless apparatus which receives messages through vibrations in the ether, so does the human mind receive impressions from without.

Thoughts are things, are entities, have form and substance and are eternal. Thoughts impinge upon your consciousness and unless you are able to reject them they will enter the subconscious mind and bring forth action in your life and conduct.

If therefore the thought be evil, then evil will result, if of weakness then failure will follow, you cannot prevent the action once you have entertained the thought.

In the same way if you entertain a noble thought, a noble action will result. If thoughts of success and power are dwelt upon, then success and power to accomplish will be manifested in your life, and circumstances. It is thought that rules your life, therefore if you govern your thoughts you control your life.

Henry Thomas Hamblin

Man's inner body is as real in the world of subjective experience as his outer physical body is real in the world of external realities, but the inner body expresses a more fundamental part of reality. This existing inner body of man must be consciously exercised and directed. The inner world of thought and feeling to which the inner body is attuned has its real structure and exists in its own higher space.

There are two kinds of movement, one that is according to the inner body and another that is according to the outer body. The movement which is according to the inner body is causal, but the outer movement is under compulsion. The inner movement determines the outer which is joined to it, bringing into the outer a movement that is similar to the actions of the inner body. Inner movement is the force by which all events are brought to pass. Outer movement is subject to the compulsion applied to it by the movement of the inner body.

Whenever the actions of the inner body match the actions which the outer must take to appease desire, that desire will be realized.

Construct mentally a drama which implies that your desire is realized and make it one which involves movement of self. Immobilize your outer physical self. Act precisely as though you were going to take a nap, and start the predetermined action in imagination.

A vivid representation of the action is the beginning of that action. Then, as you are falling asleep, consciously imagine yourself into the scene. The length of the sleep is not important, a short nap is sufficient, but carrying the action into sleep thickens fancy into fact.

At first your thoughts may be like rambling sheep that have no shepherd. Don't despair. Should your attention stray seventy times seven, bring it back seventy times seven to its predetermined course until from sheer exhaustion it follows the appointed path. The inner journey must never be without direction. When you take to the inner road, it is to do what you did mentally before you started. You go for the prize you have already seen and accepted.

Neville Goddard

We have within us a power that is greater than anything that we shall ever contact in the outer, a power that can overcome every obstacle in our life and set us safe, satisfied and at peace, healed and prosperous, in a new light, and in a new life.

Mind, all Mind is right here. It is God's Mind, God's creative Power, God's creative Life. We have as much of this Power to use in our daily life as we can believe in and embody.

The store house of nature is filled with infinite good awaiting the touch of our awakened thought to spring forth into manifestation in our life; but the awakening must be on our part and not on the side of life. We stand at the gateway of limitless opportunity in the eternal and changeless NOW. Now is the day in which to begin the new life that is to lift us up to the greater expression of all that is wonderful.

The word that we speak (thought) is the Law of our life and nothing hinders but ourselves. We have through ignorance of our real nature misused the power of our word (thought), and behold what it has brought upon us, "the very thing that we feared." But now it shall produce a new thing, a new heaven and a new earth.

Ernest Holmes

Do we not perceive, therefore, that the substance of the invisible universe is mind: that thought produces energy or the substance of the visible universe by acting upon the invisible: and again, that thought molds this energy or matter into form? We are led, therefore, to the inevitable conclusion that the Existing Cosmos Is Thought in Form; that it exists and moves in the limitless sea of the unmanifest Mind; and that potential power lies in that Mind to create new universes and new forms when and where It will.

Fenwicke L. Holmes

The mind or the plane of thought is both conscious and unconscious. The brain is the instrument of the mind; therefore the brain possesses the machinery that registers the impressions of both conscious and unconscious mental activity. There is never an activity of the mind, whether the subject is aware or unaware of its exercise, but makes a physical impression on the nervous system or the brain. There is never a sensation, whether perceived or unperceived, which does not produce its reflex response in the mind, either conscious or unconscious. Mind and body are mutually responsive, and each reflects the passing status of the other.

If Nature had not developed in man the marvelous machinery of his complex brain and nervous system, he would not be possessed of the high intellect he enjoys. There is no such thing as a thought without a brain. There may indeed be forces in Nature, which are logically related, and which interact with responsive intelligence, but such forces become what we know as thought only when they operate through the organ of a brain.

Henry Frank

"**The things that we see, are but a very small fraction of the things that are.** The real, vital forces at work in our own lives, and in the world about us, are not seen by the ordinary physical eye. Yet they are the causes of which all things we see are merely the effects. Thoughts are forces; like builds like, and like attract like. For one to govern his thinking then is to determine his life." Therefore do not believe anyone who wants to teach you how to "overcome" other people, and to dominate them either by "will-power" or by Hypnotism. If you seek to get the better of other people and to influence them by mind domination, you are charging full tilt against the Law of the Universe, and this can only lead to the most disastrous results.

The "hypnotic gaze" and "suggestion" can never bring you success; it may bring a temporary, fleeting advantage, but this will be followed by disaster either in your business or profession, your body, your life, or your home.

By the right use of your thought-forces you can make yourself a magnet and attract to yourself all that you deserve. We each get what he or she deserves. As we improve the quality of our thoughts, so do we become deserving of better results; as we become deserving of better results, so do better things flow to us by the operation of Universal Law.

By the use of carefully graded denials and affirmations, we break the power of evil thought-habit, and in its place create a new mental attitude, hopeful, strong, cheerful, successful, confident, an attitude of mind that knows not failure, can never be discouraged; that stands firm and unafraid amid the changing scenes of life; an attitude of mind that overcomes, conquers and achieves. An attitude of mind that lives in a sea of positive, helpful, stimulating thoughts, that are the products of the best minds of all ages.

Thus it all comes down to this. It is by the use of denials and affirmations, and by persevering in their use, that the life can be changed, circumstances altered, and ambitious realized. By denials and affirmations we can direct our thought-stream into the right channel; by denials and affirmations we can impress upon our subconscious mind thoughts which, becoming translated into actions, lead to success and all accomplishment. By denials and affirmations we can break down the force of evil habit, and in its place install habits that ennoble and enrich our lives. By denials and affirmations we can build up our characters, changing what was weak and vacillating into that which is powerful and stable.

By denials and affirmations we can concentrate our consciousness upon thoughts of Power, Success and Courage and these, in turn, will attract to us multitudes of other thoughts of a similar nature. Do you realize, dear

Reader, the extent of the wonderful power that you hold in your hands?

Henry Thomas Hamblin

Man is master, and can still every tempest by his "Peace, be still," when he comes to know himself as Soul. Ignorant of his heir ship to the Crown of Life, he yields himself a slave where he should reign as king. He manifests all his power in those ' 'Fundamental facts" of Fiske, Thought and Feeling. He can control all that is not himself, and also himself, by those laws that Buchner calls "Laws of the Universe," for they are only the Laws of Thought. Since man can control thought, he is the Master of the Universe and "a Law unto himself." His Universe is his body and his environment. He is as supreme in his individual Universe as God is in the Absolute Universe.

Henry Harrison Brown

The men who have climbed up in the world have seen themselves climbing, have pictured themselves actually in the position they longed to be in. They have climbed up mentally first. They have kept a vision of themselves as ever climbing to higher and higher things. They have continually affirmed their ability to climb, to grow up to their ideal. If we ever hope to make our dreams come true, we must do as they did; we must actually live in the conscious realization of our ideal. This is the entering wedge which will split the difficulties ahead of us, which will open the doors which shut us from our own. If you are discouraged by repeated failures and disappointments, suffering the pangs of thwarted ambition; if you are not doing the thing you long to do; if life is not yielding the satisfaction, the success and joy of happy service; if your plans do not prosper; if you are hampered by poverty and a narrow, crude, uncongenial environment, there is something wrong . . not with the world, or the Creator's beneficent plans for His children, but with yourself.

You are not thinking right. You are not visualizing yourself as you long to be. We are, every one of us, both ourselves and our environment, true pictures of what we have thought, believed, and done in the past. Every moment of our lives we are experiencing the result of thought. The outward things that have been acting on us, shaping the conditions in which we live, are chiefly the fruits of our own motives, thoughts and acts. What we believe, what we think, what we expect, shapes our lives. Through the control and direction of our thoughts, backed up with corresponding efforts on the physical plane, we can attract to us all our heart's desires.

Orison Swett Marden

The dreamers are the saviors of the world. As the visible world is sustained by the invisible, so men, through all their trials and sins and sordid vocations, are nourished by the beautiful visions of their solitary dreamers. Humanity cannot forget its dreamers. It cannot let their ideals fade and die. It lives in them. It knows them in the realities which it shall one day see and know.

Composer, sculptor, painter, poet, prophet, sage, these are the makers of the afterworld, the architects of heaven. The world is beautiful because they have lived; without them, laboring humanity would perish.

He who cherishes a beautiful vision, a lofty ideal in his heart, will one day realize it. Columbus cherished a vision of another world, and he discovered it. Copernicus fostered the vision of a multiplicity of worlds and a wider universe, and he revealed it. Buddha beheld the vision of a spiritual world of stainless beauty and perfect peace, and he entered into it.

Cherish your visions. Cherish your ideals. Cherish the music that stirs in your heart, the beauty that forms in your mind, the loveliness that drapes your purest thoughts, for out of them will grow all delightful conditions, all heavenly environment; of these, if you but remain true to them, your world will at last be built.

To desire is to obtain; to aspire is to achieve. Shall man's basest desires receive the fullest measure of gratification, and his purest aspirations starve for lack of sustenance? Such is not the Law. Such a condition of things can never obtain . . "Ask and receive."

Dream lofty dreams, and as you dream, so shall you become. Your Vision is the promise of what you shall one day be. Your Ideal is the prophecy of what you shall at last unveil.

James Allen

I wish to direct your attention to one other very important thing about thought, and that is the Adductive Power of Thought. Pay attention to this; please as it is of the highest importance. Avoiding all attempts at a scientific explanation, and keeping away from technical terms, I will state the matter concisely thus: Thoughts attract like thoughts; the good thought attracts other good thoughts; the bad thought, the bad; thought of strength, likewise; thoughts of discouragement and doubt follow the rule, and so on through the entire gamut of thoughts. Your thought attracts to it the corresponding thought of others and increases your stock of that particular kind of thought. Do you see the point?

Think Fear thoughts, and you draw to yourself all the Fear thought in that neighborhood. The harder you think it, the greater supply of undesirable thought flocks to you. Think "I AM Fearless," and all the courageous thought force within your radius will move towards you, and will aid you. Try it. That is, try the latter. Don't think Fear thought.

William Walker Atkinson

The body is composed of billions of cells, each cell being an individual unto itself with its own intelligence. Cells can live in peace only as they harmonize with each other. Love is the force which brings peace and harmony into an organization, and the body is no exception to the rule. When man has charged his thoughts with the universal principal of love, the solar plexus immediately becomes relaxed and the energies are charged with the healing force of love principles. The cells of the body take the impression of mind and at once harmony begins to prevail where discord and its side partner . . disease . . once held sway.

When love and its many modifications predominate, emotion is radiated to every part of the being through the force of energy, and builds the principle into the cells until the body is completely charged with love which is the greatest healing force of mind. If we want to be well we must think constructive thoughts; if we want to be strong we must think strong thoughts; if we want to be happy we must think happy thoughts; for, "As a man thinketh in his heart so is he," is ever true.

It is an immutable law that works for our good as well as for our destruction. A thought that does not affect the emotions does not leave a definite impression. We might well paraphrase that old adage, "As a man thinketh" to "as a man thinketh and is impressed emotionally, so is he."

Mrs. Evelyn Lowes Wicker

Verse ten (Book of John) points out that your consciousness is the creator of your world, but the majority of people do not know that the cause of all is their own state of consciousness. A state of consciousness means what you think, feel, believe, and mentally assent to.

Joseph Murphy

Man's Greatest Discovery enables him now to say: Thought is a form of Energy! The Universe is one Substance, whose manifestation is Motion. "One God, one Law, one Element, And one divine, far off event, Toward which the whole creation moves," says a later poet than Paul, from the same intuition. What is the limit of Power? The limit of wind, wave, water, steam, electric power? What is the limit of light, magnetism, X-ray, heat, and gravity? They are limitless. By the use of musical tones, Keely raised a power he could not control. It destroyed his every machine, softening Bessemer steel to the consistency of putty.

He no more knew the Power he had evoked, than did Franklin know that which he drew from the cloud to make chips and straws dance between his key and the ground. Where is the limit to Electricity? There is none. What is the limit to its application? Human ignorance!

All limitations to Power in any direction are those imposed by man. Nature in one form of motion is as limitless as in any other. Behind each manifestation of Power lies Infinity. Deep and enduring as the glacial marks on the granite ledge, let this truth be etched upon your intellect, then you will have no trouble with my thought. All is One and that One is Omnipresent; not omnipresent in any one manifestation of Power, but in all. The possibility of Infinity lies behind every manifestation. There is no limit to Ever-present Power. Beyond all dream of man, is the possibility of the One.

As sand-grain to a world, is any dream of achievement compared to the Possible. Beyond the possibilities which man has found in the lower pitched vibrations, lie those which he now dimly sees in the vibrations of Thought and Love. To know Power, to apply Power is the whole possible endeavor of man. From cave to "White City," he has only learned how to apply Power. What Power can do, he can do, for he is Power!

Henry Harrison Brown

To the ordinary "man in the street" a thought is an "airy nothing " . . a mere flash in the consciousness . . it comes, it goes, and there is an end to it. To the student of Mind however, thought is known to be the power that is greater than any other power . . a force that controls all other forces. An American writer speaking of Universal Mind says:

"It thinks, and Suns spring into shape;
It wills, and Worlds disintegrate;
It loves and Souls are born."

It will thus be seen that thought is the origin of the visible Universe. All that we see around us is the result of thought. We may even go further, and say that all the invisible forces, which keep the wonderful machinery of the Universe working perfectly and smoothly, are but the thought-energies of the same Universal Mind.

As in the macrocosm so is it in the microcosm; the subliminal mind of man is the same in essence as the Universal Mind of the Universe; the difference is not one of kind but of degree.

In our world, our circumstances, our life, our bodies, we stand supreme, or rather we have within us the power, which properly directed, can make us supreme. This power is "Thought." Thought is so subtle, so elusive, that it has by the majority of men, been considered impossible of control, but the greatest philosophers, seers and leaders in the World's history have known differently. All that they achieved, they accomplished through the power of thought; and this was possible because they had learned the art of thought control.

"What man has done, man can do." This was never so true as it is today, because the science of Mind is now being spread abroad, and that it is possible for quite ordinary people to learn how to control their thoughts, is now known to be a scientific possibility.

Henry Thomas Hamblin

Man is made by circumstances. True. But it is also true that Man makes circumstances. We are not mere machines and automaton. We are rational, self-conscious free, and self-determining beings. We can make of ourselves what we choose. We may shape our destiny as we will. "It is not in our stars, but in ourselves, that we are underlings." So shape your thoughts, your resolves, your persistence, that your life shall reflect all that you choose.

Henry Frank

Thought is everything: action and things are only the externalized result of thought.

That is what Emerson meant when he said, "My children, you will never see anything worse than yourselves." Your own thought about a thing is all you see of it: if your own thought is ugly, that which you look upon becomes to you as your thought.

That is what is meant by, "My children, you will never see anything more lovely than yourselves." All things are lovely to all who are possessed of the vision of loveliness.

That is what Shakespeare meant in Hamlet when he said, "There is nothing either good or bad, but thinking makes it so."

All of which is to say:

You, O Man, carry the world in your heart!

All of the world you see is the reflection of your inner mental condition. You are the manner of man your mental attitudes . . your viewpoint . . have made you.

Reflect and see if what you really are isn't the result of what you have loved to think about when you have been free to follow your heart's desire.

Frank Waller Allen

The mind CREATES the body, and everything the body does. Remember this, remember that everything you do, think, say, or feel, is Created By the Mind. You cannot hide your mind or your thoughts. Watch the lowest laborer at his work. The better mind manifests or creates the best work. Study the vibrations of the minds about you. Watch them unfold to you their every thought or idea in their work.

The truly great soul does the best he can in everything he does.

F. E. Gariner and Dr. R. Swineburne Clymer

Creative Mind receives our thought and cannot stop creating, it must always be making something for us. What it will make depends absolutely and only upon what we are thinking, and what we will attract will depend entirely upon our holding thought to the complete exclusion of all that would contradict it. It is not enough that we should sit down and say, 'I AM one with Infinite Life."

This must mean more than mere words; it must be felt, it must become an embodiment of a positive mental attitude. It is not claiming something to be true which is going to happen; it is not sending out an aspiration, or a desire, or a supplication, or a prayer; it must be the embodiment of that which knows that now it is. This is more than holding a thought.

Our ability to attract will depend upon the largeness of our thought as we feel that it flows out into a great Universal Creative Power. We are dealing with the form in thought, and not with the form in matter. We have learned that when we get the true form in thought and permeate it with the spirit of belief we will see the thought made flesh without any further effort on our part. Thought can attract to us only that which we first mentally embody.

We cannot attract to ourselves that which we are not. We can attract in the outer only that which we have first completely mentally embodied within, that which has become a part of our mental make-up, a part of our inner understanding.

Ernest Holmes

All growth and life is from within outward; all decay and death is from without inward; this is a universal Law. All evolution proceeds from within. All adjustment must take place within. He who ceases to strive against others, and employs his powers in the transformation, regeneration, and development of his own mind, conserves his energies and preserves himself; and as he succeeds in harmonizing his own mind, he leads others by consideration and charity into a like blessed state, for not by assuming authority and guidance over other minds is the way of enlightenment and peace discovered, but by exercising a lawful authority over one's own, and by guiding one's self in pathways of steadfast and lofty virtue.

A man's life proceeds from his heart, his mind; he has compounded that mind by his own thoughts and deeds: it is in his power to refashion that mind by his choice of thought: he can therefore transform his life.

James Allen

Right thinking means right action. If we would only hold the right thought, the constructive thought, the happy thought, the joy thought, the helpful thought, the unselfish thought each day, we should all soon become supremely happy, because, finally, happiness is a mental state. Your degree of happiness or misery today is merely a resultant of your thought. If such a large part of our days were not filled with discordant thoughts, worry thoughts, fear thoughts, envy, jealousy, hatred thoughts, perhaps half unconsciously much of the time, we would be happy instead of miserable. "Seek ye first the kingdom of God and His righteousness; and all these things shall be added unto you."

When we realize the kingdom of God or heaven, that is, the kingdom of harmony, we are in a position to attract everything else that is desirable. Christ meant that when we have put ourselves into harmony with the great Source of supply, when we have become conscious of our oneness with the One, in other words, when we reach the cosmic consciousness, we are right in the midst of the all-supply. One would think that after all these centuries of searching for happiness it would have been found by the great mass of human beings, but how few have yet found it! We have not found it because we have not understood the perfect truth of Christ's philosophy, "The kingdom of God is within you."

All through history man has been hunting for this kingdom of God outside of himself. Multitudes have thought that wealth would furnish the key to this kingdom, which would supply all of his wants. He has looked for this marvelous paradise everywhere but the right place, . . within himself. Divinely fathered and mothered by his Maker, placed in an earthly paradise, infinitely more beautiful, more glorious than any human imagination could conceive, made lord over a world filled with everything necessary to make human beings ideally happy and ideally successful, yet, after centuries of race evolution, centuries of groping after ideal conditions, centuries of searching for his highest good, man is still dissatisfied. The average man is a god playing the fool.

He is still looking for happiness outside of himself. If we had found the kingdom of heaven within, our faces would be so lighted up that we would give the impression to everybody we met that we had just come into possession of some great good fortune, something that had made us exquisitely happy.

You know how pleased people appear when they have come into possession of that which they have struggled for all their lives, people who have perhaps been poor and tried hard to get on, but who barely managed to make a living, and have suddenly fallen heirs to a fortune. How changed the appearance of the whole family! There is an unwonted light in their eyes. Hope has taken the place of despair. Buoyancy and gayety have taken the place of heaviness and gloom. In other words, they have all at once become new creatures. The light of happiness shines through their flesh, looks out of their eyes.

This is how we should all impress one another. Instead of looking miserable and forlorn, God's children ought to look as though they were supremely happy. Their physical eyes should reflect an entrancing beauty which their inward eyes should behold. Through their faces should shine that inner vision which the soul should sense. If we had found the kingdom of heaven within us the countenance of every human being would reflect a superb satisfaction, a harmony, a blessedness which only very few mortals have ever yet reflected.

Orison Swett Marden

Now you begin to realize that your own thought and feeling are your destiny; this is the third and fourth generation spoken of in the Bible. It represents a state of mind wherein you know that you fashion, mold, and direct your own destiny by transforming your mind. You begin to reject all the thoughts and beliefs of the past. As you begin to realize the Omnipotence of the Spirit within and the power of your own thought, you cease giving power to anything else. You enthrone the concepts of freedom, peace, and health in your mind, and you live with these ideas, entering into the reality of them.

In other words you sense and feel you are a son of God, and heir to all the qualities, powers, and attributes of God. You declare your freedom, and write your declaration of independence and freedom in your heart. You begin to love all things good; the law responds accordingly by opening for you the windows of heaven, and pouring out a blessing that there is not room enough to receive.

Joseph Murphy

Through the thoughts we think and the words we speak, we are continually bringing forth into evidence either the Word of God or our false beliefs. One or the other must illumine or darken our mental atmosphere.

Mrs. C. L. Baum

The spoken word creates conditions. It conveys meaning to the listener, and from this arises nearly everything that is accomplished by man. But behind the word is the thought which is the real creative force. The thought must precede the word. The reality must first be pictured and worked out in the architect's mind. Thought, then, is the prime mover in all creation. "As a man thinketh in his heart, so is he."

Kathleen M. H. Besly

To the student who has realized that all is mind and that everything is governed by law, there comes another thought: it is that he can create, or have created for him, from his own thinking. He can create such a strong mental atmosphere of success that its power of attraction will be irresistible. He can send his thought throughout the world and have it bring back to him whatever he wants.

He can so fill his place of business with the power of success that it will draw from far and near. Thought will always bring back to us what we send out. First we must clear our thought of all unbelief.

Without mental clearness on the part of the thinker there can be no real creative work done. As water will reach only its own level, so mind will return to us only what we first believe. We are always getting what we believe but not always what we want. Our thought has the power to reach, in the outer form of conditions, an exact correspondence to our inner convictions.

By thinking, you set in motion a power that creates. It will be exactly as you think. You throw out into mind an idea, and mind creates it for you and sets it on the path of your life. Think of it, then, as your greatest friend. It is always with you wherever you may be. It never deserts you. You are never alone. There is no doubt, no fear, no wondering; you know. You are going to use the only power that there is in the universe. You are going to use it for a definite purpose. You have already fixed this purpose in your thought; now you are going to speak it forth.

You are speaking it for your own good. You desire only the good and you know that only the good can come to you. You have made your unity with life, and now life is going to help you in your affairs.

You are going to establish in your rooms such an atmosphere of success that it will become an irresistible power; it will sweep everything before it as it realizes the greatness and the All-Mightiness of the One. You are so sure, that you will not even look to see if it is going to happen; you KNOW.

And now your word, which is one with the Infinite Life, is to be spoken in calm, perfect trust. It is to be taken up, and at once it is to be operated on. Perfect is the pattern and perfect will be the result. You see yourself surrounded by the thing that you desire. More than this, you are the thing that you desire.

Your word is now establishing it forever; see this, feel it, know it. You are now encompassed by perfect life, by infinite activity, by all power, by all guidance. The power of the Spirit is drawing to you all people; it is supplying you with all good; it is filling you with all life, truth and love.

Wait in perfect silence while that inner power takes it up. And then you know that it is done unto you. There goes forth from this word the power of the Infinite. "The words which I speak, they are spirit and they are life."

Ernest Holmes

Happy, contented and optimistic thoughts soon crystallize into similar conditions in our lives. While unhappy, discouraged and discontented thoughts just as surely and naturally create after their kind.

Elinor S. Moody

The question is always asked, "Where did the first thought of evil come from and why did God allow evil and suffering in the world? Why does He permit war, famine, and death?" And the answer is: He does not permit it. He has nothing to do with it. He gives us the power to think as individuals. He gives us free will and choice and then leaves it up to us as to what we shall think. If we choose to think in terms of limitation that is our affair, but we must bear the consequences of the Law that we get what we think.

We must realize that there is supply enough in the world to satisfy the needs of all. If we fail to take it, it is not the fault or work of God. If we bring pain and loss upon ourselves, it does not involve Him.

Fenwicke L. Holmes

When once the "Great Discovery" was made, through telepathy, that thought is, like heat, sound, light, a mode of motion, identical in principle with all other forms of motion, then was the way open for the study of Life also as a mode of motion. Until then, Life was outside the possibility of study. Its phenomena could be catalogued, but Life itself was an unknown quantity.

Thought is Life transformed in accordance with Nature's one unerring law of Conservation. Force is transformable but non-destructible, non-creatable. Thought, being a form of force, had an antecedent form. In this antecedent form, which we term Life, it passes through the brain and becomes thought. As it passes out of the brain, it ceases to be thought. It becomes some other form of Vibration. It is not lost. Though we may not follow it now, we shall sometime do so. It is safe to infer that part of this force is changed to Will, and from Will is changed into the power to do, into that power which acts in unison with chemical power.

Henry Harrison Brown

Psychology is teaching us that all forms of discouragement, despondent thoughts, thoughts of doubt, of fear, of worry, must be kept out of the mind, for it cannot create while these enemies are in possession of the mental kingdom.

We are finding that in order to create, to build, we must hold a constructive mental attitude all the time, that we must keep all negatives, all thoughts of discouragement, despondency, of possible failure out of the mind. We are learning through psychology that we can produce only that which we concentrate upon, that which we constantly think of; that only that which is dominant in our mind, whether it is beneficial or injurious will be reproduced in our lives.

Your mental attitude will lead you into the light or hold you in darkness. It will lead you to hope or despair, to a glorious success or a miserable failure, and it is entirely within your own power to choose which it shall be.

Successful people, without knowing it, perhaps, are constantly giving themselves prosperity treatments, success treatments, by encouraging themselves, by making their minds positive, so that they will be immune from all negative, discouraging, poverty thought currents. Holding the success thought, the prosperity ideal, constantly dwelling upon one's successful future, expecting it, working for it, . . these are, whether you know it or not, success, prosperity treatments.

Orison Swett Marden

Man can no more get outside the law of habit, than he can get outside the law of gravitation, but he can employ it wisely or unwisely. As scientists and inventors master the physical forces and laws by obeying and using them, so wise men master the spiritual forces and laws in the same way. While the bad man is the whipped slave of habit, the good man is its wise director and master. Not its maker, let me reiterate, nor yet its arbitrary commander, but its self-disciplined

user, its master by virtue of knowledge grounded on obedience. He is the bad man whose habits of thought and action are bad. He is the good man whose habits of thought and action are good. The bad man becomes the good man by transforming or transmuting his habits. He does not alter the law; he alters himself; he adapts himself to the law.

Instead of submitting to selfish indulgences, he obeys moral principles. He becomes the master of the lower by enlisting in the service of the higher. The law of habit remains the same, but he is changed from bad to good by his readjustment to the law.

James Allen

No thought of form can be impressed upon original substance without causing the creation of the form. A person is a thinking center and can originate thought. All the forms that a person fashions with his hands must first exist in his thought. He cannot shape a thing until he has thought that thing. So far, humankind has confined its efforts wholly to the work of its hands, applying manual labor to the world of forms and seeking to change or modify those already existing. Humankind has never thought of trying to cause the creation of new forms by impressing thought upon formless substance.

When a person has a thought-form, he takes material from the forms of nature and makes an image of the form which is in his mind. People have, so far, made little or no effort to cooperate with formless intelligence . . to work "with the Father." The individual has not dreamed that he can "do what he seeth the Father doing." An individual reshapes and modifies existing forms by manual labor and has given no attention to the question of whether he may produce things from formless substance by communicating his thoughts to it. We propose to prove that he may do so . . to prove that any man or woman may do so . . and to show how. As our first step, we must lay down three fundamental propositions.

First, we assert that there is one original formless stuff or substance from which all things are made. All the seemingly many elements are but different presentations of one element. All the many forms found in organic and inorganic nature are but different shapes, made from the same stuff. And this stuff is thinking stuff . . a thought held in it produces the form of the thought. Thought, in thinking substance, produces shapes. A human being is a thinking center, capable of original thought. If a person can communicate his thought to original thinking substance, he can cause the creation, or formation, of the thing he thinks about. To summarize this:

There is a thinking stuff from which all things are made, and which, in its original state, permeates, penetrates, and fills the interspaces of the universe.

A thought in this substance produces the thing that is imaged by the thought.

A person can form things in his thought, and, by impressing his thought upon formless substance, can cause the thing he thinks about to be created.

You must lay aside all other concepts of the universe, and you must dwell upon this until it is fixed in your mind and has become your habitual thought. Read these statements over and over again. Fix every word upon your memory and meditate upon them until you firmly believe what they say. If a doubt comes to you, cast it aside. Do not listen to arguments against this idea. Do not go to churches or lectures where a contrary concept of things is taught or preached. Do not read magazines or books which teach a different idea. If you get mixed up in your understanding, belief, and faith, all your efforts will be in vain. Do not ask why these things are true nor speculate as to how they can be true. Simply take them on trust. The science of getting rich begins with the absolute acceptance of this.

Wallace Wattles

Whatever we dwell upon in thought becomes a reality to us. That which we dwell upon most and strongest is soonest realized. We are in a continuous growth of realization, getting tangible results of our thoughts. If we are dwelling much on healthy harmony, peace and happiness, we will find that they will become such a reality to us that they will exclude sin, sickness and evil from our thought. This should always be our attitude. "I have set before you life and death, blessing and cursing; therefore choose life, that both thou and thy seed may live." We need to inquire diligently into our own minds and see what we are dwelling on most, and choose life that we may live.

If we hold strongly to the idea of the power of the Omnipresence and our unity with it, we must ultimately realize truth and forget the shadows of unreality. This applies to our attitude towards others as well as to ourselves. We should always see only the good in others, and purify our own conscious thought so that our very presence will be a blessing. Remember that the sun goes on its way expressing nothing but its own perfect light; it knows no darkness, neither can anything else know darkness in its presence.

Another strong aid to realization is what is called the silence. This, as the name indicates, is a silent period of meditation and concentration for the purpose of coming face to face with the invisible Presence within; that in this inner stillness we may be able to feel and know this Presence with us always.

No one can get the consciousness of this presence for us and we cannot get it without effort. It is by thus training the thought to concentration, that we come to know the reality of the universe in which we as Spirit Substance, live, move and have our being. It is in the silence that we realize that we are one with this reality that lies back of all external form.

Mrs. C. L. Baum

Besides affecting others, our thoughts affect us, not only temporarily, but also permanently. We are what we think ourselves into being. The biblical statement that "as a man thinketh in his heart, so is he," is literally correct. We are all creatures of our own mental creating. You know how easy it is to think yourself into a "blue" state of mind, or the reverse, but you do not realize that repeated thought upon a certain line will manifest itself not only in character (which it certainly does), but also in the physical appearance of the thinker. This is a demonstrable fact, and you have but to look around you to realize it. You have noticed how a man's occupation shows itself in his appearance and general character.

What do you suppose occasions this phenomenon? Nothing more or less than that thought. If you've have changed your occupation, your general character and appearance kept pace with your changed habits of thought. Your new occupation brought out a new train of thought, and "Thoughts take form in Action." You may have never taken this view of the matter, but it is true nevertheless, and you may find ample proof of its correctness by merely looking around you.

William Walker Atkinson

Who shall limit the Power of thought? Faith can move mountains. Faith is only Thought united with, and directing, all the Soul forces. Faith is the Self-Suggestion of Power. Faith is a Suggestion of the Conscious man dropped into the Infinity of the Unconscious. Faith is telling the Soul what to manifest. Faith is the Conscious Power of God. Faith is the Power of the Conscious God.

Henry Harrison Brown

The Objective or Conscious Mind is the outer or surface mind of mind. It is the finite mind of very close limitations. It receives impressions through the organs of sight, hearing, taste, touch and smell. It learns from books, speech, experience and experiment.

We have seen that the subliminal mind is one with the Infinite Mind of the Universe, differing only in degree and not in kind, yet this is useless if the objective mind does not make use of the potential powers lying dormant within.

We have also seen that the so called subconscious mind is pregnant with tremendous power, and that it is a wonderful intelligence far exceeding anything that the objective consciousness can grasp or understand. Further that this is regulated and controlled by thoughts, impressions and suggestions, coming through the conscious mind. Therefore this great intelligence is ruled and governed, or ought to be, by the objective mind. Yet of what use is all this if the mind of the senses does not govern wisely or does not govern at all, but lets the subconscious mind run amuck, as it were, and acting upon instincts and false impressions, untruths and harmful suggestions, turn the whole life into an inferno of trouble and difficulty?

Therefore you will see that the objective mind, although very limited, is, in a way, the most important of all, at any rate as far as this life and consciousness are concerned, for through it the Ego governs or can govern the whole of the submerged mind.

Henry Thomas Hamblin

Mastery of self-control of your thoughts and feelings is your highest achievement

Neville Goddard

The upper brain is controlled by conscious thought. The middle brain consists of the residual of the impressions

left by the passing thought once resident in the consciousness. Thus the middle brain is the product of the upper brain. But only so in part.

For, as we are at present constituted, myriads of impressions leave their residual effects in the middle brain in which the upper brain has no part. The dynamic or active mind is the motor of the upper brain. The latent or static mind is the motor of the middle brain. As the middle brain results largely from the activities of the upper brain, so to a very large extent the static mind is subject to the control of the dynamic mind.

Hence, the conscious thoughts we entertain are themselves responsible for the subconscious forces that prevail. If the conscious mind undertake seriously to hold in its leash of power the activities of the latent mind, it may cause the subconscious or subliminal energies to respond to its commands and make for the good, the health, and the happiness of the individual.

Henry Frank

Prosperity is in our own hands to do with as we will, but we will never reach it until we learn to control our thought. We must see only what we want and never allow the other things to enter. If we wish activity we must be active in our thought, we must see activity and speak it into everything that we do. The spoken word shall bring it to pass. We speak the word, it is brought to pass of the Power that we speak it into. We can only speak the word that we understand, the activity will correspond to our inner concepts. If they are large the results will be large. The thing to do is to unify ourselves with all the biggest ideas that we can compass; and realizing that our ideas govern our power of attraction, we should be constantly enlarging within ourselves. We must realize our at-one-ment with All Power and know that our word will bring it to pass.

We speak the word, it is brought to pass of As consciousness grows it will manifest in enlarged opportunities and a greater field of action. Most people think in the terms of universal powers. Feel that you are surrounded by all the power that there is when you speak and never doubt but that what you say will spring into being.

We should speak right out into mind all that we desire, and believe that it will be done unto us. Never take the time to listen to those who doubt. We observe that their philosophy has done but little to save the world or themselves. here again let the dead bury the dead and see to it that you maintain in your own thought what you want, letting go of all else.

Think only what you want to happen and never let yourself get mentally lazy and sluggish taking on the suggestions of poverty and limitation. See yourself as being in the position that you desire, mentally dwell upon it and then speak with perfect assurance that it is done; and then forget it and trust in the law. This will answer all needs.

Ernest Holmes

Fears and doubts repel prosperity. Abundance cannot get to a person who holds such a mental attitude. Things that are unlike in the mental realm repel one another. Trying to become prosperous while always talking poverty, thinking poverty, dreading it, predicting that you will always be poor, is like trying to cure disease by always thinking about it, picturing it, visualizing it, believing that you are always going to be sick, that you never can be cured.

Nothing can attract prosperity but that which has an affinity for it, the prosperous thought, the prosperous conviction, the prosperity faith, the prosperity ambition. Opulence follows a law as strict as that of mathematics. If we obey the law we get the opulent flow. If we disobey the law, we cut off the flow. Most of us tap the great life supply by inserting a half-inch pipe, and then pinch even this with our doubts, fears and uncertainties. There is no lack in Him in whom all fullness lies. The pinching, the limitation is in ourselves, "for He satisfieth the longing soul and filleth the hungry soul with good things."

We must conquer inward poverty before we can conquer outward poverty. True prosperity is the inward consciousness of spiritual opulence, wholeness, completeness; we cannot feel poor when we are conscious of being enveloped in the all-supply, that God is our partner, our Shepherd, and that we cannot want.

Orison Swett Marden

Each man moves in the limited or expansive circle of his own thoughts, and all outside that circle is non-existent to him. He only knows that which he has become. The narrower the boundary, the more convinced is the man that there is no further limit, no other circle. The lesser cannot contain the greater, and he has no means of apprehending the larger minds; such knowledge comes only by growth.

The man who moves in a widely extended circle of thought knows all the lesser circles from which he has emerged, for in the larger experience all lesser experiences are contained and preserved; and when his circle impinges upon the sphere of perfect manhood, when he is fitting himself for company and communion with them of blameless conduct and profound understanding, then his wisdom will have become sufficient to convince him that there are wider circles still beyond of which he is as yet but dimly conscious, or is entirely ignorant.

James Allen

A man who thinks Energy manifests Energy. The man, who thinks Courage manifests courage. The man who thinks, "I can and I will," "gets there", while the "I can't" man "gets left." You know that to be true. Now, what causes the difference? Thought . . just plain thought. But why? Just because it cannot help itself. Action follows as the natural result of vigorous thinking. You think in earnest, and action does the rest.

Thought is the greatest thing in the world. If you do not know it now, you will. You may say that this is no new thing to you . . that you know all about "making up your mind," and all that sort of thing, long ago. Then why did you not put it into practice and make something of yourself? I will tell you the trouble.

You thought "I Can't" instead of "I Can." Now, I am going to change that "I Can't" into a big "I Can" and a bigger "I Will." That is what I am here for, and I intend to "make you over," before I am through with you. I suppose that you thought I would give you an elaborate, transcendental discourse on things away up in the clouds, and hoped that I would tell you how to charge yourself up with a lot of magnetism, so that you would be able to light the gas with the tips of your fingers, or draw everybody to you like a piece of steel to a magnet, now, didn't you? Well, I am not. But I intend to tell you how you can generate in yourself a force, compared with which magnetism is weak; a force that will make a man of you; a force that will make you realize the I AM within you; a power that will enable you to be a man of strong personal qualities; a man of influence; a successful man.

I will tell you how you can acquire that which you have been calling Personal Magnetism, providing you will start at it in earnest. It is worth working for, and when you feel your new strength developing within you, you would not exchange your newfound knowledge for a fortune.

William Walker Atkinson

Of the vital power of thought and the interior forces in molding conditions, and more, of the supremacy of thought over all conditions, the world has scarcely the faintest grasp, not to say even idea, as yet. The fact that thoughts are forces, and that through them we have creative power, is one of the most vital facts of the universe, the most vital fact of man's being. And through this instrumentality we have in our grasp and as our rightful heritage, the power of making life and all its manifold conditions exactly what we will.

Through our thought-forces we have creative power, not in a figurative sense, but in reality. Everything in the material universe about us had its origin first in spirit, in thought, and from this it took its form. The very world in which we live, with all its manifold wonders and sublime manifestations, is the result of the energies of the Divine Intelligence or Mind, . . God, or whatever term it comes convenient for each one to use. And God said, Let there be, and there was, . . the material world, at least the material manifestation of it, literally spoken into existence, the spoken word, however, but the outward manifestation of the interior forces of the Supreme Intelligence.

Every castle the world has ever seen was first an ideal in the architect's mind. Every statue was first an ideal in the sculptor's mind. Every piece of mechanism the world has ever known was first formed in the mind of the inventor. Here it was given birth to. These same mind-forces then dictated to and sent the energy into the hand that drew the model, and then again dictated to and sent the energy into the hands whereby the first instrument was clothed in the material form of metal or of wood. The lower negative always gives way to the higher when made positive. Mind is positive: matter is negative.

Each individual life is a part of, and hence is one with, the Infinite Life; and the highest intelligence and power belongs to each in just the degree that he recognizes his oneness and lays claim to and uses it. The power of the word is not merely an idle phrase or form of expression. It is a real mental, spiritual, scientific fact, and can become vital and powerful in your hands and in mine in just the degree that we understand the omnipotence of the thought forces and raise all to the higher planes.

The blind, the lame, the diseased, stood before Christ, who said, "receive thy sight, rise up and walk, or, be thou healed;" and lo! it was so. The spoken word, however, was but the outward expression and manifestation of His interior thought forces, the power and potency of which He so thoroughly knew. But the laws governing them are the same today as they were then, and it lies in our power to use them the same as it lay in His.

Ralph Waldo Trine

Love, remember, is the creative power. If you ever get to the place where you love everything and everybody every hour of every day of your life, all the problems of your life will be solved. Love heals, and the world wants love like that, a love which goes out through the very pores of the skin, emanating with the magnetic currents of the body.

When you have that much love you will think love and speak love and love will be the impulse back of everything you do. Love is the great constructive current. Hatred is the destructive current of thought.

Mary C. Ferriter

The conscious mind of man is personal and selective. It chooses, selects, weighs, analyzes, dissects, and investigates. It is capable of inductive and deductive reasoning. The subjective or subconscious mind is subject to the conscious mind. It might be called a servant of the conscious mind. The subconscious obeys the order of the conscious mind. Your conscious thought has power. The power you are acquainted with is thought. Back of your thought is Mind, Spirit, or God. Focused, directed thoughts reach the subjective levels; they must be of a certain degree of intensity. Intensity is acquired by concentration.

To concentrate is to come back to the centre and contemplate the Infinite Power within you which lies stretched in smiling repose. To concentrate properly you still the wheels of your mind, and enter into a quiet, relaxed, mental state. When you concentrate, you gather your thoughts together, and you focus all your attention on your ideal, aim, or objective. You are now at a focal or central point, where you are giving all your attention and devotion to your mental image.

The procedure of focused attention is somewhat similar to that of a magnifying glass, and the focus it makes of the rays of the sun. You can see the difference in the effect of scattered vibrations of the sun's heat, and the vibrations which emanate from a central point. You can direct the rays of the magnifying glass, so it will burn up a particular object upon which it is directed. Focused, steadied attention of your mental images gains a similar intensity, and a deep, lasting impression is made on the sensitive plate of the subconscious mind.

You may have to repeat this drama of the mind many times before an impression is made, but the secret of impregnating the deeper mind is continuous or sustained imagination. When fear or worry comes to you during the day, you can always immediately gaze upon that lovely picture in your mind, realizing and knowing you have operated a definite, psychological law which is now working for you in the dark house of your mind. As you do this, you are truly watering the seed and fertilizing it; thereby accelerating its growth.

The conscious mind of man is the motor; the subconscious is the engine. You must start the motor, and the engine will do the work. The conscious mind is the dynamo that awakens the power of the subconscious.

Joseph Murphy

For men live in spheres low or high according to the nature of their thoughts. Their world is as dark and narrow as they conceive it to be, as expansive and glorious as their comprehensive capacity. Everything around them is tinged with the color of their thoughts.

Consider the man whose mind is suspicious, covetous, envious. How small and mean and drear everything appears to him. Having no grandeur in himself, he sees no grandeur anywhere; being ignoble himself, he is incapable of seeing nobility in any being. Even his God is a covetous being that can be bribed, and he judges all men and women to be just as petty and selfish as he himself is, so that he sees in the most exalted acts of unselfishness only motives that are mean and base.

Consider again the man whose mind is unsuspecting, generous, magnanimous. How wondrous and beautiful is his world. He is conscious of some kind of nobility in all creatures and beings. He sees men as true, and to him they are true. In his presence the meanest forget their nature, and for the moment become like himself, getting a glimpse, albeit confused, in that temporary upliftments of a higher order of things, of an immeasurably nobler and happier life.

James Allen

Mind is the Creator, the Creator of all thought and desire. These thoughts and desires unfold and manifest the mind. The desire, or love, hidden WITHIN the mind's Center is what gives power to produce, or create.

If a man is selfish, he lavishes all his thoughts on himself. He creates and produces for self, because there is where his love is centered and his power is selfish love. Love for money, home, country, children, worldly goods, or fame, gives the power to create the thing desired. Authors spend hours and labor indefatigably to produce the idea their minds have created.

They have the power according to their love. All men are Creators. They love what they create. And their love gives them power to create. No matter what it is, good or bad.

F. E. Gariner and Dr. R. Swineburne Clymer

Creative mind cannot force itself upon us because we have the power of self-choice. It recognizes us when we recognize it. When we think that we are limited or have not been heard, it must take that thought and bring it into manifestation for us.

When we look about us and see nature so beautiful, lavish and so limitless, when we realize that something, some power, is behind all, and sees to it that plenty obtains everywhere, so that in all things manifest there is more than could be used; and when on the other hand we see man so limited, sick, sad and needy, we are disposed to ask this question: "Is God good after all? Does He really care for the people of His creation? Why am I sick? Why am I poor?" Little do we realize that the answer is in our own mouths, in the creative power of our own thought. The average person when told the Truth will still seek some other way.

Ernest Holmes

When you long for anything that it is right for you to have, affirm in perfect confidence that the thing is already yours; claim it as a reality; do what you can on the material plane to make it yours, and soon you will reap what you have sown in thought and in positive creative affirmation.

Say to yourself, "God is no respecter of persons. Our Father is not and could not be, partial in His treatment of His children. To all, without distinction, He gives the same love, the same rights and privileges. He will give me, through my own effort, what I need, what I ask for. I can and I will do what I long to do. I will be what I desire to be."

Make these affirmations again and again, and do not wait for an opportunity to begin the thing you want to do. Make your opportunity. The power of affirmation will work miracles for you.

Orison Swett Marden

That which we call Personal Magnetism is the subtle current of thought-waves, or thought-vibrations, projected from the human mind. Every thought created by our minds is a force of greater or lesser intensity, varying in strength according to the impetus imparted to it at the time of its creation. When we think, we send from us a subtle current, which tables along like a ray often far removed from us by space, a forceful thought will go on its errand charged with a mighty power, and will often bear down the instinctive resistance of the minds of others to outside impressions, whilst a weak thought will be unable to obtain an entrance Trance to the mental castle of another, unless that castle be but poorly guarded.

Repeated thoughts along the same lines sent one after the other, will . . often effect . . an entrance where a single thought-wave, although much stronger, will be repulsed. It is an exhibition of a physical law in the Psychical world, and exemplifies the old saying about steady dripping wearing away a stone.

William Walker Atkinson

Most of us strangle our supply by our pinching thoughts, our stingy, poverty thought, our doubt and fear thoughts. We pinch or entirely cut off the inflow of prosperity by our poverty-stricken mental attitude. The stream of plenty flows toward the open mind, the expectant mind. It flows toward faith and confidence and away from doubt. It will not flow toward a stingy, pessimistic unbelieving mind, a fearing, worrying, anxious mind. We must keep the current open or the supply will be cut off. We cannot get a sixty or a hundred candle power supply through a four or eight candle power bulb.

The stream of plenty, of unlimited opulence, is flowing right past your door, carrying an infinite, never-ending supply of all the good things that heart could wish for. If you have the faith that creates, the faith that believes the best is coming to you, you can reach out mentally into this great stream of plenty . . the universal supply . . and get material aid to build what you will. The supply is there. It rests with you to make the connection that will draw it to you, the opulent thought.

Orison Swett Marden

In our very laboratory experiments we are demonstrating the great fact that thoughts are forces. They have form, and duality, and substance, and power, and we are beginning to find that there is what we may term a science of thought. Everything in the material universe about us, everything the universe has ever known, had its origin first in thought. From this it took its form. Every castle, every statue, every painting, every piece of mechanism, everything had its birth, its origin, first in the mind of the one who formed it before it received its material expression or embodiment. The Very universe in which we live is the result of the thought energies of God, the Infinite Spirit that is back of all. And if it is true, as we have found, that we in our true selves are in essence the same, and in this sense are one with the life of this Infinite Spirit, do we not then see that in the degree that we come into a vital realization of this stupendous fact, we, through the operation of our interior, spiritual, thought forces, have in like sense creative power?

Everything exists in the unseen before it is manifested or realized in the seen, and in this sense it is true that the unseen things are the real, while the things that are seen are the unreal. The unseen things are cause; the seen things are effect. The unseen things are the eternal; the seen things are the changing, the transient. The "power of the word" is a literal scientific fact. Through the operation of our thought forces we have creative power. The spoken word is nothing more nor less than the outward expression of the workings of these interior forces.

The spoken word is then, in a sense, the means whereby the thought-forces are focused and directed along any particular line; and this concentration, this giving them direction, is necessary before any outward or material manifestation of their power can become evident. Much is said in regard to "building castles in the air," and one who is given to this building is not always looked upon with favor. But castles in the air are always necessary before we can have castles on the ground, before we can have castles in which to live. The trouble with the one who gives himself to building castles in the air is not that he builds them in the air, but that he does not go farther and actualize in life, in character, in material form, the castles he thus builds. He does part of the work, a very necessary part; but another equally necessary part remains still undone.

There is in connection with the thought-forces what we may term, the drawing power of mind, and the great law operating here is one with that great law of the universe, that like attracts like. We are continually attracting to us from both the seen and the unseen side of life, forces and conditions most akin to those of our own thoughts.

This law is continually operating whether we are conscious of it or not. We are all living, so to speak, in a vast ocean of thought, and the very atmosphere around us is continually filled with the thought forces that are being continually sent or that are continually going out in the form of thought waves. We are all affected, more or less, by these thought forces, either consciously or unconsciously; and in the degree that we are more or less sensitively organized, or in the degree that we are negative and so are open to outside influences, rather than positive, thus determining what influences shall enter into our realm of thought, and hence into our lives.

Ralph Waldo Trine

The universe does not favor the greedy, the dishonest, the vicious, although on the mere surface it may sometimes appear to do so; it helps the honest, the magnanimous, the virtuous.

All the great Teachers of the ages have declared this in varying forms, and to prove and know it a man has but to persist in making himself more and more virtuous by lifting up his thoughts.

Intellectual achievements are the result of thought consecrated to the search for knowledge, or for the beautiful and true in life and nature. Such achievements may be sometimes connected with vanity and ambition but they are not the outcome of those characteristics. They are the natural outgrowth of long an arduous effort, and of pure and unselfish thoughts.

Spiritual achievements are the consummation of holy aspirations. He who lives constantly in the conception of noble and lofty thoughts, who dwells upon all that is pure and unselfish, will, as surely as the sun reaches its zenith and the moon its full, become wise and noble in character, and rise into a position of influence and blessedness.

James Allen

The word spoken once from the mind that knows is immediately taken up by the Mind in which we live, and this Mind begins to create around the word, which is the seed, the thing thought of. We must speak that word with authority. There can be no wondering if it is going to work. When we plant a seed in the ground and water and care for it, we never doubt but a plant will spring into being. So it is with the word. It is acted upon by some power which we do not see, but that the power is there, there is no doubt, since all who go about it get results.

As Thomas Edison says of electricity, "It Is; use it;" so we say of mind, "It Is; use it." Always remember that your every thought is the way that you are creating, since it is the way that you are thinking.

Ernest Holmes

The Mind is invisible, but its form of expression and thoughts are daily manifested and felt, because there is a communication between mind and matter, and matter conveys to a more compact, tangible form the ideas and workings of the mind. Within the ether and spaces about us, recognized and felt by the finer substance, Mind, dwells ideas, thoughts, a manifestation of the workings of some greater or force.

This is conveyed to matter (darkness) and is developed into a more compact and tangible form. The very fact that the idea or thought becomes tangible is but greater proof that a Supreme Force exists and dwells in and with and illuminates matter, or man.

F. E. Gariner and Dr. R. Swineburne Clymer

Metaphysics, therefore, teaches us how we may govern our bodies, our world, and our happiness by the thoughts we think; for it declares that man reproduces the creative method and that what is true in the macrocosm or universe is true in the microcosm or individual, that thoughts become things.

And it claims that by acquiring the knowledge of the law, and by working in harmony with it, man can be freed from limitations of all kinds.

Fenwicke L. Holmes

Man, like God, has the power to create. He is the architect of his character and the molder of his destiny. Thoughts are the tools man uses to bring about whatever condition or change he desires. The lowest manifestation of mind is sensation . . the highest, imagination. There are beings higher than man as man is higher than an insect. All are partakers of universal mind.

There is only mind . . Universal Mind. Our mind is the use we make of this mind.

Frank L. Hammer

If you will insist upon mentally seeing yourself surrounded by things and conditions as you wish them to be you will understand that the Creative Energy sends its substance in the direction indicated by the tendency of your thoughts. Herein lies the advantage of holding your thought in the form of a mental picture.

Genevieve Behrend

The great Teacher said, "Man shall give an account for every idle word that he speaks." Your day of judgment is now, and at this very time you may be having to face your own thoughts in the form of flesh and blood. "The word became flesh." I can speak my body into a state of health, power or any other condition . . either negative or positive.

"In the beginning was the Word and the Word was with God and the Word was God." As you go to the office with thoughts of financial depression, you are vibrating this wonderful universal thinking Substance . . Mind . . and you are causing it to take negative forms. I cannot think without having the results of that thought. It is always cause and effect.

Franklin Fillmore Farrington

Thoughts are not only things; they are also incarnate characters. They become organized into living beings which betimes control us. The novel writer may create his characters, but, once created, they become his guide and inspiration.

They speak from the pages to him and answer the problems that confront him. Like spiritual forms they make their entrances and exits to the solitary auditor who indites their deeds on the excited pages. They become to him as real, yea, more real, than the men and women he meets in the streets and shops. A literary critic was recently amazed to find a character he well knew, a demoralized poet, so literally portrayed in a current novel, that he was sure the writer must have known him. Yet he could not bring himself to believe that the woman who wrote the novel in view could have intimately known a character so degenerate and debased. Such a fact alone would compromise and defame her.

Yet he made bold to ask her, for he could not imagine how the writer, an Englishwoman, could know this dreamy and unhappy wight whom she depicted as one of her conspicuous characters. What was the critic's amazement to learn from her own lips that she had never seen him in the flesh nor knew that he had a bodily existence. " Yet," she said, " he is better known to me than a man in the flesh could be . . he is more real, more consciously present, than any physical being I ever knew."

Henry Frank

Articles in your daily paper on diet, Influenza and other topics again suggest illness to you; even the advertisements suggest that you have Kidney disease or worse, and that to save your life it is necessary for you to take certain tablets or pills. The newspapers themselves do their best to suggest evil to you. The columns are full of the seamy sordid side of life. If any man commits a crime, it is reported in the papers. If however he resists temptation and instead does a good deed, no notice is taken. Therefore newspapers give an entirely false presentation of life. The press closes its eyes to the good and presents the evil and thus suggests evil to you, which if you do not watch it, will produce evil in your life.

For every bad deed reported in the papers, a thousand good actions go unrecorded.

The world is full of noble deeds and gracious thoughts, and they can be seen and realized by those who look for them.

Therefore be very careful what newspapers you read and how you read them.

Avoid reading of the evil, seamy side of life; instead, look for the good, and you will find it. When reading your paper devote your attention to the large things, those which will go down in history. Avoid that which is mean and petty . . thus will you avoid unwholesome and dangerous suggestion.

Newspapers, periodicals and some books would have you believe that life is an unlovely thing. Even some hymn writers have dared to describe the world as a vale of tears and life as a long drawn out woe. Do not believe these wicked suggestions. Life is a gracious and lovely thing. It is full of beauty and love and peace and happiness. Life is what we make it, we can make it sublime or we can make it savor of Hell. It is in our own hands.

Therefore do not read either papers, books or magazines that do not present life in a joyous and optimistic way. Avoid low class scrappy reading. Read instead good books by great minds. Imbibe noble thoughts. Read good poetry if you can. Seek the beautiful, the noble, the true, in your reading and in your fellow men, and you will find them and be richly blessed thereby.

Henry Thomas Hamblin

The spiritual healer cures by awakening the sympathetic vibration in the Soul, through love. When the love nature is awakened and Thought, by Suggestion, directs it, then is the healing power, strongest. This can be a fact only in those most highly developed spiritually. In these it is limitless in its power for good. It is typified in Jesus, who spent his whole life in doing good; loving so much, that those who came into His presence were healed. This development is possible to all. We have only to raise the pitch of our radiations from those we now have to those of a higher octave. Love will develop this. If we Love enough, we shall not only be whole ourselves but will be wholesome to all who meet us, to all of whom we think.

Henry Harrison Brown

Think evil, evil follows; think good, good follows. Your mind is like water which takes the shape of any vessel in which it is poured. The vessel is your thought patterns and mental imagery which the Creative Power flows through and brings to pass in your experience. Your deeper mind called the subconscious is the fabricator which weaves the pattern of your thoughts into your experience and conditions.

Feed the mind with premises which are true, noble, and Godlike, and you will find the subconscious is your best friend providing that which is beautiful, lovely, and glorious in your outer world.

Joseph Murphy

How often do we hear it said of some man, "Everything he undertakes succeeds," or "Everything he touches turns to gold?" Why? Because the man is constantly picturing to himself the success of his undertakings and he is backing up his vision by his efforts. By clinging to his vision, by vigorous resolution and persistent, determined endeavor he is continually making himself a powerful magnet to draw his own to him. Consciously or unconsciously, he is using the divine intelligence or force by the use of which every human being may mold himself and his environment according to the pattern in his mind.

Why don't you use your divine power to make yourself what you long to be? Why don't you cling to the vision of yourself which you see in your highest moment, and resolve to make the vision a reality? By persistent right thinking, backed by the steady exercise of your will, you can, if you desire, remake yourself and your environment. Since we can "for one transcendent moment" be the thing we long for, you and I and every human being can make that transcendent or highest moment permanent. It is purely a matter of right thinking.

Every time we visualize the thing we long for, every time we see ourselves in imagination in the position we long to fill, we are forming a habit which will tend to make our highest moments permanent, to bring our vision out of the ideal into the actual.

Orison Swett Marden

Achievement, of whatever kind, is the crown of effort, the diadem of thought. By the aid of self-control, resolution, purity, righteousness, and well-directed thought a man ascends. By the aid of animality, indolence, impurity, corruption, and confusion of thought a man descends.

A man may rise to high success in the world, and even to lofty altitudes in the spiritual realm, and again descend into weakness and wretchedness by allowing arrogant, selfish, and corrupt thoughts to take possession of him.

Victories attained by right thought can only be maintained by watchfulness. Many give way when success is assured, and rapidly fall back into failure.

All achievements, whether in the business, intellectual, or spiritual world, are the result of definitely directed thought, are governed by the same law and are of the same method; the only difference lies in the object of attainment.

He who would accomplish little must sacrifice little. He who would achieve much must sacrifice much. He who would attain highly must sacrifice greatly.

James Allen

I AM as Conscious Law that which I think I AM, and since Thought is creative. I live in the world I think into existence. The real world of imagination, the subconscious world of Mind.

Henry Harrison Brown

The spiritual mind will know in time that your thought influences people for or against your interests, though their bodies are thousands of miles distant. The material mind does not regard its thought as an actual element as real as air or water. The spiritual mind knows that every one of its thousand daily secret thoughts are real things acting on the minds of the persons they are sent to.

The spiritual mind knows that matter or the material is only an expression of spirit or force; that such matter is ever changing in accordance with the spirit that makes or externalizes itself in the form we call matter, and therefore, if the thought of health, strength and recuperation is constantly held to in the mind, such thought of health, strength and rejuvenation will express itself in the body, making maturity never ceasing, vigor never ending, and the keenness of every physical sense ever increasing.

Prentice Mulford

We live and move and have our being in what we call an Infinite Mind, an Infinite Creative Mind, also infinitely receptive, operative, omnipotent, and all-knowing; and we have learned that this mind presses against us on all sides, flows through us, and becomes operative through our thinking. The human race, ignorant of the laws of this mind, ignorant of the power of its own thought, has through its ignorance misused and abused the creative power of its thought, and brought upon itself the thing it feared.

This is true because all thought is law, and all law is mind in action, and the word which you speak today is the law which shall govern your life tomorrow, as the word which you spoke, ignorantly or innocently, consciously or unconsciously yesterday, is absolutely governing your life today.

As metaphysicians, then, we are not dealing with a material, nor denying a manifest universe, but we are claiming that the manifestation is the result of the inner activity of the mind; and if we wish for a definite manifestation, we must produce a definite inner activity. You and I, then, are not dealing with conditions, but with mental and spiritual law. We are dealing with the power of thought, the power of mind, and the more spiritual the thought the higher the manifestation. The more our reliance upon what we call God, the greater the power.

Ernest Holmes

We speak our thoughts every time we utter a word, and an unspoken thought may be just as Powerful. A thought is a thing . . a vibration, just the same as an electrical current from a charged wire, or the ripple of the water created by throwing a pebble across its surface.

A true scientist will begin practicing with HIMSELF. He will purify his body from all gross material, and will purge his mind of all unclean, evil, lustful thoughts. His creed is: "As a man thinketh in his heart so is he," and he will begin by keeping his heart pure, noble and clean. You can think good or you can think evil. You know what is wrong, and you know what is right. Every bit of knowledge that comes to you, if used for humanity, will lead you into the Right, but every bit you accumulate for selfish desires lead you far from the greater Truths and Powers which are yours by Divine Right.

The Power of Thought Is Mighty, It is the foundation of ALL things. It is the secret force of all Creation and all science.

Thoughts grow into beauty or evil just as the heart guides, for the heart brings forth all thoughts, and "as you sow so shall you reap."

F. E. Gariner and Dr. R. Swineburne Clymer

All power lies in creative thought. Thought is the key to life; for as a man thinketh in his heart, so is he. People are beginning to understand today something of the power of thought to shape the individual's destiny . . they know vaguely that thoughts are things . . but how the Great Law of thought is to be applied they do not know.

Emmet Fox

If we expect to get a message from the Father of Love we must see that the receiving apparatus is pure and vibrant with love. Any unloving thought clogs the flow of God's love, just as rusty pipes retard or prevent the even flow of life-giving waters from the great reservoirs in the mountains.

Glen Clark

Jesus made a remarkable statement at one time. He said, "The Prince of this World cometh and findeth nothing in me." What did He mean? He meant that no thought of lack, or evil, or fear could enter His mind because there was nothing in Him to attract it. The negative thought comes blowing along but it cannot "blow in" on the mind that is positive for there is nothing in that mind to attract or hold it. Hence evil cannot become a reality to that soul. This is the reason why we should place the mind on the highest things because it holds the mind positive only to the best and the worst can "have no part in us" for it does not "find anything in us."

Fenwicke L. Holmes

It is easy for the average person to see how it is that mind can control, and to a certain extent govern, the functions of the body. Some can go even further than this and see that the body is governed entirely by consciousness. This they can see without much difficulty, but it is not so easy for them to see how it is that thought governs their conditions and decides whether they are to be successes or failures.

Here we will stop to ask the question: If our conditions are not controlled by thought, by what, then, are they controlled? Some will say that conditions are controlled by circumstances. But what are circumstances? Are they cause or are they effect?

Of course they are always effect; everything that we see is an effect. An effect is something that follows a cause, and we are dealing with causation only; effects do not make themselves, but they are held in place by mind, or causation.

If this does not answer your thought, begin over again and realize that behind everything that is seen is the silent cause. In your life you are that cause. There is nothing but mind, and nothing moves except as mind moves it. We have agreed that, while God is love, yet your life is governed absolutely by mind, or law. In our lives of conditions we are the cause, and nothing moves except as our mind moves it.

The activity of our mind is thought., We are always acting because we are always thinking. At all times we are either drawing things to us or we are pushing them away from us. In the ordinary individual this process goes on without his ever knowing it consciously, but ignorance of the law will excuse no one from its effects.

Ernest Holmes

As thought has the power to make people violently ill, and even kill them, which it often has by bad news such as the passing of a loved one, it assuredly has the power to alleviate and heal. All things have a mental origin, and disease and its cure are no exceptions. Thought is the creative power and can be used either constructively or destructively. People can think themselves ill, unhappy and unsuccessful, or they can create the opposite conditions. By changing your opinion of yourself, you change yourself; and you certainly won't accomplish much until you think you can.

Frank L. Hammer

The great trouble with all of us who are struggling with unhappy or unfortunate conditions is, that we have separated ourselves in some way from the great magnetic center of creation. We are not thinking right, and so we are not attracting the right things. "Think the things you want." The profoundest philosophy is locked up in these few words.

Think of them clearly, persistently, concentrating upon them with all the force and might of your mind, and struggle toward them with all your energy. This is the way to make yourself a magnet for the things you want. But the moment you begin to doubt, to worry, to fear, you demagnetize yourself, and the things you desire flee from you. You drive them away by your mental attitude. They cannot come near you while you are deliberately separating yourself from them.

You are going in one direction, and the things you want are going in the opposite direction. "A desire in the heart for anything," says H. Emilie Cady, "is God's sure promise sent beforehand to indicate that it is yours already in the limitless realm of supply." No matter how discouraging your present outlook, how apparently unpromising your future, cling to your desire and you will realize it. Picture the ideal conditions, visualize the success, which you long to attain; imagine yourself already in the position you are ambitious to reach.

Do not acknowledge limitations, do not allow any other suggestion to lodge in your mind than the success you long for, the conditions you aspire to. Picture your desires as actually realized, and hold fast to your vision with all the tenacity you can muster. This is the way out of your difficulties; this is the way to open the door ahead of you to the place higher up, to better and brighter conditions.

Orison Swett Marden

It is not external things, but our thoughts about them, that bind us or set us free. We forge our own chains, build our own dungeons, take ourselves prisoners; or we loose our bonds, build our own palaces, or roam in freedom through all scenes and events. If I think that my surroundings are powerful to bind me, that thought will keep me bound. If I think that, in my thought and life, I can rise above my surroundings, that thought will liberate me. One should ask of his thoughts, Are they leading to bondage or deliverance? and he should abandon thoughts that bind, and adopt thoughts that set free.

If we fear our fellow-men, fear opinion, poverty, the withdrawal of friends and influence, then we are bound indeed, and cannot know the inward happiness of the enlightened, the freedom of the just; but if in our thoughts we are pure and free, if we see in life's reactions and reverses nothing to cause us trouble or fear, but everything to aid us in our progress, nothing remains that can prevent us from accomplishing the aims of our life, for then we are free indeed.

James Allen

We are all influenced much more than we are aware by the thoughts of others. I do not mean by their opinions but by their thoughts. A great writer on this subject very truly says: "thoughts are things." They are things, and most powerful things at that. Unless we understand this fact, we are at the mercy of a mighty force, of whose nature we know nothing, and whose very existence many of us deny. On the other hand, if we understand the nature and laws governing this wonderful force, we can master it and render it our instrument and assistant. Every thought created by us, weak or strong, good or bad, healthy or unhealthy, sends out its vibratory waves, which affect, to a greater or lesser extent all with whom we come in contact, or who may come within the radius of our thought vibrations.

Thought waves are like the ripples on a pond caused by the casting in of a pebble, they move in constantly widening circles, radiating from a central point. Of course, if an impulse projects the thought waves forcibly toward a certain object, its force will be felt more strongly at that point.

William Walker Atkinson

The first thing to realize is that since any thought manifests it necessarily follows that all thought does the same, else how should we know that the particular thought we were thinking would be the one that would create? Mind must cast back all or none. Just as the creative power of the soil receives all seeds put into it, and at once begins to work upon them, so mind must receive all thought and at once begin to operate upon it. Thus we find that all thought has some power in our lives and over our conditions. We are making our environments by the creative power of our thought. God has created us thus and we cannot escape it.

By conforming our lives and thought to a greater understanding of law we shall be able to bring into our experience just what we wish, letting go of all that we do not want to experience and taking in the things we desire. Every person is surrounded by a thought atmosphere. This mental atmosphere is the direct result of thought which in its turn becomes the direct reason for the cause of that which comes into our lives. Through this power we are either attracting or repelling. Like attracts like and we attract to us just what we are in mind. It is also true that we become attracted to something that is greater than our previous experience by first embodying the atmosphere of our desire.

Ernest Holmes

Man like God has the power to create and thoughts are his tools. Thought is the ancestor of all manifested things, for to think is to create. Man's use of his creative power makes his happiness, health, success, or their opposites. Thought projects itself in like conditions to material things, and all things on this earth are effects of man's thinking.

Frank L. Hammer

The habit of seeing only that which our senses permit, renders us totally blind to what we otherwise could see. To cultivate the faculty of seeing the invisible, we should often deliberately disentangle our minds from the evidence of the senses and focus our attention on an invisible state, mentally feeling it and sensing it until it has all the distinctness of reality.

Earnest, concentrated thought focused in a particular direction shuts out other sensations and causes them to disappear. We have but to concentrate on the state desired in order to see it. The habit of withdrawing attention from the region of sensation and concentrating it on the invisible develops our spiritual outlook and enables us to penetrate beyond the world of sense and to see that which is invisible. "For the invisible things of him from the creation of the world are clearly seen."

Neville Goddard

Watch and Pray. Student of Truth, you must watch your thoughts diligently, always striving to raise the vibrations and create purer atmospheres of love and tenderness for all things. The Kingdom within yields to prayer and concentration. It is said that to labor is to pray, to ask is to receive, and to knock is to have opened, but not without the effort and action of the seeker.

Your treasure is within yourself. When the recognition of self comes to the soul the Divine Spirit enlightens and instructs, illuminating and revealing the treasure within.

Grace M. Brown

Before a man can achieve anything, even in worldly things, he must lift his thoughts above slavish animal indulgence. He may not, in order to succeed, give up all animality and selfishness, by any means; but a portion of it must, at least, be sacrificed. A man whose first thought is bestial indulgence could neither think clearly nor plan methodically. He could not find and develop his latent resources, and would fail in any undertaking. Not having commenced manfully to control his thoughts, he is not in a position to control affairs and to adopt serious responsibilities. He is not fit to act independently and stand alone, but he is limited only by the thoughts which he chooses.

There can be no progress, no achievement without sacrifice. A man's worldly success will be in the measure that he sacrifices his confused animal thoughts, and fixes his mind on the development of his plans, and the strengthening of his resolution and self reliance. And the higher he lifts his thoughts, the more manly, upright, and righteous he becomes, the greater will be his success, the more blessed an enduring will be his achievements.

James Allen

Man's word, (spoken or thought) spoken forth into creative mind, is endowed with power of expression. "By our words we are justified and by our words we are condemned." Our word has the exact amount of power that we put into it. This does not mean power through effort or strain but power through absolute conviction, or faith. It is like a little messenger who knows what he is doing and knows just how to do it. We speak into our words the intelligence which we are, and backed by that greater intelligence of the Universal Mind our word becomes a law unto the thing for which it is spoken. Jesus understood this far better than we do. Indeed, He absolutely believed it, for He said, "Heaven and earth shall pass away but my words shall not pass away till all be fulfilled."

This makes our word inseparable from Absolute Intelligence and Power. Now if any word has power it must follow that all words have power. Some words may have a greater power than others, according to our conviction, but all words have some power. How careful, then, we should be what kind of words we are speaking.

All this goes to prove that we really are one with the Infinite Mind, and that our words have the power of life within them; that the word is always with us and never far off. The word is within our own mouth. Every time we speak we are using power.

We are one in mind with the whole universe; we are all eternally united in this mind with real power. It is our own fault if we do not use this truth after we see it.

We should feel ourselves surrounded by this mind, this great pulsating life, this all-seeing and all-knowing reality. When we do feel this near presence, this great power and life, then all we have to do is to speak forth into it, speak with all the positive conviction of the soul that has found its source, and above all else never fear but that it will be done unto us even as we have believed.

What wonderful power, what a newness of life and of power of expression, is waiting for those who really believe. What may the race not attain to when men wake up to the real facts of being? As yet the race has not begun to live, but the time is drawing near. Already thousands are using this great power, and thousands are eagerly watching and waiting for the new day.

Ernest Holmes

Your destiny depends entirely upon your own mental conduct. It is the thoughts that you allow yourself to dwell upon all day long that make your mentality what it is, and your circumstances are made by your mentality.

You may think that you know this already, but if you do not act upon it, it is certain that you do not really know it. As a matter of fact, most people would be amazed to discover how much negative thinking they do indulge in, in the course of a day. Thought is so swift, and habit is so strong that, unless you are very careful, you will constantly transgress. Even your conversation may be much more negative than you suspect.

Emmet Fox

The cause of all man's weakness, mistakes and failures, has been that he has not realized the Power within; instead, he has thought himself to be separate and friendless, weak and helpless, adrift, without chart or compass upon the sea of life. He has thought himself to be the victim of circumstance, the sport of fate, and the puppet of forces outside himself. He has called himself a worm instead of looking upon himself as a king. He has thought himself to be worthless and insignificant instead of realizing his wonderful interior POWERS and the grandeur of his being.

Instead of being a worm, man is a king. Potentially all the powers of the Infinite Mind are his. Instead of being the victim of circumstances he can control them. Instead of being the puppet of forces outside himself, he has within him the Power to be what he will; to do what he will; to accomplish all that he desires.

Now at last the darkness is being pierced and man realizes that he is a mental creature, and that he is MIND as well as matter, that is, as Mind, is one with the Universal or Infinite MIND. That the difference between him and the Infinite or Universal MIND is not one of kind, but of degree.

This is the greatest discovery in the history of the World; this is the crowning revelation of all the ages; this is the blinding knowledge that dwarfs every other knowledge THAT WITHIN MAN DWELLS THE INFINITE AND UNFATHOMABLE MIND OF THE UNIVERSE.

Call how he may on these hidden forces, they can never fail to respond, for they are infinite and inexhaustible. Man stands alone and apart from all other creatures, in this visible world around him, in that he has the power to govern his own actions, choose right or wrong, to mold his own fate, and create his own life and circumstances.

To other creatures, life and the visible world are fixed quantities. To man, life and the world are reflexes of inward mental states. Thus, can he make life what he will; thus can he live in a world of his own creating.

Man alone has the power to realize and recognize the inward Power of the Infinite, and to consciously bring It into objectivity.

Henry Thomas Hamblin

Imagine whatsoever things are lovely, noble, and of good report, and your entire emotional attitude toward life will change. What do you imagine about life? Is it going to be a happy life for you? Or is it one long series of frustrations? "Choose ye whom ye will serve."

You mold, fashion, and shape your outer world of experience according to the mental images you habitually dwell on. Imagine conditions and circumstances in life which dignify, elevate, please, and satisfy. If you imagine life is cold, cruel, hard, bitter, and that struggle and pain are inevitable, you are making life miserable for yourself.

Joseph Murphy

The new philosophy teaches us how to get hold of our resources, and how to use them, so as to get just what we want. It teaches us that the source from which all things spring is in the great cosmic intelligence which fills all space, and that in this vast cosmic ocean riches inconceivable are waiting to be objectified and utilized by man.

It teaches us that all these things will respond to the right thought, the right motive, and that we can call out everything we desire from this All Supply.

It holds that the reason why our lives are so lean, so pinched and poor, why our achievement is so limited, so picayune, in comparison with what we are capable of, is because we do not draw upon the All Supply. Our narrow, limited, dwarfed ideals, our poverty-stricken view of things, the limitations our own thought imposes . . these are the things that rob us of power and keep us in poverty. Our achievements or our possessions can never outrun our convictions or our ideals. We fix our own limitations.

Orison Swett Marden

Circumstances, however, are so complicated, thought is so deeply rooted, and the conditions of happiness vary so vastly with individuals, that a man's entire soul condition (although it may be known to himself) cannot be judged by another from the external aspect of his life alone.

A man may be honest in certain directions, yet suffer privations. A man may be dishonest in certain directions, yet acquire wealth. But the conclusion usually formed that the one man fails because of his particular honesty, and that the other prospers because of his particular dishonesty, is the result of a superficial judgment, which assumes that the dishonest man is almost totally corrupt, and honest man almost entirely virtuous. In the light of a deeper knowledge and wider experience, such judgment is found to be erroneous. The dishonest man may have some admirable virtues which the other does not possess; and the honest man obnoxious vices which are absent in the other. The honest man reaps the good results of his honest thoughts and acts; he also brings upon himself the sufferings which his vices produce. The dishonest man likewise garners his own suffering and happiness.

It is pleasing to human vanity to believe that one suffers because of one's virtue. But not until a man has extirpated every sickly, bitter, and impure thought from his mind, and washed every sinful stain from his soul, can he be in a position to know and declare that his sufferings are the result of his good, and not of his bad qualities. And on the way to that supreme perfection, he will have found working in his mind and life, the Great Law which is absolutely just, and which cannot give good for evil, evil for good. Possessed of such knowledge, he will then know, looking back upon his past ignorance and blindness, that his life is, and always was, justly ordered, and that all his past experiences, good and bad, were the equitable outworking of his evolving, yet unevolved self.

Good thoughts and actions can never produce bad results. Bad thoughts and actions can never produce good results. This is but saying that nothing can come from corn but corn, nothing from nettles but nettles. Men understand this law in the natural world, and work with it. But few understand it in the mental and moral world (though its operation there is just as simple and undeviating), and they, therefore, do not cooperate with it.

James Allen

Here is something worth remembering. Unless we are working with people who think as we do, we had better be working alone. One stream of thought, even though it may not be very powerful, will do more for us than many powerful streams that are at variance with each other. This means that, unless we are sure that we are working with people who harmonize, we would better work alone. Of course we cannot retire from business simply because people do not agree with us, but what we can do is to keep our thoughts to ourselves. We do not have to leave the world in order to control our thought; but we do have to learn that we can stay right in the world and still think just what we want to think, regardless of what others are thinking.

One single stream of thought, daily sent out into Creative Mind, will do wonders. Within a year the person who will practice this will have completely changed his conditions of life. The way to practice this is daily to spend some time in thinking and in mentally seeing just what is wanted; see the thing just as it is wished and then affirm that this is now done. Try to feel that what has been stated is the truth.

Words and affirmations simply give shape to thought; they are not creative. Feeling is creative and the more feeling that is put into the word the greater power it will have over conditions. In doing this we think of the condition only as an effect, something that follows what we think. It cannot help following our thought. This is the way that all creation comes into expression.

It is a great help to realize mentally that at all times a great stream of thought and power is operating through us; it is constantly going out into Mind, where it is taken up and acted upon. Our business is to keep that stream of thought just where we want it to be: to be ready at any time to act when the impulse comes for action. Our action must never be negative, it must always be affirmative, for we are dealing with something that cannot fail. We may fail to realize, but the power in itself is Infinite and cannot fail. We are setting in motion in the Absolute a stream of thought that will never cease until it accomplishes its purpose. Try to feel this, be filled with a great joy as you feel that it is given to you to use this great and only power.

Keep the thought clear and never worry about the way that things seem to be going. Let go of all outer conditions when working in Mind, for there is where things are made;

there creation is going on, and it is now making something for us. This must be believed as never believed before; it must be known as the great reality; it must be felt as the only Presence. There is no other way to obtain.

Though all the Infinite may want to give, yet we must take, and, as far as we are concerned, that taking is mental. Though people may laugh at this, even that does not matter, "He laughs best who laughs last." We know in "What we believe," and that will be sufficient.

Ernest Holmes

Our word or thought is literally "made flesh and dwells among us." We get out of our universe what we put into it, for it reflects our moods and thoughts. Good and evil are alike real, as effects, but they are simply the outer expression of inner concepts. And you live in an eternal, undying universe, for though form and thought may change, the primary substance can never pass away. The primary substance is Mind, and as you share in It, you too are eternally at one with It. As the Infinite Responsive Intelligence, It is your Father leading you in green pastures and beside the still waters.

Fenwicke L. Holmes

If the subconscious mind believes in lack of any kind, such conditions of lack will be vibrated to the individual who entertains the thought.

Franklin Fillmore Farrington

To change your world, you must first change your conception of it. To change a man, you must change your conception of him. You must first believe him to be the man you want him to be and mentally talk to him as though he were. All men are sufficiently sensitive to reproduce your beliefs of them. Therefore, if your word is not reproduced visibly in him toward whom it is sent, the cause is to be found in you, not in the subject.

As soon as you believe in the truth of the state affirmed, results follow. Everyone can be transformed; every thought can be transmitted; every thought can be visibly embodied.

Subjective words . . subconscious assumptions . . awaken what they affirm.

Neville Goddard

Suffering is always the effect of wrong thought in some direction. It is an indication that the individual is out of harmony with himself, with the Law of his being. The sole and supreme use of suffering is to purify, to burn out all that is useless and impure. Suffering ceases for him who is pure.

There could be not object in burning gold after the dross had been removed, and perfectly pure and enlightened being could not suffer.

The circumstances which a man encounters with suffering are the result of his own mental inharmony. The circumstances which a man encounters with blessedness, not material possessions, is the measure of right thought. Wretchedness, not lack of material possessions, is the measure of wrong thought. A man may be cursed and rich; he may be blessed and poor. blessedness and riches are only joined together when the riches are rightly and wisely used. And the poor man only descends into wretchedness when he regards his lot as a burden unjustly imposed.

Indigence and indulgence are the two extremes of wretchedness. They are both equally unnatural and the result of mental disorder. A man is not rightly conditioned until he is a happy, healthy, and prosperous being. And happiness, health, and prosperity are the result of a harmonious adjustment of the inner with the outer, of the man with his surroundings.

A man only begins to be a man when he ceases to whine and revile, and commences to search for the hidden justice which regulates his life. And as he adapts his mind to that regulating factor, he ceases to accuse others as the cause of his condition, and builds himself up in strong and noble thoughts. He ceases to kick against circumstances, but begins to use them as aids to his more rapid progress, and as a means of discovering the hidden powers and possibilities within himself.

Law, not confusion, is the dominating principle in the universe. Justice, not injustice, is the soul and substance of life. And righteousness, not corruption, is the molding and moving force in the spiritual government of the world. This being so, man has but to right himself to find that the universe is right; and during the process of putting himself right, he will find that as he alters his thoughts toward things and other people, things and other people will alter toward him.

James Allen

The Law of Thought Attraction is one name for the law, or rather for one manifestation of it. Again I say, your thoughts are real things. They go forth from you in all directions, combining with thoughts of like kind . . opposing thoughts of a different character . . forming combinations . . going where they are attracted . . flying away from thought centers opposing them. And your mind attracts the thought of others, which have been sent out by them conscious or unconsciously. But it attracts only those thoughts which are in harmony with its own. Like attracts like, and opposites repel opposites, in the world of thought.

William Walker Atkinson

There are some bodies which are wholly immune to zymotic germs, but there are also some minds which are immune to the reception of a disease thought, and in some such minds there resides the force that may nullify the power of the disease germs in the body. The British Medical Journal " (Autumn, 1897) said: "Disease of the body is so much influenced by the mind that in each case we have to understand the patient quite as much as the malady. This is not learnt at the hospitals." Van Norden, in his "Twentieth Century Practice of Medicine," remarks: There are many carefully observed cases of diabetes on record, in which the disease followed a sudden fright, or joy, or some other disturbance of mental equilibrium."

One of the most baneful and secret diseases of the human system is cancer. It is always fatal, and is to a very large degree beyond the control of the physician's skill. We need not therefore be surprised to learn that cancer is chiefly induced by mental conditions. " I have been surprised," says Dr. Murchison, " how often patients with primary cancer of the liver have traced the cause of their ill-health to protracted grief or anxiety. The cases have been far too numerous to be accounted for as mere coincidences."

Here we see how the entire body is eaten away, beginning its deadly emasculation usually in the most vital centers, as the direct result not of a bacillus-invasion, but of the projection of a mental germ into the blood. Dr. Snow (London "Lancet," 1880) asserts his conviction that " the vast majority of the cases of cancer, especially of breast and uterine cancer, are due to mental anxiety."

Henry Frank

We can never stand still in our thought. Either we will be growing or else we will be going back. As we can attract to ourselves only what we first have a mental likeness of, it follows that if we wish to attract larger things we must provide larger thoughts. This enlarging of consciousness is so necessary that too much cannot be said about it.

Most people get only a short way and then stop: they cannot seem to get beyond a certain point; they can do so much and no more. Why is it that a person in business does just about so much each year? We see people in all walks of life, getting so far, never going beyond a certain point. There must be a reason for everything; nothing happens, if all is governed by law, and we can come to no other conclusion.

When we look into the mental reason for things we find out why things happen. The man who gets so far and never seems to go beyond that point is still governed by law; when he allows his thoughts to take him out into larger fields of action, his conditions come up to his thought; when he stops enlarging his thought he stops growing. If he would still keep on in thought, realizing more and still more, he would find that in the outer form of things he would be doing greater things.

There are many reasons why a man stops thinking larger things. One of them is a lack of imagination. He cannot conceive of anything more to follow than that which has already happened. Another thought works like this: "This is as far as anyone can go in my business." Right here he signs his own death warrant. Often a person will say, "I am too old to do bigger things." There he stops. Someone else will say, "Competition is too great"; and here is where this man stops; he can go no further than his thought will carry him.

All this is unnecessary when we realize that life is first of all Consciousness, and then conditions follow. We see no reason why a man should not go on and on, and never stop growing. No matter what age or what circumstance, if life is thought, we can keep on thinking bigger things. There is no reason why a man who is already doing well should not be able mentally to conceive of a still better condition. What if we are active? There is always a greater activity possible. We can still see a little beyond what has come before. This is just what we should do, see, even though it be but a little beyond our former thought. If we always practice this, we will find that every year we shall be growing, every month we shall be advancing; and as time goes on we shall become really great. As there is no stopping in that power which is Infinite, as the Limitless is without bounds, so should we keep on trying to see more and greater possibilities in life.

We should definitely work every day for the expansion of thought. If we have fifty customers a day we should endeavor to believe that we have sixty. When we have sixty we should mentally see seventy. This should never stop; there is no stopping place in mind.

Let go of everything else, drop everything else from your thought, and mentally see more coming to you than has ever come before; believe that Mind is establishing this unto you, and then go about your business in the regular way. Never see the limitation; never dwell upon it, and above all things else never talk limitation to any one; this is the only way, and there is no other way to grow a larger thought. The man with the big thought is always the man who does big things in life. Get hold of the biggest thing that you can think of and claim it for your own; mentally see it and hold it as a thing already done, and you will prove to yourself that life is without bounds.

Ernest Holmes

There has been a lot of nonsense written and spoken about the Law of Attraction. People have been solemnly taught that all they need to do is to adopt a certain mental attitude, think thoughts of success and abundance, and then to sit and wait for abundance of all good things to drop from the skies at their feet. The folly of it is seen when we find that these teachers of "abundance" and "opulence" have themselves to work for a living, by teaching the very thing which, if true, would save them from all necessity of working.

Supposing it were true, then what is possible for one would be possible for all, and if all adopted this method of getting a living then who would till the soil or make our clothes? Would everything we need. come from the skies?

Even if these were true and man could draw all that he needed by the power of thought from the blue vault of heaven, then no one would have anything to do, life would become stagnant, and the race would perish from inaction.

Life is action, and if a man ceases to work he at once begins to disintegrate and soon requires six feet of earth wherein to cover his bones. When business men retire they quickly die, and those who, being born with riches have no necessity to work for a living, have to find work and interest of some sort in order to prevent themselves from mental and physical decay.

There is no such thing as getting something for nothing. The principle of the "square deal" runs right through life and the Universe. A business man who tries to get something for nothing, who, in other words, fails to give value for money, finally finds himself without a customer.

Those who try to evade this law by creating trusts and combines will find that their ill gotten gains will be confiscated by a power greater than themselves.

The "square deal," reasonable profits, fair wages, honest straight-forward business integrity, all these will succeed and continue to succeed, as long as there remain people to do business with; but the "ring" or "combine" or "trust," squeezing its swollen, dishonest profits out of the life and blood of the common people, can only do business so long as the community allows them to. All who read history know what has been the fate of tyrants in the past, and there is no reason for believing that the profiteers and extortioners of the present day will fare any better.

Even if, however, a man can filch a fortune by unfair means, i.e., by not giving good value for money, by extortion or profiteering, he will lose in one direction exactly in proportion to that which he gains in another. Let him make a fortune by sharp practice; let him snap his fingers and sneer at integrity and honor and universal law; let him rejoice at what he has done; let him think himself a fine, clever fellow; nevertheless nemesis awaits him. He will lose in love, peace of mind, happiness and health in exact proportion to his dishonest gain. He makes money, granted, but he loses that which money cannot buy.

The writer has known men to be happy until they became wealthy, then they became of all men the most miserable. He has known them to be healthy while they were comparatively poor, and full of sickness and trouble when they became passing rich. There is a Law of Compensation running through life and the Universe and you cannot avoid it. If you are to succeed you must work and accomplish; if you are to receive the riches of the world you must give of your best in exchange.

"Then give to the world the best you have, And the best will come back to you."

This is where the Law of Attraction operates, not by your sitting still and expecting the impossible to happen, but by the giving in faith and confidence of your best efforts to the World. By calling upon your hidden powers, and by creating powerful thoughts, you attract to yourself armies of thoughts of a similar kind, which passing into your subconscious mind are translated into actions of the highest type, the type that glories in achievement, and that wins Success.

Thus if you give your best to the world, then in the form of a rich and abundant success "the best will come back to you."

Henry Thomas Hamblin

The subconscious mind is the universal conductor which the operator modifies with his thoughts and feelings. Visible states are either the vibratory effects of subconscious vibrations within you or they are vibratory causes of the corresponding vibrations within you.

Neville Goddard

Some of the possibilities of Thought are shown in the transference of messages from mind to mind, the transference of pictures by Clairvoyance or of individuality by Psychometry. When I hold the letter of an absent person, a stranger, and once come into sympathetic vibration with him, I become him for the time being. I feel as he feels, I think as he thinks, I act as he acts, for I LET his thought act through me and I become transformed for the time being into his image. Mental Healing, which is only Thought and Love transference, is a fact, testified to by thousands. Healing by Suggestion is testified to by other thousands; Magnetic Healing, by millions.

Success in every walk of life, born from Right Thinking, is testified to by thousands more. Success by dollars, books and arms is giving way to Success by Thought alone.

Henry Harrison Brown

To change your mind is to change your world and you do this by trusting the One Spiritual Power which you can contact through your thought rejecting completely all belief in powers outside your own consciousness. You will come to the conclusion that your consciousness is God relative to your world, and that everything you experience comes forth from your consciousness which is the sum total of your conscious and subconscious beliefs.

Joseph Murphy

Circumstance does not make the man; it reveals him to himself. No such conditions can exist as descending into vice and its attendant sufferings apart from vicious inclinations, or ascending into virtue and its pure happiness without the continued cultivation of virtuous aspirations. And man, therefore, as the Lord and master of thought, is the maker of himself, the shaper and author of environment.

Even at birth the soul comes to its own, and through every step of its earthly pilgrimage it attracts those combinations of conditions which reveal itself, which are the reflections of its own purity and impurity, its strength and weakness.

Men do not attract that which they want, but that which they are. Their whims, fancies, and ambitions are thwarted at every step, but their inmost thoughts and desires are fed with their own food, be it foul or clean. The "divinity that shapes our ends" is in ourselves; it is our very self. Man is manacled only by himself.

Thought and action are the jailers of Fate . . they imprison, being base. They are also the angels of Freedom . . they liberate, being noble. Not what he wishes and prays for does a man get, but what he justly earns. His wishes and prayers are only gratified and answered when they harmonize with his thoughts and actions.

James Allen

Some time ago I was talking to a man about the Attractive Power of Thought. He said that he did not believe that Thought could attract anything to him, and that it was all a matter of luck. He had found, he said, that ill luck relentlessly pursued him, and that everything he touched went wrong. It always had, and always would, and he had grown to expect it. When he undertook a new thing he knew beforehand that it would go wrong and that no good would come of it. Oh, no! There wasn't anything in the theory of Attractive Thought, so far as he could see; it was all a matter of luck!

This man failed to see that by his own confession he was giving a most convincing argument in favor of the Law of Attraction. He was testifying that he was always expecting things to go wrong, and that they always came about as he expected. He was a magnificent illustration of the Law of Attraction . . but he didn't know it, and no argument seemed to make the matter clear to him. He was "up against it," and there was no way out of it . . he always expected the ill luck. and every occurrence proved that he was right, and that the Mental Science position was all nonsense.

There are many people who seem to think that the only way in which the Law of Attraction operates is when one wishes hard, strong and steady. They do not seem to realize that a strong belief is as efficacious as a strong wish. The successful man believes in himself and his ultimate success, and, paying no attention to little setbacks, stumbles, tumbles and slips, presses on eagerly to the goal, believing all the time that he will get there. His views and aims may alter as he progresses, and he may change his plans or have them changed for him, but all the time he knows in his heart that he will eventually "get there." He is not steadily wishing he may get there . . he simply feels and believes it, and thereby sets to operation the strongest forces known in the world of thought.

William Walker Atkinson

Thoughts of failure, limitation or poverty are negative and must be counted out of our lives for all time. Somebody will say, "But what of the poor; what are you going to do with them; are they to be left without help?" No; a thousand times no. The same power is in them that is in all men. They will always be poor until they awake and realize what life is. All the charity on earth has never done away with poverty, and never will; if it could have done so it would have done so; it could not, therefore it has not. It will do a man a thousand times more good to show him how to succeed than it will to tell him he needs charity.

We need not listen to all the calamity howlers. Let them howl if it does them any good. God has given us a power and we must use it.

We can do more toward saving the world by proving this law than all that charity has ever given it. Right here, in the manifold world today, there is more money and provision than the world can use. Not even a fraction of the wealth of the world is used. Inventors and discoverers are adding to this wealth every day; they are the real people. But in the midst of plenty, surrounded by all the gifts of heaven, man sits and begs for his daily bread. He should be taught to realize that he has brought these conditions upon himself; that instead of blaming God, man or the devil for the circumstances by which he is surrounded, he should learn to seek the truth, to let the dead bury their dead.

We should tell every man who will believe what his real nature is; show him how to overcome all limitations; give him courage; show him the way. If he will not believe, if he will not walk in the way, it is not our fault, and having done all we can, we must go our way.

We may sympathize with people but never with trouble, limitation or misery. If people still insist upon hugging their troubles to themselves, all the charity in the world will not help them. Remember that God is that silent power behind all things, always ready to spring into expression when we have provided the proper channels, which are receptive and positive faith in the evidence of things not seen with the physical eye but eternal in the heavens. All is mind, and we must provide a receptive avenue for it as it passes out through us into the outer expression of our affairs. If we allow the world's opinion to control our thinking, then that will be our demonstration. If, on the other hand, we rise superior to the world, we shall do a new thing. Remember that all people are making demonstrations, only most of them are making the ones they do not desire, but the only ones they can make with their present powers of perception.

Ernest Holmes

The Creative process is simply Mind in action, or Mind thinking its Life, Love and Wisdom into form. Mind in action is always creative, but it is also thought. Thought acts in Mind to create. Or mind first produces thought and then reacts to it to become that which it has thought. This is the whole law of creation. Mind creates what it thinks. The many forms pass out of the one Mind, but each form has a corresponding thought which produces and sustains it.

Fenwicke L. Holmes

As we by the power of thought-control develop our subliminal powers, we become conscious of a new Self developing and manifesting itself within us. This is our Subliminal Self. Not only do we become increasingly conscious of the new powers within, but we also are aware of powers without us. As we develop our inward powers along correct lines, so do we come into harmony with the powers without. There are powers within and powers without, all of which will help and bless us, if we only come into line with them.

Henry Thomas Hamblin

There is no limit to the power of the thought current you can attract to you nor limit to the things that can he done through the individual by it. In the future some people will draw so much of the higher quality of thought to them, that by it they will accomplish what some would call miracles. In this capacity of the human mind for drawing a thought current ever increasing in fineness of quality and power lies the secret of what has been called "magic."

Prentice Mulford

Reason is for the objective life. The Soul knows. It perceives Truth. The intellect applies Truth thus perceived to the needs of the objective life. But to try to live by reason is like man trying to live off of stones for bread. Man does not live by material food, but by every thought that cometh from the Subconscious (The Inner God) into the conscious life. Love and Thought, by the conversion of energy, are only transformed Life. Therefore, to think, and to love, is the all of Life. When the Human Soul came to say, "I think and I feel," then, because it had power to decide upon its manifestations and to choose pleasure from pain, it became Self-conscious.

Through this choice, it became self-creative. It therefore cannot die. Every act of self-consciousness is an act of recreation. It may change its environment; may, through this Law of Conservation, change the manner of manifestation, but "I" must henceforth ever be "I," because it must ever know that it is not something else.

Henry Harrison Brown

If you set your mind to the keynote of courage, confidence, strength and success, you attract to yourself thoughts of like nature; people of like nature; things that fit in the mental tune. Your prevailing thought or mood determines that which is to be drawn toward you . . picks out your mental bedfellow. You are today setting into motion thought currents which will in time attract toward you thoughts, people and conditions in harmony with the predominant note of your thought. Your thought will mingle with that of others of like nature and mind, and you will be attracted toward each other, and will surely come together with a common purpose sooner or later, unless one or the other of you should change the current of his thoughts.

Fall in with the operations of the law. Make it a part of yourself. Get into its currents. Maintain your poise. Set your mind to the keynote of Courage, Confidence and Success.

Get in touch with all the thoughts of that kind that are emanating every hour from hundreds of minds. Get the best that is to be had in the thought world. The best is there, so be satisfied with nothing less. Get into partnership with good minds. Get into the right vibrations. You must be tired of being tossed about by the operations of the Law . . get into harmony with it.

William Walker Atkinson

To nothing else touching his life can the aphorism "As a man thinketh in his heart so is he" be more fittingly applied than to a man's health. Health can be established only by thinking health, just as disease is established by thinking disease. Just as you must think success, expect it, visualize it, make your mind a huge success magnet to attract it if you are to attain it, so if you want to be healthy, you must think health, you must expect it, you must visualize it, you must attract it by making your mind a huge health magnet to attract more health, abundant health.

As long as physical defects, weaknesses, or diseased conditions exist in the imagination, as long as the mind is filled with visions of ill health the body must correspond, because our bodies are but an extension of our thoughts, our minds objectified.

Orison Swett Marden

Of all the beautiful truths pertaining to the soul which have been restored and brought to light in this age, none is more gladdening or fruitful of divine promise and confidence than this . . that man is the master of thought, the molder of character, and maker and shaper of condition, environment, and destiny.

As a being of Power, Intelligence, and Love, and the lord of his own thoughts, man holds the key to every situation, and contains within himself that transforming and regenerative agency by which he may make himself what he wills.

Man is always the master, even in his weakest and most abandoned state; but in his weakness and degradation he is the foolish master who misgoverns his "household." When he begins to reflect upon his condition, and to search diligently for the Law upon which his being is established, he then becomes the wise master, directing his energies with intelligence, and fashioning his thoughts to fruitful issues. Such is the conscious master, and man can only thus become by discovering within himself the laws of thought; which discovery is totally a matter of application, self-analysis, and experience.

James Allen

You have to get acquainted with the fact that there is but one Creative Principle, and then realize that when you think the One Power is responding to you, as you contemplate the great truth that the Supreme Power is now functioning in your behalf, you are assured of success and triumph. When negative thoughts or opposing factors come to your mind, reject them completely by recalling that they are shadows of the mind, and a shadow has no real home.

They are illusions of power; the power is in your own thought and consciousness. Fear, doubt, and worry are merely suggestions of power and cannot do any harm to you except you give them power.

Joseph Murphy

Remember that thought is the most powerful and wonderful power in the Universe, and that you can control your thought; therefore by controlling your thought you have perfect mastery over the most potent force of which we have any knowledge. Having perfect mastery over these most potent forces you therefore have control over your life and circumstances, and there is nothing that can prevent your ultimate success, save your own lack of faith and staying power.

Your mind actually has creative power, not in a figurative sense but in reality. All that you see with your bodily eyes is matter vibrating at different rates. The matter that you can see in this way is coarse matter. With your mind's eye you can see other matter of a finer nature. With your mind you can mold this finer matter into any pattern you please. What you create in your mind in this way, in other words, that which you visualize, if persistently held to, will form the matrix out of which will grow your outer life.

The coarser particles of the outer life are shaped on the model of the pattern formed in the finer matter of the mind. This is why these lessons have persistently taught you to cast your mind in a certain attitude of thought and to visualize all that you wished to accomplish. By the use of affirmations which is thought control in its most practical form you have learned to make the most powerful use of the greatest of all powers, viz.: Thought; by visualization you put into operation a power known to the old occultists but withheld from the multitude until now.

Visualization is a form of concentrated thought. It is only possible as a result of intense concentration. It is thought materialized in fine matter of mind-stuff. Therefore the more real and clear and sharply defined your mental image is, the greater your powers of concentration.

Henry Thomas Hamblin

Man is just what he thinks himself to be; he is big in capacity if he thinks big thoughts; he is small if he thinks small thoughts. He will attract to himself what he thinks most about. He can learn to govern his own destiny when he learns to control his thoughts. In order to do this he must first realize that everything in the manifest universe is the result of some inner activity of Mind. This Mind is God, producing a universe by the activity of His own divine thoughts; man is in this Mind as a thinking center, and what he thinks governs his life, even as God's thought governs the Universe, by setting in motion all the cosmic activities.

This is so easy to understand, and so plain as to use that we often wonder why we have been so long finding out this, the greatest of all truths of all the ages. Believing; thinking what is believed to be true; thinking into Mind each day that which is wished to be returned; eliminating negative thoughts; holding all positive thoughts; giving thanks to the Spirit of Life that it is so trusting always in the higher law; never arguing with one's self or with others; using; these are the steps which, when followed, will bring us to where we shall not have to ask if it be true, for, having demonstrated, we shall know.

The seed that falls into the ground shall bear fruit of its own kind; and nothing shall hinder it.

"He that hath ears to hear, let him hear."

Ernest Holmes

Think right thoughts NOW and the future can take care of itself. There is NOTHING to fear, henceforth there is nothing capricious or uncertain in your life, all is according to Eternal Law. All that you have to do is to think aright and to act aright, and all things will be added unto you.

As you bring your life, by the control of your thoughts, into harmony with the unseen higher forces, you enter into a life of peace and power. There is nothing whatever about which you need fear or worry, because you are in harmony with all the Universe. The power that maintains the stars in their places and guides the planets in their courses, is the same power that animates you. Nothing can come by chance into your life, only that which is the result of your thinking.

Now is given into your hands the power and the knowledge whereby you can control your thinking; the power and the knowledge by which you can choose those thoughts which will build up your life in beauty and strength, and ensure an harmonious future. Nothing can go wrong in your life if your thoughts are right. Right cannot produce wrong, neither can wrong produce right. Get your thoughts under control and all evil must flee away.

Henry Thomas Hamblin

NEVER BEGIN TO DO A THING UNTIL YOU ARE READY. And you are not ready until, like the engine on the track, you are filled with Power. The hasty, the worried, the fearful, the irritable, the impatient, the doubtful, the fault-finding, are all like the engine that has punctures in the boilers, or has no fire. They are not ready. Get ready by first filling up with Thought. As in the experiment, breathe and think. Consider what to do; think of it; and breathe slowly, with this concentrated thought. All calm, patient, concentrated persons do this.

All happy, healthful and successful persons do this. It is the secret of their success. Before they move to do, they let the Thought fill them, possess them. The Suggestion and the Affirmation must have time and opportunity to fill the organism with its power. This done, then this Power, this Thought, does the work. Think and breathe before you act! This is the Law of Power. This is the conquering force in man that will give him dominion over all things.

Henry Harrison Brown

Each man is as low or high, as little or great, as base or noble as his thoughts; no more, no less. Each moves within the sphere of his own thoughts, and that sphere is his world. In that world in which he forms his habits of thought, he finds his company. He dwells in the region which harmonizes with his particular growth.

But he need not perforce remain in the lower worlds. He can lift his thoughts and ascend. He can pass above and beyond into higher realms, into happier habitations. When he chooses and wills he can break the carapace of selfish thought, and breathe the purer airs of a more expansive life.

James Allen

Each time we indulge in an undesirable thought or habit, the easier does it become for us to repeat that thought or action. Mental scientists are in the habit of speaking of desirable thoughts or mental attitudes as "positive," and of the undesirable ones as "negative." There is a good reason for this. The mind instinctively recognizes certain things as good for the individual to which it belongs, and it clears the path for such thoughts, and interposes the least resistance to them.

They have a much greater effect than an undesirable thought possesses, and one positive thought will counteract a number of negative thoughts. The best way to overcome undesirable or negative thoughts and feelings is to cultivate the positive ones. The positive thought is the strongest plant, and will in time starve out the negative one by withdrawing from it the nourishment necessary for its existence.

Of course the negative thought will set up a vigorous resistance at first, for it is a fight for life with it. In the slang words of the time, it "sees its finish" if the positive thought is allowed to grow and develop; and, consequently it makes things unpleasant for the individual until he has started well into the work of starving it out. Brain cells do not like to be laid on the shelf any more than does any other form of living energy, and they rebel and struggle until they become too weak to do so.

The best way is to pay as little attention as possible to these weeds of the mind, but put in as much time as possible watering, caring for and attending to the new and beautiful plants in the garden of the mind.

William Walker Atkinson

To assume, as in the common belief, that all man can do is to direct physical force, or to relegate, as does Prof. Crooks, Life to some other origin than that of ordinary force, is to limit man to the use of external force, and this to the neglect of himself as force. It is to shut the gates of the "Kingdom." "Lift up your heads, O ye eternal gates, and the King of Glory shall come in! Who is the King of Glory?" MAN. Man recognizing himself as Power.

Henry Harrison Brown

In the Infinity of mind, which is the principle of all metaphysics and of all life, there is nothing but mind, and that which mind does.

That is all there is in the Universe. That is all there ever was or ever will be. This mind is acted upon by our thought, and so our thought becomes the law of our lives. It is just as much a law in our individual lives as God's thought is in the larger life of the Universe.

For the sake of clearness, think of yourself as in this Mind, think of yourself as a center in it. That is your principle. You think, and Mind produces the thing. One of the big points to remember is that we do not have to create; all that we have to do is to think. Mind, the only Mind that there is, creates.

Ernest Holmes

If you entertain "pure" thoughts you will attract thoughts of a similar kind from out the ether, and be strengthened and blessed thereby. By the same law you will attract other people of lofty minds who will aid you in your upward climb.

If you entertain beautiful thoughts, you will draw to yourself a constant stream of thoughts of a like nature, and you will attract to yourself friends of a noble and inspiring character.

In the same way, if you allow thoughts of success only to be held in the mind, and chase away all thoughts of failure, you will attract to yourself a full measure of successful thoughts. These will strengthen your determination and inspire you to greater effort. By the same law you will also attract to yourself men and women of a successful type of mind. You will find yourself sought after by successful people, and they will bring with them opportunities for your more abundant success.

Again, if you will only think thoughts of Health and Perfection, and kill by denial all thoughts of disease, if you will raise yourself into your Perfect World of Mind, and realize that there is no such thing as sickness, illness, ill-health or disease, but that instead there is only infinite Perfection and abounding Health, then not only will Health manifest itself in your body, but you will also attract to yourself, happy, radiant, healthy minded, and healthy bodied people, who will inspire and help you in every department of your life.

Therefore you will readily see how important it is that only the right type of thoughts should be allowed to enter the subconscious mind.

Henry Thomas Hamblin

Man is buffeted by circumstances so long as he believes himself to be the creature of outside conditions. But when he realizes that he may command the hidden soil and seeds of his being out of which circumstances grow, he then becomes the rightful master of himself.

That circumstances grow out of thought every man knows who has for any length of time practiced self-control and self-purification, for he will have noticed that the alteration in his circumstances has been in exact ratio with his altered mental condition. So true is this that when a man earnestly applies himself to remedy the defects in his character, and makes swift and marked progress, he passes rapidly through a succession of vicissitudes.

James Allen

New Thought people often have much to say about "holding the thought;" and, indeed, it is necessary to "hold the thought" in order to accomplish results. But something more is needed. You must "act out" the thought until it becomes a fixed habit with you. Thoughts take form in action; and in turn actions influence thought. So by "acting out" certain lines of thought, the actions react upon the mind, and increase the development of the part of the mind having close relation to the act. Each time the mind entertains a thought, the easier becomes the resulting action . . and each time an act is performed, the easier becomes the corresponding thought.

So you see the thing works both ways . . action and reaction. If you feel cheerful and happy, it is very natural for you to laugh. And if you will laugh a little, you will begin to feel bright and cheerful. Do you see what I am trying to get at? Here it is, in a nutshell: if you wish to cultivate a certain habit of action, begin by cultivating the mental attitude corresponding to it.

And as a means of cultivating that mental attitude, start in to "act-out " or go through, the motions of the act corresponding to the thought. Now, see if you cannot apply this rule. Take up something that you really feel should be done, but which you do not feel like doing. Cultivate the thought leading up to it . . say to yourself: "I like to do so and so," and then go through the motions (cheerfully, remember!) and act out the thought that you like to do the thing. Take an interest in the doing . . study out the best way to do it . . put brains into it . . take a pride in it . . and you will find yourself doing the thing with a considerable amount of pleasure and interest . . you will have cultivated a new habit.

William Walker Atkinson

"Son thou are ever with me, and all that I hath is thine." All things you need are in the invisible. It could be said, that all things needed are in the abstract. You must desire to be greater than you are, in order to advance in life. Desire comes first followed by a recognition of the Power within you enabling you to manifest what you want. The subconscious mind is the medium through which all that you desire can be brought into objectivity.

You are the one giving orders in the form of habitual thinking, feeling, opinions, and beliefs. The subconscious mind obeys the orders given by the conscious mind. If your conscious mind is opposed to all negative thoughts, they can make no impression upon your subconscious mind. You become immunized.

Joseph Murphy

Think evil thoughts, and you will assuredly attract others just as evil, which will help to drag you down. If a man thinks evil thoughts he will become evil in word and deed. Let him think evil thoughts and he will attract other people even worse than himself. In the same way if you entertain thoughts of failure, if you doubt your ability to succeed, if you feel that circumstances will arise which will "swamp" your business, then you will attract streams of "failure" thoughts which will help to keep success away. Not only so, but you will attract other people of a similar nature, whose pessimism will help to complete your final discomfiture.

Like always attracts like. Thus it is that "failures" always drift together, just as men of a successful type always draw to themselves others of the same type of mind. "Birds of a feather flock together" has behind it an unalterable law.

Henry Thomas Hamblin

Principle itself is simplicity, yet it is infinite . . it is Infinite Mind and manifestation of Mind. We live in a Spiritual universe governed through thought, or the word which first becomes law; this law creates what we call matter. Jesus Christ discerned the truth about spiritual principles more than any other man who ever lived, and he proclaimed the eternal reign of law and understanding, absolute, complete, perfect; and he found that law to be operative through his own thought and the power of his own word.

And when you and I shall cease looking outside ourselves to any person and shall realize that whatever truth and whatever power we shall have must flow through us; when we begin to interpret our own natures, we shall begin to understand God and law, and life, and not until then.

Ernest Holmes

Get your mind into this attitude and all will be well. By thinking in this way you create currents and vibrations which will bring you blessing, happiness, health, healing and success.

It may seem strange to insist upon forgiveness and love in lessons on mind training and success development, but believe me there can be no true all-round success, no happiness or harmony in life, so long as hatred, malice and uncharitableness are cherished. These are negative qualities, and success, real, lasting and true, can come only to those who overcome and cast out, root and branch, all negative thoughts, beliefs and habits.

Great minds are above all such petty, mean feelings as hatred, spite and malice. It is the truly great who can best afford to be magnanimous. By regulating and controlling your thinking, by casting out fear and hate and all other negative states, you, too, can become great in mind, and noble in action.

Henry Thomas Hamblin

A man's mind may be likened to a garden, which may be intelligently cultivated or allowed to run wild; but whether cultivated or neglected, it must, and will, bring forth. If no useful seeds are put into it, then an abundance of useless weed seeds will fall therein, and will continue to produce their kind.

Just as a gardener cultivates his plot, keeping it free from weeds, and growing the flowers and fruits which he requires, so may a man tend the garden of his mind, weeding out all the wrong, useless, and impure thoughts, and cultivating toward perfection the flowers and fruits of right, useful, and pure thoughts, By pursuing this process, a man sooner or later discovers that he is the master gardener of his soul, the director of his life.

He also reveals, within himself, the laws of thought, and understands with ever-increasing accuracy, how the thought forces and mind elements operate in the shaping of his character, circumstances, and destiny.

James Allen

Some scientists have claimed that something that might as well be called "Love" is at the bottom of the whole of life. They claim that the love of the plant for water causes it to send forth its roots until the loved thing is found. They say that the love of the flower for the sun causes it to grow away from the dark places, so that it may receive the light. The so-called "chemical affinities" are really a form of love. And Desire is a manifestation of this Universal Life Love. So I am not using a mere figure of speech when I tell you that you must love the thing you wish to attain. Nothing but intense love will enable you to surmount the many obstacles placed in your path.

Nothing but that love will enable you to bear the burdens of the task. The more Desire you have for a thing, the more you Love it; and the more you Love it, the greater will be the attractive force exerted toward its attainment . . both within yourself, and outside of you. So love but one thing at a time . . don't be a mental Mormon.

William Walker Atkinson

Thoughts are unexpressed words and are to be guarded and kept pure if all inharmony in the external is to be overcome forever. Our beliefs are continually "bearing witness" in the external, and the visible reveals the invisible thought. "There is nothing hidden that shall not be revealed" False beliefs reveal themselves as negation in various forms, as the absence of Truth.

Mrs. C. L. Baum

We must remember that we create our own world after the image and likeness of our own mental pictures and thought patterns.

Joseph Murphy

"It is the contention of the authors and also of thousands of such teachers through all the march of the centuries that thoughts are things; actually physical entities, created by the brain as the child is created by another physical process. From this theory came the old saying, 'Coming events cast their shadows before!' Those who accept this theory contend that these thoughts work out an astral, or thought-pattern, before they ever manifest in actual happenings.

"It is their contention that we are standing before the mighty portals, waiting for the curtain of time to rise on the new age, wherein wonders greater than the radio will seem commonplace to the eyes of our descendants.

"If all this seems but the fevered dream of an enthusiast, stop and consider for a moment our present position, as contrasted with that of our grandparents a hundred years ago.

Harriette Augusta Curtiss

Again let us say that the Spirit creates by becoming the thing that it thinks. There is no other possible way in which it could work. Since it is all and there is no other, the thought of opposing forces never enters into its mental working; when we are judging from the outer we are not working in line with the power that we should be using.

We must come to see that there is only One Power and that we are touching it at all points, for there is not a power of poverty and a power of prosperity. There is the one becoming the many; it makes and it unmakes that a higher form may appear to express through it. All that is not in line with its forward movement will soon pass away, for it recognizes no opposite.

As far as we are concerned what we are and what we are to become depends only upon what we are thinking, for this is the way that we are using creative power. The sooner we get away from the thought that we have to create, the sooner we will be able to work in line with the Spirit. Always man uses; he never creates anything. The united intelligence of the human race could not make a single rosebud; it does not know enough. But our slightest thought adrift in mind causes the same power that makes all things to create for us.

Ernest Holmes

A knowledge of the psychology incident to protecting the mind from undesirable thoughts during our waking hours is no small accomplishment, and to protect ourselves from them during sleep requires a knowledge of the psychology of sleep mastered only by the earnest student who has come into a knowledge of the law.

The value of "sleep-knowledge," to those who have come to an understanding of the law, is inestimable, a fact now so universally recognized by all mentalists that only a mention of it is necessary to call attention to the desirability of consciously acquiring it. The current saying, "I will sleep over it," having reference to any impending proposition, is not without its deeper significance. "Sleep-knowledge" is the court of final appeal to the higher Self whose wisdom has ever been regarded as conclusive.

To expect to enjoy good health and happiness, to acquire success while the mind is in the turmoil caused by selfish and unclean thoughts, or choked with weak and useless ones, would be like polluting the fountain and expecting the waters of the stream to remain pure and uncontaminated.

Every cell in your body is a vital, throbbing center of intelligence, and it must be fed with normal, clean thought in order to keep it aglow with the flame of radiant life.

You, the Thinker, are responsible for the alertness, the awareness, the harmony and health which your thoughts express to, in and through every cell of your body. If it is not normal and healthy, you can make it so by thinking constructively; holding the picture of health and strength clearly in your mind. Your thoughts determine your state of health. You can and do think yourself into states of disease or into that of health in a far greater degree than you are aware of; primarily there is no other force that enters into the matter. When we come to know and realize, even in a general way, the structure, and use of our bodies; the forms and expressions of Nature, the trees, plants, flowers, fruits and the animal kingdom, as well as that of the earth itself; that it is a living, moving organism, keeping time to the constant flow of the cosmic life, we are impressed with the thought that all things of the material world are the agents through which the Universal Mind, Ultimate Reality or God is expressing omnipotent power.

Charles Wesley Kyle

This matter of Thought Attraction is a serious one. When you stop to think of it you will see that a man really makes his own surroundings, although he blames others for it. I have known people who understood this law to hold a positive, calm thought and be absolutely unaffected by the inharmony surrounding them. They were like the vessel from which the oil had been poured on the troubled waters . . they rested safely and calmly whilst the tempest raged around them. One is not at the mercy of the fitful storms of Thought after he has learned the workings of the Law.

William Walker Atkinson

As the plant springs from, and could not be without, the seed, so every act of a man springs from the hidden seeds of thought, and could not have appeared without them. This applies equally to those acts called "spontaneous" and "unpremeditated" as to those which are deliberately executed.

Act is the blossom of thought, and joy and suffering are its fruits; thus does a man garner in the sweet and bitter fruitage of his own husbandry.

Thought in the mind hath made us. What we are
By thought we wrought and built. If a man's mind
Hath evil thoughts, pain comes on him as comes
The wheel the ox behind . . . If one endure in purity
of thought joy follows him as his own shadow . . sure.

James Allen

Just imagine yourself surrounded by mind, so plastic, so receptive, that it receives the slightest impression of your thought. Whatever you think it takes up and executes for you. Every thought is received and acted upon. Not some but all thoughts. Whatever the pattern we provide, that will be our demonstration. If we cannot get over thinking that we are poor then we will still remain poor. As soon as we become rich in our thought then we will be rich in our expression.

These are not mere words, but the deepest truth that has ever come to the human race. Hundreds of thousands of the most intelligent thinkers and the most spiritual people of our day are proving this truth. We are not dealing with illusions but with realities; pay no more attention to the one who ridicules these ideas than you would to the blowing of the wind.

In the center of your own soul choose what you want to become, to accomplish; keep it to yourself. Every clay in the silence of absolute conviction know that it is now done. It is just as much done, as far as you are concerned, as it will be when you experience it in the outer. Imagine yourself to be what you want to be. See only that which you desire, refuse even to think of the other. Stick to it, never doubt. Say many times a day, "I AM that thing," realize what this means. It means that the great Universal power of Mind is that, and it cannot fail.

Ernest Holmes

The Soul is seeking freedom and self-determination, but its thought binds and enslaves it at every turn in its holding to conceptions that have been handed down through the ages. As one divests himself of these enslaving conceptions, and reaches a fuller consciousness of freedom, more health is expressed; and with full realization of freedom, and therefore of power, complete health would be attained. It is for this purpose that humanity now seeks to free itself from the chains with which it has long since bound itself.

Eugene Del Mar

Beethoven, in the creation of his deathless symphonies, experienced the power of thought to control and heal the body as evidenced by his writing these words: "I do not fear for my works. No evil can befall them; and whosoever shall understand them, he shall be freed from all the miseries that burden mankind." The wonderful power of music as a healing agent, now universally recognized, is accounted for by its tendency to make us concentrate.

Everyone has, doubtless, realized the truth expressed by Balzac where he says: "Music alone of all the arts, has power to make us live within ourselves." This quality of music is its greatest worth, as it teaches us that the dominant object of life is the recognition of the true self . . the only way by which we may unfold . . as all growth is from within.

Charles Wesley Kyle

Like a stone thrown into the water, thought produces ripples and waves which spread out over the great ocean of thought. There is this difference, however: the waves on the water move only on a level plane in all directions, whereas thought waves move in all directions from a common center, just as do the rays from the sun. Just as we here on earth are surrounded by a great sea of air, so are we surrounded by a great sea of Mind.

Our thought waves move through this vast mental ether, extending, however, in all directions, as I have explained, becoming somewhat lessened in intensity according to the distance traversed, because of the friction occasioned by the waves coming in contact with the great body of Mind surrounding us on all sides.

These thought waves have other qualities differing from the waves on the water. They have the property of reproducing themselves; in this respect they resemble sound waves rather than waves upon the water. Just as a note of the violin will cause the thin glass to vibrate and "sing," so will a strong thought tend to awaken similar vibrations in minds attuned to receive it.

Many of the "stray thoughts" which come to us are but reflections or answering vibrations to some strong thought sent out by another. But unless our minds are attuned to receive it, the thought will not likely affect us. If we are thinking high and great thoughts, our minds acquire a certain keynote corresponding to the character of the thoughts we have been thinking.

And, this keynote once established, we will be apt to catch the vibrations of other minds keyed to the same thought. On the other hand, let us get into the habit of thinking thoughts of an opposite character, and we will soon be echoing the low order of thought emanating from the minds of the thousands thinking along the same lines.

We are largely what we have thought ourselves into being, the balance being represented by the character of the suggestions and thought of others, which have reached us either directly by verbal suggestions or telepathically by means of such thought waves.

Our general mental attitude, however, determines the character of the thought waves received from others as well as the thoughts emanating from ourselves. We receive only such thoughts as are in harmony with the general mental attitude held by ourselves; the thoughts not in harmony affecting us very little, as they awaken no response in us.

William Walker Atkinson

Thought and character are one, and as character can only manifest and discover itself through environment and circumstance, the outer conditions of a person's life will always be found to be harmoniously related to his inner state. This does not mean that a man's circumstances at any given time are an indication of his entire character, but that those circumstances are so intimately connected with some vital thought element within himself that, for the time being, they are indispensable to his development.

Every man is where he is by the law of his being. The thoughts which he has built into his character have brought him there, and in the arrangement of his life there is no element of chance, but all is the result of a law which cannot err. This is just as true of those who feel "out of harmony" with their surroundings as of those who are contented with them.

As the progressive and evolving being, man is where he is that he may learn that he may grow; and as he learns the spiritual lesson which any circumstance contains for him, it passes away and gives place to other circumstances.

James Allen

"For the thing which I greatly feared has come upon me," lamented Job. Of course it did. Nothing in the universe could have prevented it, for through the immutable law of attraction we draw to ourselves whatever we have been thinking. All thoughts eventually assume objective form and we then are surrounded by our mental creations. We can attract friends, health, wealth, success, happiness; or we can draw to us their opposites.

One often hears persons say, when speaking of unfortunate events, "I knew that was going to happen," or "I expected to have bad luck." Their expectant attitude coupled with fear attracted and later materialized the conditions.

Frank L. Hammer

Here are a few simple rules for prosperity that are as sure of working as that water is sure to be wet. First remember that nothing happens by chance. All is law and all is order. You create your own laws every time you think. There is something, call it what you will, but there is a Power around you that knows and that understands all things.

This Power works like the soil; it receives the seed of your thought and at once begins to operate upon it. It will receive whatever you give to it and will create for you and throw back at you whatever you think into it.

Ernest Holmes

It is always possible to pass from thinking of the end you desire to realize, to thinking from the end. But the crucial matter is thinking from the end, for thinking from means unification or fusion with the idea: whereas in thinking of the end, there is always subject and object – the thinking individual and the thing thought. You must imagine yourself into the state of your wish fulfilled, in your love for that state, and in so doing, live and think from it and no more of it. You pass from thinking of to thinking from by centering your imagination in the feeling of the wish fulfilled.

Neville Goddard

The only thing that really matters is what is in the mind or what is not in the mind. If we have a belief in evil, and thoughts of evil, in our mind, then we have evil in our life. If, however, we can cast the thought of, and belief in, evil out of our mind then it will cease to appear in our life.

By raising ourselves above the sensuous life and realizing our permanent world of Mind and there denying evil, poverty, failure, pain, sickness, unhappiness, or whatever our trouble may be, we kill the thought which is the cause of all our troubles. Then whatever we affirm will take their place. If we deny "evil," then we follow by affirming "good," if we deny sickness, then we affirm prosperity and affluence. By denials we can take out all the evil, care, fear and worry out of our lives and build up in their place by means of affirmations, perfect good, success, affluence, happiness, health, love, peace and courage.

Everything being in the mind, then everything that is taken out of the mind is taken out of the life, and everything that is put into the mind, comes into the life.

Thus it is possible with mathematical accuracy and certainty to recreate the life, to cast out all the undesirable and to build up in its place only the beautiful, the good, the true.

Henry Thomas Hamblin

Anger and impatience are natural and easy to thousands of people, because they are constantly repeating the angry and impatient thought and act, and with each repetition the habit is more firmly established and more deeply rooted.

Calmness and patience can become habitual in the same way . . by first grasping, through effort, a calm and patient thought, and then continuously thinking it, and living in it, until "use becomes second nature," and anger and impatience pass away forever. It is thus that every wrong thought may be expelled from the mind; thus that every untrue act may be destroyed; thus that every sin may be overcome.

James Allen

Your thoughts are either faithful servants or tyrannical masters . . just as you allow them to be. You have the say about it; take your choice. They will either go about your work under direction of the firm will, doing it the best they know how, not only in your waking hours, but when you are asleep . . some of our best mental work being performed for us when our conscious mentality is at rest, as is evidenced by the fact that when the morning comes we find troublesome problems have been worked out for us during the night, after we had dismissed them from our minds . . apparently; or they will ride all over us and make us their slaves if we are foolish enough to allow them to do so.

More than half the people of the world are slaves of every vagrant thought which may see fit to torment them.

William Walker Atkinson

Negative thinking and indulging the emotional nature to excess is the primary cause of all these disturbances.

The present condition of the race attests how very inadequate is the attempt to treat these disorders from the physical side of life only. The normal relations of these bodies must be brought about before harmonious results may be expected, and as disordered thoughts caused the inharmony, constructive thought must be aroused that order may be restored. This is best done, as is well known, by inducing natural rest and sleep during which undisturbed condition the life force readjusts the disordered relations and normal action ensues.

During sleep the negative thought no longer disturb and the results of their former action are most easily overcome by giving Nature's restoring powers the opportunity to work their will unhindered; the patient sleeps, perspires, and the danger is past. What has occurred? The negative mind has been stilled, and the exterior forces have ceased to trouble, giving the inner forces of the man the opportunity to do the healing and restoring work. This is the object of all methods of drugless healing.

The power by which you govern all of this marvelous machinery through which life is expressed is THOUGHT. "As a man thinketh in his heart so is he." If you desire health, THINK HEALTH; if you desire wealth THINK WEALTH, and if you desire LOVE, THINK LOVE, always THINK LOVE for it fulfills every requirement of the law; it meets every possible demand that may be made upon you, and it clears the way of all obstructions.

Concentration is the method by, which you will win the desire of your heart; it matters not what your trouble may be, concentrated thought will bring you sure and perfect relief. By the positive exercise of thought are you made just what you are and by its exercise you may become whatsoever you will to be.

The object and purpose of going into the Silence is that we may contact the higher vibrations . . to come in touch with the Source of Universal Energy and*'Power. Herein lies the secret of all becoming, for here we are enabled to catch all that we may be enabled to express of the Divinity of being. Happy is he who has found this never failing oasis in the otherwise comparatively lifeless desert of human experience.

When you contact this supreme state you will know it; you will never have a doubt about that experience, for no "flash of lightning, however vivid, could have impressed you so much as will this first experience. When you once have experienced the effect of contacting this powerful voltage, you will no longer be enslaved by the bonds of the psychic mind. From the indolent state of the subjective . . the world of idle fancies and dreams, in which the many are content to dwell . . you will be carried into a practical, sane and sensible plane of life where the power which you have received will call into activity every energy of your whole nature, and your life of action and genuine worth to yourself and others will begin.

"We awake to the consciousness of it, we are aware of it (this indefinable plus) coming forth in our mind; but we feel that we did not make it, that it is discovered to us, that it is whether we will or no.

Thoughts are things of force and power, I feel and know this saying true, For but within the present hour, They swift have flown to me from you.

Charles Wesley Kyle

All thought energy produces a thought atmosphere that is instantly perceived by anyone who is in the least sensitive. Just as the magnet attracts certain metals and repels others, so you, by your harmonious or inharmonious mental condition, either attract or repel the people in sympathy with your mood.

Benjamin Johnson

Each man is circumscribed by his own thoughts, but he can gradually extend their circle; he can enlarge and elevate his mental sphere. He can leave the low, and reach up to the high; he can refrain from harboring thoughts that are dark and hateful, and can cherish thoughts that are bright and beautiful; and as he does this, he will pass into a higher sphere of power and beauty, will become conscious of a more complete and perfect world.

James Allen

All is law, and cause and effect obtain through all life. Mind is cause, and what we term matter, or the visible, is effect. As water will freeze into the form that it is poured, so mind will solidify only into the forms that our thought takes.

Thought is form. The individual provides the form; he never creates or even manifests, . . that is, of himself; there is something that does all this for him. His sole activity is the use of this power. This power is always at hand ready to be spoken into and at once ready to form the words into visible expression. But the mold that most of us provide is a very poor one, and we change it so quickly that it is more like a motion picture than anything else.

Ernest Holmes

Whatever thought we allow to pass into the subconscious mind is translated into action. This is why a thought has been described as "an action in the process of being born."

Henry Thomas Hamblin

Each person has the power, by his thought, to depress or raise the dominant note of his life; that each person can raise or lower the pitch of his expression; that he can control himself in all his being, thus becoming self-controlled. The possibilities of this discovery cannot as yet be dreamed, but that it is the Greatest of all human discoveries, the century will demonstrate. Thought will yet control, where now we use the lesser forces. Nature's finer forces will need no crude machinery; will need no dynamos, no locomotives, no wires. The only dynamo is the Human Soul; its wires and tracks will be Thoughts. But the material world will be the playground of the Conscious Life in Man, and he, because he is "Conscious Law," be "King of Kings."

Henry Harrison Brown

Man is a growth by law, and not a creation by artifice, and cause and effect is as absolute and undeviating in the hidden realm of thought as in the world of visible and material things. A noble and Godlike character is not a thing of favor or chance, but is the natural result of continued effort in right thinking, the effect of long-cherished association with Godlike thoughts. An ignoble and bestial character, by the same process, is the result of the continued harboring of groveling thoughts.

James Allen

Fear and Worry must go before we can do much. One must proceed to cast out these negative intruders, and replace them with Confidence and Hope. Transmute Worry into keen Desire. Then you will find that Interest is awakened, and you will begin to think things of interest to you.

Thoughts will come to you from the great reserve stock in your mind and you will start to manifest them in action. Moreover you will be placing yourself in harmony with similar thoughts of others, and will draw to you aid and assistance from the great volume of thought waves with which the world is filled. One draws to himself thought waves corresponding in character with the nature of the prevailing thoughts in his own mind . . his mental attitude.

Then again he begins to set into motion the great Law of Attraction, whereby he draws to him others likely to help him, and is, in turn, attracted to others who can aid him. This Law of Attraction is no joke, no metaphysical absurdity, but is a great live working principle of Nature, as anyone may learn by experimenting and observing.

William Walker Atkinson

You realize that there is more than enough air for everyone to breathe, and that pure air supplies the blood with oxygen and revitalizes the body . . yet not one person in ten remembers to take advantage of this abundance of air! Hence thousands of people die daily . . because they do not think about breathing properly every time they have the opportunity.

Benjamin Johnson

We shall learn the power, the laws, of thought, and shall harness it to Human Will and Desire. Thought as Force means the Redemption of the world from all old conditions. Almighty Power lies in thought, and, unlike all other power, it cannot be monopolized. It is open alike to all men. Its only limit is human ignorance. As the Without has been made to serve man's will through knowledge, so now will the Within become subject to him. The mighty realm of Mind will become the theatre of human activity and all its power be consciously used to bless.

Henry Harrison Brown

One of the master thinkers of the age just past, whose mental impress stamps itself indelibly upon the highest form of the civilization of the present, in speaking of this state of consciousness said: "Any person who has made observations on the state and progress of the human mind, by observing his own, cannot but have observed that there are two distinct classes of what are called Thoughts; those that we produce in ourselves by reflection and the act of thinking, and those that bolt into the mind of their own accord.

I have always made it a rule to treat those voluntary visitors with civility, taking care to examine, as well as I was able, if they were worth entertaining; and it is from them I have acquired almost all the knowledge that I have.

Charles Wesley Kyle

The reason man is so weak and unhappy is because he lives the whole of his time in the objective life, the shallow material life of the senses, and neglects the deeper, grander and transcendental life of the inner mind. It is the inner life that gives power and peace and satisfaction. The outer material life of the infinite mind of the senses only bring worry and care, the inner life of the deeper mind brings strength, wisdom, understanding and ability to accomplish and achieve.

It is a proved scientific fact that you grow into the likeness of that upon which you meditate. If you meditate upon evil then evil will come into your life; if you meditate upon revenge, your life will be turned into an inferno of trouble; on the other hand, if you meditate upon happiness and other higher mental states, then happiness will be yours, and if you let your thoughts dwell upon "peace" then peace of mind will result. All these states and many others are within you; they can be called forth by meditation. You can call forth either good or evil, success or failure, strength or weakness, happiness or woe, everything is in your own hands.

Henry Thomas Hamblin

Man is surrounded by a great universal thought power which returns to him always just as he thinks. So plastic, so receptive is this mind, that it takes the slightest impression and molds it into conditions. There are two things in man which his thought affects, his body and his environment. At all times he is given absolute control over these two things, and from the effect of his thought upon them he cannot hope to escape.

At first, being ignorant of this fact, he binds himself by a misuse of the laws of his being; but as he begins to see that he himself is responsible for all that comes to him on the path of life, he begins to control his thought, which in its turn acts on the universal substance to create for him a new world.

Ernest Holmes

You will know what to expect if you plant wonderful seeds (thoughts) of peace, health, happiness, joy, good will, and humor in your mind regularly and systematically. The future is always the present grown up, the invisible thoughts we dwell on become visible in experience and events. When you meditate on whatsoever things are lovely and of good report, you are assured of a wonderful future. Cause is your mental action and effect is the automatic response of your subconscious mind called the Law.

Joseph Murphy

In time of adversity prepare for prosperity. The blue is always back of the clouds and all we have to do is to dissipate the latter. In times of depression prepare for joy. Never hold on to depression or feel that such a belief is going to stay with you permanently.

Any condition which is opposed to joy is but a belief in your own thought which is depressing you by crowding joy out of your consciousness; so realize the unreality of it and prepare for joy which is real and eternal.

Mrs. C. L. Baum

Your mind is given you for your good and for your own use . . not to use you. There are very few people who seem to realize this and who understand the art of managing the mind. The key to the mystery is Concentration. A little practice will develop within every man the power to use the mental machine properly. When you have some mental work to do concentrate upon it to the exclusion of everything else, and you will find that the mind will get right down to business . . to the work at hand . . and matters will be cleared up in no time. There is an absence of friction, and all waste motion or lost power is obviated. Every pound of energy is put to use, and every revolution of the mental driving wheel counts for something. It pays to be able to be a competent mental engineer.

And the man who understands how to run his mental engine knows that one of the important things is to be able to stop it when the work has been done. He does not keep putting coal in the furnace, and maintaining a high pressure after the work is finished, or when the day's portion of the work has been done, and the fires should be banked until the next day. Some people act as if the engine should be kept running whether there was any work to be done or not, and then they complain if it gets worn out and wobbles and needs repairing. These mental engines are fine machines, and need intelligent care.

To those who are acquainted with the laws of mental control it seems absurd for one to lie awake at night fretting about the problems of the day, or more often, of the morrow. It is just as easy to slow down the mind as it is to slow down an engine, and thousands of people are learning to do this in these days of New Thought. The best way to do it is to think of something else . . as far different from the obtruding thought as possible.

There is no use fighting an objectionable thought with the purpose of "downing" it . . that is a great waste of energy, and the more you keep on saying, "I won't think of this thing!" the more it keeps on coming into your mind, for you are holding it there for the purpose of hitting it. Let it go; don't give it another thought; fix the mind on something entirely different, and keep the attention there by an effort of the will. A little practice will do much for you in this direction. There is only room for one thing at a time in the focus of attention; so put all your attention upon one thought, and the others will sneak off. Try it for yourself.

William Walker Atkinson

One of the master thinkers of the age just past, whose mental impress stamps itself indelibly upon the highest form of the civilization of the present, in speaking of this state of consciousness said: "Any person who has made observations on the state and progress of the human mind, by observing his own, cannot but have observed that there are two distinct classes of what are called Thoughts; those that we produce in ourselves by reflection and the act of thinking, and those that bolt into the mind of their own accord. I have always made it a rule to treat those voluntary visitors with civility, taking care to examine, as well as I was able, if they were worth entertaining; and it is from them I have acquired almost all the knowledge that I have.

To raise our consciousness to a plane where by reason of that which it has come to be, it attracts "voluntary visitors" from the higher planes of intelligence, is to make the most of our abilities, demonstrating as it does, the truth of the saying, "To him that hath more shall be given," not as a favor, but because he has complied with the law governing the growth of consciousness.

Do you wish wisdom? Do you wish for health, for wealth, for happiness, for power, for peace, for love? Here is the only avenue open to you whereby you may obtain the actual realization of your desires. It is the one thing in all the whole world worth striving for, for in grasping this, in making sure of your connection with the Source of All, you are placed in possession of "Aladdin's Lamp" and the "Philosopher's Stone.' In other words, you have arrived.

There is nothing mysterious about this method of bringing the mind to function consciously within all of these separate states of consciousness . . separate only in the sense of an ever increasing realization of power. It is the plain, normal advancement of the intellect, absolutely sane, and in the most exacting sense scientific. You may come to know it for yourself; to realize in the most practical way the truth of it, and to receive and enjoy for yourself all of the inestimable powers and benefits this mastership of mind confers. It is all you can ever wish for or expect in the human consciousness. It is not difficult of attainment, if you determine to possess yourself of it. It requires the exercise of all your common sense in a concentrated degree, for it includes thinking, expressing and living your highest conceptions of truth.

Nothing wants you unless you first want it. You attract what you are. If you want anything you must, in essence, become that thing, when the supreme law of attraction, of growth, will be put in operation against which there is no power that can keep you from the thing you may desire. You are a supreme magnet in the great field of cosmic energy, charged with the power to draw your own to yourself.

The result of the highest revelation, using that word in the plain sense and meaning that whenever any fact that was unknown to us is made known, that it is revealed, shows that there is but one substance; that mind is universal, and, consequently in everything; that thought is the creator, and that all that is, is the product of thought.

All things spring from one source, and that source being infinite, it follows that nothing ever was or ever can be separated from it; space when used in this connection being an illusion. Everything, percept, concept, thought, form and act is included in the infinite. Infinity can have nothing opposed to it. We only oppose ourselves from a lack of the knowledge of Unity. The expression of Jesus, "I and my Father are one," clearly sets out his understanding of the truth of Unity. Harmony, peace and perfection are meaningless words unless founded upon the presupposition of Unity, and a lack of the understanding of this law and its application, has been the cause of all the trouble in the world. A comprehension of this law constitutes the supreme lesson for man to learn.

Charles Wesley Kyle

Man is made or unmade by himself; in the armory of thought he forges the weapons by which he destroys himself. He also fashions the tools with which he builds for himself heavenly mansions of joy and strength and peace. By the right choice and true application of thought, man ascends to the Divine Perfection; by the abuse and wrong application of thought, he descends below the level of the beast. Between these two extremes are all the grades of character, and man is their maker and master.

James Allen

As Power is unlimited, and as manifestations differ only in the pitch of vibrations, we may learn to so raise the pitch in which we manifest that we may become invisible to those who can manifest only upon the Lower-Octaves-of-Humanity. That this is possible, that it is scientific, note what Art is already doing. The solid iron becomes liquid when man, by applying heat, raises its pitch. Applying still more heat, it is so raised in its vibrations that it passes from sight. But it is not destroyed. It still IS.

Henry Harrison Brown

See to it that we think only positive, constructive thoughts. A calm determination to think just what we want to think regardless of conditions will do much to put us on the highway to a greater realization of life.

Of course we will fall, of course the road is not easy, but we will be growing. Daily we will be giving to the Creative Mind a newer and a greater concept to be worked out into the life around us. Daily we will be overcoming some negative tendency. We must stick to it until we gain the mastery of all our thought and in that day we will rise never to fall again. We must be good-natured with ourselves, never becoming discouraged or giving up until we overcome. Feel that you are always backed by an Omnipotent power and a kind Father of Love and the way will become easier.

Ernest Holmes

The mind has many degrees of pitch, ranging from the highest positive note to the lowest negative note, with many notes in between, varying in pitch according to their respective distance from the positive or negative extreme.

When your mind is operating along positive lines you feel strong, buoyant, bright, cheerful, happy, confident and courageous, and are enabled to do your work well, to carry out your intentions, and progress on your roads to Success. You send out strong positive thought, which affects others and causes them to cooperate with you or to follow your lead, according to their own mental keynote.

When you are playing on the extreme negative end of the mental keyboard you feel depressed, week, passive, dull, fearful, cowardly. And you find yourself unable to make progress or to succeed. And your effect upon others is practically nil. You are led by, rather than leading others, and are used as a human doormat or football by more positive persons.

William Walker Atkinson

The thought world and the material world are the same in this respect . . "two objects cannot occupy the same place at the same time."

Benjamin Johnson

When Clifton Crawford, the actor, started on his career in America, he played in one week performances in small towns and cities. One night he was told by a prominent member of the company that his work wasn't much good, that he would never be successful, and had better go back home to Scotland. Notwithstanding this discouraging but well-meant criticism and advice, young Crawford remained in America, continued in his profession and in a comparatively short time reached the coveted position of a Broadway "star." After his first success in New York he had the satisfaction of meeting the friend who had advised him to return to his own country, and reminded him of the incident.

Clifton Crawford won out because he related himself mentally to the thing he wanted, because he listened to the voice in his own soul rather than to the pessimistic predictions of outside voices. Why has the heart restless yearnings For heights and steps untrod? Some call it the voice of longing And others the voice of God. That something within you which longs to be brought out, to be expressed, is the voice of God calling to you. Don't disregard it. Don't be afraid of your longings; there is divinity in them. Don't try to strangle them because you think they are much too extravagant, too Utopian. The Creator has not given you a longing to do that which you have no ability to do.

Orison Swett Marden

Some people visualize everything that they think of and many think that it is impossible to make a demonstration unless they possess the power to visualize. This is not the case. While a certain amount of vision is necessary, on the other hand it must be remembered that we are dealing with a power that is like the soil of the ground, which will produce the plant when we plant seed. It does not matter if we have never before seen a plant like the one that is to be made for us.

Our thought is the seed and mind is the soil. We are always planting and harvesting. All that we need to do is to plant only that which we want to harvest. This is not difficult to understand. We cannot think poverty and at the same time demonstrate plenty. If a person wants to visualize let him do so, and if he sees himself in full possession of his desire and knows that he is receiving, he will make his demonstration. If, on the other hand, he does not visualize, then let him simply state what he wants and absolutely believe that he has it and the result will always be the same.

Remember that you are always dealing with law and that this is the only way that anything could come into existence. Don't argue over it. That means that you have not as yet become convinced of the truth or you would not argue. Be convinced and rest in peace.

Ernest Holmes

Man can do anything, because he is Conscious Law, and his creative power is Thought. All he has now to learn is how to use Thought intelligently learn as he has learned to use steam, and he will have "dominion over all things.

Henry Harrison Brown

We must therefore think of God in other terms than that of the ordinary concept of personality. The ancients found this in the law itself, saying, "Verily the Law is a Person," for they found that the Law reflected their faith with infinite exactness. If one looks to the Law with thoughts of faith and love, he finds a response in it to his mood. If he looks with hate and skepticism into his universe, it appears tragic to him. This is why Jesus spoke of it as the Father giving bread to His children because they asked for bread; and again as the adversary, casting the debtor into prison until he pays the utmost farthing.

To those whose faith turns heavenward expecting good, it comes; to those who think in terms of limitation and fear and want the law becomes the adversary. It is therefore like a person, said the Jewish rabbis, for it reflects our moods with utmost exactness.

Fenwicke L. Holmes

Remember, you possess the power to raise the keynote of your mind to a positive pitch by an effort of the will. And, of course, it is equally true that you may allow yourself to drop into a low, negative note by carelessness or a weak will. There are more people on the negative plane of thought than on the positive plane, and consequently there are more negative thought vibrations in operation in our mental atmosphere. But, happily for us, this is counterbalanced by the fact that a positive thought is infinitely more powerful than a negative one, and if by force of will we raise ourselves to a higher mental key we can shut out the depressing thoughts and may take up the vibrations corresponding with our changed mental attitude. This is one of the secrets of the affirmations and autosuggestions used by the several schools of Mental Science

William Walker Atkinson

It is of supreme importance that we learn to control our impulses, impressions and motives, many of which arise from sources most difficult to discover, as well as the many thoughts bent on straying; our vain imaginings, and the endless repetition of thoughts that worry and annoy. What a disorderly band of stragglers they present, to say nothing of those stray thoughts that drift in from the highways and byways, the "tramps" of the mental world at large, idle, unkempt and wholly disreputable. You can put them out and refuse to entertain them, but to get your own thoughts under definite control; to hold your mind in such a state of poise as to effectually bar them from entrance, requires long and purposeful concentration.

Charles Wesley Kyle

The soul attracts that which it secretly harbors; that which it loves, and also that which it fears. It reaches the height of its cherished aspirations. It falls to the level of its unchastened desires . . and circumstances are the means by which the soul receives its own.

Every thought seed sown or allowed to fall into the mind, and to take root there, produces its own, blossoming sooner or later into act, and bearing its own fruitage of opportunity and circumstance. Good thoughts bear good fruit, bad thoughts bad fruit.

The outer world of circumstance shapes itself to the inner world of thought, and both pleasant and unpleasant external conditions are factors which make for the ultimate good of the individual. As the reaper of his own harvest, man learns both by suffering and bliss.

James Allen

When fifty-one percent of your thinking is health and life and power, that day the fifty-one percent will swallow up, erase, kill out the rest. The day you, as an individual, through fifty-one percent of your thought, pass beyond the perception of limitation, you will draw out of the universe everything you desire; poverty will desert you and you will be emancipated forever. The day you think fifty-one percent of happiness, misery shall depart and never return.

Is it not then worth your time and your effort, and should it not be the greatest purpose in the life of any awakened soul so to depict this principle as to emancipate himself?

Ernest Holmes

By the power of the adductive qualities of thought, which works upon the theory "like attracts like." By holding certain thoughts constantly, in your mind, you attract to you thoughts and influences of the like nature, from the great body of thought surrounding us, unseen, but all powerful.

This power is one of the strongest forces in nature, and if properly used will attract assistance from the most unexpected quarters. "Thoughts are Things," and possess a wonderful power of attracting to themselves other thought waves of the same vibratory pitch and quality.

William Walker Atkinson

If we do not choose and select our thoughts, ideas, and mental images, the race mind, or the newspapers, or other people will control our thinking and our moods.

Joseph Murphy

Life is what we like to make it. We can make it like heaven itself, full to the brim with all that is good and beautiful, or we can turn it into a perfect hell. Therefore do not accept the suggestions of those, who having failed in life, proceed to call it hard names.

We can make life a continual joy, if we create a heaven within us by the quality of our thinking and mental processes.

All that we see in life, all that we experience, yea, even life itself, is but the outward expression of the life within. The life within is built up by our thinking.

Henry Thomas Hamblin

When we think we send out vibrations of a fine ethereal substance, which are as real as the vibrations manifesting light, heat, electricity, magnetism. That these vibrations are not evident to our five senses is no proof that they do not exist. A powerful magnet will send out vibrations and exert a force sufficient to attract to itself a piece of steel weighing a hundred pounds, but we can neither see, taste, smell, hear nor feel the mighty force.

These thought vibrations, likewise, cannot be seen, tasted, smelled, heard nor felt in the ordinary way; although it is true there are on record cases of persons peculiarly sensitive to psychic impressions who have perceived powerful thought-waves, and very many of us can testify that we have distinctly felt the thought vibrations of others, both whilst in the presence of the sender and at a distance. Telepathy and its kindred phenomena are not idle dreams.

William Walker Atkinson

If, at some period of life, circumstances drive to discord and disharmony, till all the chords of our being twang with distress, seek swiftly such occupation as shall invite harmony to the mind and rest to the nerves. Why dwell on thoughts that make one miserable, knowing how they precipitate disease in the body and disaster in life? By force of habit conjure such ideas and thoughts that generate hopefulness and courage. Let occupation wait on appetite. Let what interests be the guide to what we do.

Henry Frank

All things come to us through the use of our thought. If we have a small concept of life we will always be doing small things. First in the creative series is the Word, but the Word carries us no further than our consciousness back of it. Unless we are constantly expanding our thought we are not growing. Growth is the law of life and it is necessary. We cannot stand still. If you want to do a new thing, get a new thought and then you will have the power of attraction which has the possibility of drawing to you the circumstances which will make for the fulfillment of your desires. Get over the old idea of limitation.

Ernest Holmes

We are sending out thoughts of greater or less intensity all the time, and we are reaping the results of such thoughts. Not only do our thought waves influence ourselves and others, but they have a drawing power . . they attract to us the thoughts of others, things, circumstances, people, "luck," in accord with the character of the thought uppermost in our minds. Thoughts of Love will attract to us the Love of others; circumstances and surroundings in accord with the thought; people who are of like thought. Thoughts of Anger, Hate, Envy, Malice and Jealousy will draw to us the foul brood of kindred thoughts emanating from the minds of others; circumstances in which we will be called upon to manifest these vile thoughts and will receive them in turn from others; people who will manifest inharmony; and so on.

A strong thought or a thought long continued, will make us the center of attraction for the corresponding thought waves of others. Like attracts like in the Thought World . . as ye sow so shall ye reap. Birds of a feather flock together in the Thought World . . curses like chickens come home to roost, and bringing their friends with them.

William Walker Atkinson

Power is, and mind is, and life is; but they have to flow through us in order to express in our lives. We are dealing with law; and nature must be obeyed before it will work for us. Just realize that this law is as natural a law as any other of God's laws, and use it with the same intelligence that you would use the law of electricity; then you will get the desired results. We provide the thought form around which the divine energies play and to which they attract the conditions necessary for the fulfillment of the thought.

Ernest Holmes

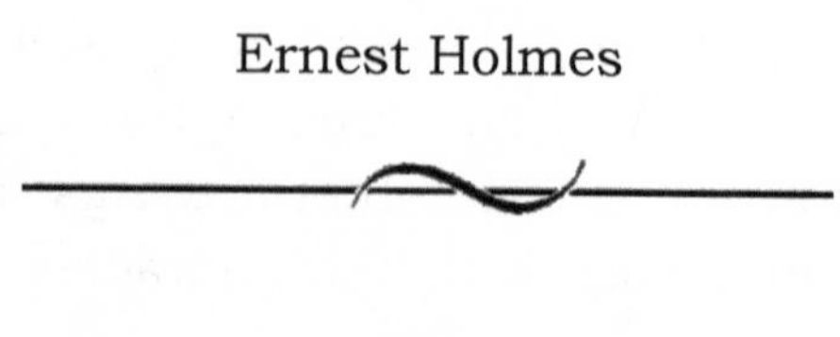

"In the beginning was the Word"; but Professor Drummond tells us that it should not be "Word," but "Thought" . . "In the beginning was Thought, and Thought was with God, and Thought was God, and without Thought nothing was made that is made, and Thought was made flesh and dwelt among us."

Henry Harrison Brown

All is good, and all good is mine. I have health now, because the power dwells within me to compel the perfect action of every function of my body; and all I need to do is to recognize this truth in order to send the negative forces (weakness, disease, pain, etc.) flying, and to utilize my unlimited power. Why, I tell you that you who read these lines have nothing to fear, for no sickness, no tyranny, no negative conditions, no fetter or slavery of any kind whatever can hold or even detain for one moment the growing soul of man after he has entered the domain of the Law of Attraction . . the Principle of Life, the all-good of limitless Being . . by the knowledge of the fact that he is one with all this infinite power; that he has this infinite power within himself, at his daily and hourly command, to set aside any hindrance in the shape of the negative forces which may rise either within or without him.

And what is required to find this power? A living recognition of it. A firm, unshaken belief that it is within you; that it is your all in all.

But this you cannot attain in a day or a week. It only comes with the daily striving after truth; the earnest thought and effort to secure truth; and constant living in, and practice of, the highest truth you know. In this way you gradually draw near to the grand results Mental Science promises and reveals; and every twenty-four hours leaves you in possession of an increased understanding.

But the increase may be so small as to be immeasurable from day to day, and only discernible at longer periods of comparison. For so it is that we journey up the heights of understanding; ever enjoying the new manifestations of the eternal revealed to our wondering eyes at each advancing step. The brain, as the most positive part of the organization, takes the lead; and because I know that this organization is all mind, I am sure that if thought . . the positive leads, the most negative parts will follow.

I am sure that my thought . . the positive part of the magnet me . . will infuse enough of its intelligence into the less intelligent part to show forth the fact that pain and sickness are not positive forces, having inherent power to conquer me, but are negative, amenable to supreme forces . . love, life, intelligence, faith, justice, courage, health, etc.

There will always be negative and positive in the magnet me; but all the time the positive part of the magnet will be getting more positive, and the negative part will keep pace with it. It will become proportionately less negative. This is our process of growth through eternity.

At the present time our reasoning powers recognize dimly the fact that all is good, and our beliefs respond in part. But presently our reasoning powers will revel unconditionally in the fullest knowledge of this great truth, and our less intelligent (or more negative) parts will be sufficiently permeated with the belief to cease to feel pain or to acknowledge disease. And from this point we will advance still farther in the glory of the knowledge of absolute good;

and our bodies will become a pleasure to us, whereas now . . under our present beliefs . . they are our most constant torments.

It is all a matter of progression or growth. While we believed in evil, our growth was retarded. We were living like the animals and dying like them. But now our belief is changed and our progress toward infinite happiness is more direct and satisfactory. It is only a question of time. Let us be patient, but at the same time leave no stone unturned that will quicken our pace.

Helen Wilmans

In the physical body, the nerves are the lines through which the Tattvas speed to their assigned field of influence, and one nerve may carry several vibrations simultaneously just as a single electric wire transmits many messages. The moment they enter the human body, however, the Tattvic vibrations encounter the disturbing influences which are ceaselessly arising in the average mind. The reasons for this, though they have so completely baffled the scientist that there are still many who deny that thought can possibly influence matter, are extremely simple, logical, and absolutely scientific. In the Tattvic law we find the solution.

It has been demonstrated beyond question that emotions of hate, passion, fear, or a guilty conscience generate poisons in the human system which, when not active enough to kill (the poisoned milk of an angry mother has been known to kill her nursing infant) are the primary cause of many disorders; and they give their distinct colors to the secretions of the perspiratory glands. These effects are caused by the abnormal vibrations into which the Tattvas are thrown by the above mental states. Thus with every thought we are molding these bodies of ours to ease or dis-ease.

Every atom, every molecule of your body is as sensitive to the thoughts within (yea, and only less sensitive to those without!) as is a feather to a riffle of air. It is only strong, positive personalities who think their own thoughts; more than half of humanity simply reflect the thoughts of other people, for the Tattvas carry them to responsive minds. They are the wings of thought.

The usurped over-lordship of the sense-directed mind is the source of most of the ills and sufferings of the body; and its crowning sin and most disastrous menace are that it stifles the soul and prevents its growth through the experiences which should be its daily and hourly portion. The sooner you recognize that you are a Soul and have a body (a worldwide difference from the ordinary conception) the sooner you will become conscious of an increased vitality and strength; for the rousing of the soul to conscious activity through this recognition raises the Tattvic vibrations to a higher, more subtle plane. The resulting sense of well-being is the proof that you are actually remaking your body of purer materials through the harmonic cooperation of all the elements needed for its up-building.

When once you have experienced the thrill that this consciousness gives you, you will never again deny the dynamic power of thought, nor the deeply significant truth that spirit works through matter.

These physical bodies of ours are always in a state of flux and reflux like molten metal or plastic gypsum every component atom taking the form that is, the vibration, which the thought of the moment gives rise to. Every thought, even the most idle and fleeting which the mind admits to its sanctum, speeds away on one of the wires centering there, to affect for good or ill the molecules influenced by that nerve.

When you banish the army of discordant warring thoughts which sense-perceptions are ever giving rise to, and declare your real self, your soul, the ruler, you are exercising a will-power which connects your soul with the great central Dynamo, the Divine Spirit; and, with channels freed for their flow, streams of vital force will speed over your nerves in full rhythmic currents, which will stimulate all the atoms to harmonious vibration. (Tattva is a Sanskrit word meaning 'thatness', 'principle', 'reality' or 'truth'.)

Ella Adelia Fletcher

All are alike; there is no difference between one person and another. Come to see all as a divine idea; stop all negative thought; think only about what you want, and never about what you do not want, as that would cause a false creation. Too much cannot be said about the fact that all are dealing with only one power, making and unmaking for man through the creative power of his own thought. If there is something in your life that you do not want there, stop fighting it . . forget it!

Ernest Holmes

But it has not known its power until recently. It accepted the race opinion, of itself, and considered itself a sort of ornamental appurtenance in the human economy. Thought has only begun to know that it is a power. It does not, even yet, know what a perfectly wonderful power it is; but it is gradually learning this. It does not yet know that it has power to renew and fashion the body, out of which it had its birth. It does not know its own power to prevent fire from consuming the body. But it has this power, and in many instances in the world's history it has done this very thing.

A man's body is the product of evolution. The thought generated by the body may be considered a later product of evolution; or, rather, that quality of thought that recognizes its own power (for in strict truth the body and the thought are coeval . . being one). But it is scientific to affirm that the riper thought of the present day is the latest product of evolution.

The relations of body and thought have always been interactive. At one time the body is the cause, and thought the effect. Then, thought will be the cause and the body the effect. This has gone on in a gradually ripening process, unnoticed by the individual, until at last thought has developed to a point where it begins to recognize its power as a factor in growth; moreover, as a free power, unfettered by the fixed beliefs which compose the body.

What a tremendous position this is!

Who doubts that we stand on the threshold of the mightiest revelations our world has yet seen? Man, self-created and self-creative; and with the knowledge of how to create self.

Helen Wilmans

I want you first to realize how powerful thought is. A thought of fear has turned a person's hair gray in a night. A prisoner condemned to die was told that if he would consent to an experiment and lived through it he would be freed. He consented. They wanted to see how much blood a person could lose and still live. They arranged that blood would apparently drop from a cut made in his leg. The cut made was very slight, from which practically no blood escaped. The room was darkened, and the prisoner thought the dropping he heard was really coming from his leg. The next morning he was dead through mental fear.

The two above illustrations will give you a little idea of the power of thought. To thoroughly realize the power of thought is worth a great deal to you.

Through concentrated thought power you can make yourself whatever you please. By thought you can greatly increase your efficiency and strength. You are surrounded by all kinds of thoughts, some good, others bad, and you are sure to absorb some of the latter if you do not build up a positive mental attitude.

If you will study the needless moods of anxiety, worry, despondency, discouragement and others that are the result of uncontrolled thoughts, you will realize how important the control of your thoughts are. Your thoughts make you what you are.

When I walk along the street and study the different people's faces I can tell how they spent their lives. It all shows in their faces, just like a mirror reflects their physical countenances. In looking in those faces I cannot help thinking how most of the people you see have wasted their lives.

The understanding of the power of thought will awaken possibilities within you that you never dreamed of. Never forget that your thoughts are making your environment, your friends, and as your thoughts change these will also. Is this not a practical lesson to learn? Good thoughts are constructive. Evil thoughts are destructive. The desire to do right carries with it a great power. I want you to thoroughly realize the importance of your thoughts, and how to make them valuable, to understand that your thoughts come to you over invisible wires and influence you.

If your thoughts are of a high nature, you become connected with people of the same mental caliber and you are able to help yourself. If your thoughts are tricky, you will bring tricky people to deal with you, who will try to cheat you.

If your thoughts are right kind, you will inspire confidence in those with whom you are dealing. As you gain the good will of others your confidence and strength will increase. You will soon learn the wonderful value of your thoughts and how serene you can become even when circumstances are the most trying.

Such thoughts of Right and Good Will bring you into harmony with people that amount to something in the world and that are able to give you help if you should need it, as nearly everyone does at times.

Theron Q. Dumont

We attract to us the thoughts of others of the same order of thought. The man who thinks success will be apt to get into tune with the minds of others thinking likewise, and they will help him, and he them. The man who allows his mind to dwell constantly upon thoughts of failure brings himself into close touch with the minds of other "failure" people, and each will tend to pull the other down still more. The man who thinks that all is evil is apt to see much evil, and will be brought into contact with others who will seem to prove his theory. And the man who looks for good in everything and everybody will be likely to attract to himself the things and people corresponding to his thought. We generally see that for which we look.

William Walker Atkinson

If we are to draw from Life what we want, we must first think it forth into Life. It always produces what we think. In order to have success, we must first conceive it in our own thought.

This is not because we are creators, but because the flow of Life into manifestation, through us, must take the form we give to it, and if we want a thing we must have within ourselves the mental equivalent before we get it.

Ernest Holmes

Thought, then, which is evolved from the great body of crude or undigested mind that the world calls matter, is the most active substance that we know anything of, and is by far the most vital and intelligent. Electricity is rapid in its movements, but it does not annihilate time and space as thought does. It is thought alone that can compass the bounds of a world in a second; and thought is generated by these human brains. Electricity is an unorganized power; thought is its master, and can organize it. The thought which our brains generate is powerful only as it counterparts universal thought, which is Life, or Being. Therefore, thought is the positive pole of the magnet man; it is the captain of the craft, and has the directing power over him.

Thought can make sick and it can make well. Thought grounded in error, or from a negative basis, and educated in the knowledge that all is good or life, can make well quite as easily. Thought, though unseen, is still a substance; a substance as much more powerful than the crude substance called matter, as steam is more powerful than water.

Thought, the captain, has never recognized its power over its own craft, nor over the thoughts of other people. And yet, being a substance, it goes out of these human brains and meets the thought emanating from other brains, and an influence is wrought which the individual as a whole (positive and negative poles together) knows almost nothing of.

The thoughts that go out and meet and influence other thoughts bring back no report of the fact, simply because they do not know that they can do so, and, therefore, do not listen for them. That sense by which we can hear these thoughts is rudimentary in us, and will only develop by use.

The time is no doubt near at hand when our thoughts will go forth to distant points and bring back to us a perfectly correct report of what has been transpiring in the place where they have been visiting. We are only beginning to be conscious of the power of thought, and we do not even imagine how much it partakes of the omniscience of the Law of Being.

Thought demonstrates its omniscience in proportion as we recognize its quality and power.

Helen Wilmans

When you are in a negative mood you attract thoughts of similar nature through the law of affinity. That is why it is so important to form thoughts of a success nature to attract similar ones. If you have never made a study of this subject, you may think this is all foolishness, but it is a fact that there are thought currents that unerringly bring thoughts of a similar nature. Many persons who think of failure actually attract failure by their worries, their anxieties, their over-activity. These thoughts are bound to bring failure.

When you once learn the laws of thought and think of nothing but Good, Truth, Success, you will make more progress with less effort than you ever made before.

Theron Q. Dumont

Whether or not we believe in them, we are constantly making affirmations. The man who asserts that he can and will do a thing . . and asserts it earnestly . . develops in himself the qualities conducive to the well doing of that thing, and at the same time places his mind in the proper key to receive all the thought waves likely to help him in the doing.

If, on the other hand, one says and feels that he is going to fail, he will choke and smother the thoughts coming from his own subconscious mentality which are intended to help him, and at the same time will place himself in tune with the Failure-thought of the world . . and there is plenty of the latter kind of thought around, I can tell you.

William Walker Atkinson

By the activity of our thought things come into our life, and we are limited because we have not known the truth; we have thought that outside things controlled us, when all the time we have had that within which could have changed everything and given us freedom from bondage.

Ernest Holmes

Not a person in the world has one atom of the body today that he had ten years ago. Indeed, so rapid is the change in the human bodies that it is now said by learned physicians that from one to three months time is sufficient to change every particle of them.

Then, since we are already replacing the worn-out atoms of our bodies day by day, let us see to it that we give the new atom the stamp of immortality from our newly revised beliefs on this point. In this way, each new supply will be better and more vital than the former supply. Thought has the power to do this, being the governing and building power of the body, and it has the power to carry with it the new externals, or bodily manifestations.

Your educated thought, which is a substance, can pour tangible invigoration into the daily new supply of atoms for your body, by earnestly dwelling upon these new truths, and trying to feel (or, what is better . . feeling) as you do, so that your body is changing under the influence. This, coupled with the recognition of the fact that the thoughts are the building power of the body, will give you the ability to mold your body as you will. For your thoughts give quality to your blood (healthful and more immortalizing quality in this instance) and your blood builds this quality into your body, where it shows forth in the measure of its strength.

This is the fountain of immortal youth which Ponce de Leon sought among the negative (physical) things of earth, but which could only be found among the positives of life.

Every growing thought has the power to carry with it its own new externals, or bodily manifestations. Do not forget this. This power of thought will enable us to carry our internal and external (soul and body) together in harmonious unison forever, not necessarily, however, always existing on this earth. We should pass into higher and still higher spheres, which would open to us as we become fitted by our enlarged being to become actors in them. For "our Father's house has many mansions."

Not understanding, at the present time, how to maintain the harmonious balance in development between our thought life and our visible (or bodily life) we are able to live so long only as the two grow in unconscious concord. Just as soon as this concord is disturbed by the negative laws which govern the body . . the law of the animal existence, which is the law of disintegration, the dropping away of the body, as it were, before the power of thought . . then the thought and the body cease to work together smoothly.

The body (or negative part of the mind) becomes an impediment to the thought (or positive part, which, as yet, does not know that it has power to retain the body) and there comes that separation we call death.

Helen Wilmans

Do not allow yourselves to be affected by the adverse and negative thoughts of those around you. Rise to the upper chambers of your mental dwelling, and key yourself up to a strong pitch, away above the vibrations on the lower planes of thought. Then you will not only be immune to their negative vibrations but will be in touch with the great body of strong positive thought coming from those of your own plane of development.

William Walker Atkinson

It is necessary that we remember that we live in two worlds at the same time, the invisible world of cause where thoughts and ideas are the creators and the material world of effect where the results or manifestations of our thoughts and ideas come into being.

Ernest Holmes

Thought is the healer. Thought educated in the knowledge of that universal truth . . all is good, or all is Life . . becomes a power not to be resisted by the negative thought of the negative individual. And the thought of every soul whose belief is grounded in the appearance of evil is negative to even the weakest, frailest thought of him whose belief is grounded in that great truth . . all is good, because all is Life.

"Eschew evil and believe in God if you would be saved." This means that we are to cease to believe in evil and to learn to believe in good; or to cease to believe in death and learn to believe in life if we are to be saved.

Saved from what? Why, saved from so-called sin, and from sickness and death; saved from the undeveloped condition which these words imply, by being lifted into the power which the knowledge of truth confers; and above all, which the knowledge of that best of all truths confers . . all is good, because all is Life.

A belief in good, or the all-prevalent Principle of Life, is the foundation rock of a world's salvation from error, sickness and death.

Helen Wilmans

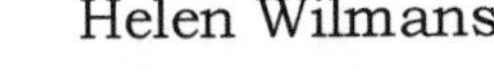

When there arises in one's consciousness an understanding of his power . . irrespective of mass help or hindrance . . to convert obstacles into opportunities, to transform failure into success, to guide and direct his own life, by himself and for himself, he has entered into the individual consciousness, and he is no longer content with dependence upon mob, mass, or class. He has risen out of the sea of mass turbulence into the open air of individual responsibility. He has come to realize the power of thought, and he has ceased to be dependent upon the mass, from which he has made his declaration of independence.

In gathering his forces to a focus he has converted himself into a powerful magnet, with ability to attract to himself that which he desires. He has entered a higher plane of consciousness, bearing the relation to his former condition somewhat akin to that between human intuition and animal instinct. Now he must think for himself, and in return there comes to him the reward of his own thinking. He has separated himself from the mass. He has allied himself with the higher thought.

He has entered a new realm of consciousness, with which it is necessary for him to become acclimated. He breathes a more rarefied atmosphere, and at first he is apt to catch his breath. As yet, he has not changed his motives, his purposes, or his ideals; he has merely taken on a new point of view, to which he is far from being adjusted completely. He notes the great material returns that have been secured by many who had been residing in this realm, and he seeks new methods whereby to satisfy the old desires.

Individual consciousness first interprets itself on the animal plane, selfishly. Its first and primary needs are physical and material, and the individual invokes the power of thought for these ends. Food, clothing, shelter, or position has been insufficient or unsatisfactory, and his new powers are concentrated on securing for himself that which formerly he lacked. He is thinking of himself alone, and cares not from whence his supply comes, nor how his appropriation of it may affect others.

He concentrates on what he wishes, and it comes; he visualizes his wants, and they manifest! As yet he is merely using his new-found powers to gratify his own animal appetites. Yes; but how tremendous an advance from his previous admission of personal slavery and subservience. What a transformation from the worm of the dust or the mass consciousness! What a splendid position to assume! Yes; and how far more glorious it is to graduate from it! For there are far higher planes of consciousness, and not a few have attained to them.

Thought is the power that moves the world. Thought creates! It does not make something out of nothing; but ever and always old forms are disappearing into the unseen, from which new forms are as constantly emerging. Thought makes visible the invisible; it gives form to that which, to the human eye, was previously formless. All energy, all power, all life is invisible; only its manifestations in form may be seen by one's so-called physical senses.

Thought makes the mold into which reality pours and is given form. The thought-mold is invisible, and the substance which fills it is invisible; but quick, presto, change! . . and form emerges. Oxygen and hydrogen are invisible gases; they combine and . . lo and behold . . water, the elixir of life. Man creates to the extent that he understands the laws of mind, and to the degree of his wisdom in manipulating the power of thought.

All known planes of existence are but way-stations to higher realms. The law of existence is eternal progress. Individual consciousness has many aspects, commencing with a personal assertiveness that is in striking contrast to its previous self-depreciation and complete dependence on others. It first uses its new instruments as weapons of offence and defense. But the law of compensation decrees that the higher the plane of living the quicker do results follow causes, and the clearer becomes the relation between action and reaction.

In time it is borne in on the individual that there is something higher and grander than this aspect of individual consciousness, that it does not induce harmony and happiness, that it ensures neither health of body nor peace of mind, that it fails to elevate character or satisfy the cravings of the soul. There comes a tune when this phase of individual consciousness spells failure instead of success, and becomes an effective bar to one's spiritual progress. The material and intellectual have ceased to satisfy, and the vision is directed to that which is real, permanent, and abiding.

And then a glorious transmutation takes place, and one enters the realm of God-consciousness . . the realization of the God within. There is no loss in this; there is only gain. The physical and mental powers are enhanced and intensified; and one's ability to secure his physical and material desires are vastly increased. One now possesses greater power to acquire what he wants, and secures deeper satisfaction from that which he creates and attracts to himself.

With God-consciousness he has secured a wider vision; he realizes the Fatherhood of God and the Brotherhood of Man; he thinks in terms of inclusiveness instead of separateness; his relations are now with the universal; he uses no weapons of offence or defense; he becomes a partner of the divine; he gives to the universal freely and wisely; and to the full measure and overflowing the universal reacts harmoniously and abundantly.

Each plane of consciousness is best in its time and place; each answers its purpose of preparation for a higher one. No one may miss any of the steps introductory to the plane he now occupies, from which in turn he must graduate. It is probable that mass consciousness will long remain predominant, but each day individual consciousness is making great numbers of converts. While God-consciousness is reserved for the comparative few, so great are its powers, that the influence of its tens of thousands will be profound throughout the confines of human existence.

One who lives in the individual consciousness is but a fraction of an individual, after all. No man may live by himself or to himself. He may exist that way, and he may die that way; but he cannot live that way. The individual consciousness pervades the intellectual realm, and dominates by personal will power. God-consciousness is on the deeper mental plane, and rules by virtue of spiritual power and the Universal Will.

Individual consciousness dominates resistance, meets and overcomes its enemies; while God-consciousness harmonizes, and finds only friendly cooperation.

This is the Era of the Brotherhood of Man! This is the Age of the League Idea! The higher thought first represents individual consciousness, and later God-consciousness; and, as these develop, the higher-thought people are coming together more and more closely into centers, associations, alliances, and leagues. The same tendency may be observed of all other progressive lines of thought.

The time has come when the progressive minds in all fields should not only come together within their own particular line of thought or activity, but should take to heart the fact that there is now in progress a great World Movement, the wondrous possibilities of which will become apparent only as each and all of its aspects . . religious, economic, scientific, philosophic, social, etc. . . are brought together in a luminous and all-embracing League of Humanity.

Eugene Del Mar

Death is simply the result of ignorance of the power of thought to save. Our bodies are our external minds. They are not to be undervalued as they have heretofore been. They are the expression of our widely diversified individualities, and are important to us as the organized expression of our present state of thought.

Our bodies are the limitation of the thought that is ourselves, just as the skin of the peach is the limitation of the substance that is the peach. We can remain in ignorance of our power over these bodies, and, in consequence, be forced to lay them down in death; or we can refine them by a consciousness of our power over them, thus rendering them so pliant that they will change in conformity with every new thought that we acquire, in this way becoming perfect manifestation of our growing, beautifying, inner selves. Which shall we do?

There is an atonement to be made, which alone has the power to arrest that breaking of the magnet man in death. The atonement, the at-one-ment of thought and body, must be made by a conscious recognition that we are all mind. It must be made either here or hereafter. We have power to make it here now, as well as any future time; and ought to make it now. The time to actualize a truth is when we recognize it. Heretofore as soon as a man arrived at that age where his intelligence began to be of benefit to the race, he died. His career was repeated in his children; and so progress has stagnated hundreds of years.

Hundreds of years ago, human intelligence had achieved almost the same success we are achieving today. Ideas were written and works were done which even now are unsurpassed, because one man has simply been a repetition of another. Men must live longer in order to widen the range of individual experience, and so increase the general stock of knowledge. We must emancipate ourselves from the old forms of thought, which have so long been our prison houses, and project better ones.

We are beginning to see the immense power of thought, to mold, not only our own bodies, but the bodies of others, and I have no hesitation in saying that as disease has become negative to him who has mastered this mind power, or Mental Science, that old age, which is only a slow aggregation of disease, can also be mastered.

Helen Wilmans

At one time man was the sport of the elements, the creature of circumstances, and the slave of environment. He was a self-acknowledged "worm of the dust." That crude plane of understanding has been passed by the developed man, who has come to recognize the power of thought in the affairs of his life. It is realized generally in the progressive philosophies of the day that it is one's thought . . with his attendant attitude of mind . . that determines his physical and material environment, attracts what comes to him, and keeps away that which it repels.

The results of man's substitution of a mental basis for a physical one, his acceptance that the mind is the realm of physical causation, has been tremendous. His understanding of the conscious and subconscious aspects of mind has opened up still another world to him. It is now realized that genius is potential generally, and may be developed intelligently. Many have already made use of the new knowledge, and demonstrated wondrous mastery of the physical body and material environment.

This is but a promise of what man's future is to be. He has yet to come to an intimate knowledge of the super-conscious aspect of mind. He is destined to as great a future revelation in his understanding of life as his past in reference to material objects. His increment of wisdom will be as extraordinary as has been his advance in thought in working out the wondrous inventions of modern days.

Man's substitution of a spiritual basis for a mental one will result in a progress even greater than followed his previous acceptance of a mental basis. Man is a spiritual being, and he may wield spiritual powers, making direct use of the energy that thought but indirectly contacts. Spiritual direction releases powers far transcending those to which thought may relate itself.

The greater powers may be exercised only by one who understands their rightful use, and comprehends the results of their misuse. The price of spiritual power is self-control, the result of wise direction of thought power when illumined by spiritual ideals. One could hardly expect to be invested with power until he knew how to control or regulate it for constructive purposes, and one may exercise outwardly only that which he already possesses inwardly. Self-control is certainly a small price to pay for spiritual dominion.

The mental realm is one of analysis, differentiation, separation, contest, conflict, and opposition. It is the amphitheater for attraction and repulsion. To the mental victor belongs the physical spoils, and the victor is one who wields his thought weapons to the greatest advantage.

Wonderful as are the methods of the thought realm, they are crude as compared with those of the spiritual. With the spiritual lever in control one accomplishes with far greater ease, for he operates in harmonious accord with the higher laws, which with the least friction turn the wheels of mental and physical activities. There is an easy way of solving difficult problems; there is a simple method of dissolving the perplexities of appearance! Its basis is spiritual realization.

Fundamentally, life is spiritual. Being expresses itself mentally and manifests physically. Physical existence is a fact, and it must be accepted as a necessity of soul unfoldment. It is the avenue of approach to one's conscious realization of innate divinity. Physical existence consists of a continuous series of experiences; and existence and experience are identical, and equally necessary.

Life manifests in individual forms environed by other forms; and that which is seemingly without, and is related to any particular form, constitutes its environment. Manifested life and its environment act and react on each other, and each one that partakes of any experience gathers such wisdom from it as it provides and to which he is receptive. In this manner each manifested form undergoes constant change; and the basic problem of any individual form of life is to maintain constant harmonious relations with an ever-changing environment.

The tendency of individualized life in general is to manifest itself in increasing accord with the ideal of its own plane of existence. As the continued existence of each plane is essential to the support of the next higher one, it is evident that only certain individuals in each group may be permitted to cross the threshold of a higher realm. The mineral, vegetable, and animal kingdoms, from which human existence has proceeded, all remain to minister to him, and are essential to his welfare. They constitute the material foundation of his physical existence.

A careful examination of the most variable and plastic forms of the mineral kingdom demonstrates clearly that the ideal of that kingdom was that of vegetation; the ideal form of the vegetable kingdom was evidently the animal; and the aspiration of the animal kingdom was the human form. Only the most progressive species were able to make these changes, even under peculiarly favorable conditions; and it is more than doubtful if conditions will ever again recur that will permit of similar graduations.

In each successive kingdom of existence the time has been shortened materially for the development of its more progressive forms into a higher realm. It took longest for the mineral kingdom to graduate into the realm of vegetation, and the time since man appeared on earth is very limited as compared with the immense intervals that elapsed before that event.

The time is now approaching when a "new" race is about to come into existence, new in the sense that its accepted foundation of thought and basis of action will be in vivid contrast with those now entertained generally by mankind. The results of such a change must be tremendous and far-reaching.

The problem now confronting the progressive individual is how to understand, comprehend, and put into activity those qualities and attributes that will entitle him to enter the new life. In order to do this it will not be necessary for him to deny his reason, or to close his eyes to facts. What is essential is a different and loftier interpretation of fundamental conceptions. The basis of this change will be his realization of himself as a spiritual being, with all of its necessary implications, including an inspired thought-consciousness and an illumined physical manifestation.

The Coming Race will neither cease to be physical nor will it dispense with any of its present faculties and functions; but its recognized motive power will be as superior to that which it now realizes, as electric and magnetic forces are to mechanical and physical ones. The Coming Race will function on a higher plane where, in the light of its greatly increased powers, its present problems will seem comparatively trivial It will mark a New Era of Human Evolution.

Eugene Del Mar

Christian Larson's 'Mastery of Fate'

The State Of Self-Supremacy

Man is inherently master over everything in his own life, because the principle of his being contains the possibility of complete mastership; and the realization of this principle produces the attitude of self-supremacy.

While mind is in this attitude, only those impressions are formed that are consciously selected; consequently, only those thoughts are created that conform to the purpose that may predominate in mind at the time.

To remain constantly in the attitude of self-supremacy, is therefore the secret of original thinking; and since the mastery of fate comes directly from original thinking, everything that interferes with the attitude of self-supremacy must be eliminated completely.

The most serious obstacle to this attitude is the belief that man is, for the greater part, the product of his environment; and that man cannot change to any extent until a change is first produced in his environment. The result of this belief is the attitude of self-submission; and the more deeply this belief is felt, the more completely does man submit himself to the influence of his surroundings.

While mind is in this attitude, it has only a partial control over the process of thinking; it accepts willingly every impression that may enter through the senses, and permits the creation of thought in the likeness of those impressions without the slightest discrimination.

To remove the attitude of self-submission, man must cease to believe that he is controlled by environment, and must establish all his thinking upon the conviction that he is inherently master over his entire domain.

This, however, may appear to be not only impossible, but absurd, when considered in the presence of the fact that man is controlled by environment. To tell a man to cease to believe as true that which he knows to be true, may not, at first sight seem to contain any reason; but at second sight it proves itself to mean the same as to tell a man to leave the darkness and enter the light.

When man ceases to believe that he is controlled by environment, he departs from a belief that is detrimental; and when he begins to realize that he has the power to completely control himself, he enters a conviction that is favorable to the highest degree.

While he is in the attitude of self-submission, he is controlled by environment, and the belief that he is thus controlled, is true to him. But when he enters the attitude of self-supremacy, he is not controlled by environment; therefore, the belief that he is controlled by environment is no longer true to him. While we are in the dark, we can truthfully say that we are in darkness; but when we enter the light, we cannot say, truthfully, that we are in darkness.

There is such a thing as being influenced by conditions that exist in our surroundings; but when we transcend that influence we are in it no more; therefore, to say that we are in it when we are out of it, is to contradict ourselves. And we equally contradict ourselves when we state that we are controlled by environment after we are convinced that we are inherently masters of everything in the personal life. What is not true to us now, we should not admit now, even though it had been true to us for all previous time.

To state that you are controlled by environment, and to permit that belief to possess your mind, is to submit yourself almost completely to the control of environment.

To recognize the principle of your being, and to realize that within that principle the power of complete supremacy does exist; to establish yourself absolutely upon that principle, and to state that you are not controlled by environment, is to depart from the control of environment. While you are conscious of the principle of self-supremacy, you are unconscious of the influence of environment; therefore, to speak the truth, you must declare that you are complete master in your own domain.

When you know that the possibility of self-supremacy is within you, you cannot state truthfully that it is not there; and to state, in the presence of your knowledge of self-supremacy, that you are controlled by environment, is the same as to state that there is no self-supremacy. The very moment that you admit the possibility of self-supremacy, the control of environment is no longer a real fact to you; because in the state of self-supremacy, it is not possible for the control of environment to exist.

When man discovers the state of self-supremacy, he can no longer believe in the control of environment as a principle; and is therefore compelled to declare that the control of environment is no longer true to him. And, as he is permitted to speak only for himself, and judge only his own life, he must refuse absolutely to believe in the control of environment under any condition whatever.

To believe that others are controlled by environment, is to judge where he has no authority, and also to place himself once again in the belief that environment controls man. To place himself in that belief is to enter the attitude of self-submission, and submit himself to the influence of everything that enters his sphere of existence.

It is therefore evident that the principal reason why those who know of self-supremacy do not master fate, is because they are not true to their own convictions. They believe that the principle of self-supremacy exists, but they also believe that the control of environment exists. They try to believe both to be true at the same time, which is impossible.

If the one exists as a living power in the life of a person, the other does not exist in the life of that person. It would be just as reasonable to believe that light and darkness could exist in the same place at the same time.

To try to believe in the idea of self-supremacy and the control of environment at the same time, is to live in confusion; and he who lives in confusion controls practically nothing. He is therefore more or less controlled by everything, When man is convinced that he is, in himself, master over his life, he can no longer believe that his life is controlled by environment. He must absolutely reject the latter belief; both cannot be true to any one mind; therefore, every mind must decide which one of these beliefs to accept as absolutely true, and which one to reject as absolutely untrue.

The mind that does not wholly reject one of the two, is trying to serve two masters, which is impossible. He who tries to serve two masters will serve the one only, and that one will be the false one; because whoever tries to serve two masters is false to himself, and will consequently serve that which is false. In this connection it may be questioned how we know that the principle of self-supremacy does exist; and how we know that complete mastership is inherent in man. But we do know; because man does exercise complete mastership over certain parts of his being at certain times; and the fact that he does this proves the existence of the principle.

If the principle of self-supremacy did not exist, man could not exercise complete control over anything at any time; but every mind demonstrates supremacy many times every hour. The mastership exercised over mind and body in various ways may be confined to limited spheres of action; but within those spheres of action the mastership is complete. And those spheres will expand constantly as the principle of self-supremacy is applied on a larger and a larger scale.

Since the principle of complete control exists in man, there is a way to apply that principle in everything, and at all times. But to accomplish this, the attitude of self-supremacy must prevail at all times, and under all conditions.

While man is in the attitude of self-supremacy, he exercises complete control over certain things in his life; but when he enters the belief that he is controlled or influenced by other things, he leaves the attitude of self-supremacy, and ceases to exercise his complete control.

In the present state of human development, the average mind is so constituted that it oscillates from one state to another, remaining the greater part of the time in the attitude of self-submission; due principally to the fact that we are seldom absolutely true to the higher conviction, and also because we try to think that both beliefs are true at the same time. Consequently, the great essential for man in his present state is to accept the high conviction as an absolute truth, and be true to that truth every moment of existence.

To be true to that truth he must refuse absolutely to believe that he can be controlled or influenced by anything or anybody. He must depart completely from the belief in the control of other powers, and must recognize in himself the only power to control . . the power to control completely, everything in his own domain.

Nor is this a contradiction, because when man enters the consciousness of self-supremacy, he cannot submit his self to any outside influence; therefore, there are no outside influences in action in his life. And when this is the case he cannot believe in the existence of outside influences, as far as he is concerned. When nothing is trying to control him, he cannot truthfully say that he is being controlled, nor even that he is liable to be controlled.

When man is in a state of self-supremacy, he is in a state where no, influence from without exists; he is in a world where the power of self-mastery is the only controlling power; therefore, he cannot truthfully recognize any other. While in the attitude of self-submission, your mind is open to all kinds of impressions from without; and consequently, your thinking will be suggested to you by your environment. The result is that you will become like your environment, and will think, act and live as your environment may suggest.

If your environment be inferior, you will think inferior thoughts, live an inferior life, and commit deeds that are low or perverse, so long as you are in the attitude of self-submission. But if you should submit yourself to a better environment, your life, thoughts, and deeds would naturally become better. In each case you would be the representation of the impressions that enter through the senses.

However, the very moment you pass from a superior environment to one that is inferior, you will begin to change for the worse, unless you have in the meantime attained a degree of self-supremacy.

To enter a superior environment will not of itself develop self-supremacy, nor the art of original thinking; because so long as you permit yourself to be influenced by environment, you prevent your mind from gaining consciousness of the principle of self-supremacy.

A change of environment, therefore, will not give man the power to master his fate. This power comes only through a change of thought.

While in the attitude of self-supremacy your mind is not open to impressions from any source; but you can place your mind, at will, in the responsive attitude, so that it may receive impressions from any source that you may select.

By proper selection, consciousness can, in this way, be trained to express itself only through those mental channels that reach the superior side of things, and thereby come in contact with the unlimited possibilities of things.

From impressions received through this contact with unlimited possibilities, mind will be able to form original thoughts that embody superior powers and attainments; and as man becomes like his thoughts, he will, through this process, become superior.

Instead of being controlled by the impressions received from environment, he will control those impressions, and use them as material in the construction of his own larger life, and the greater destiny that must follow.

While mind is in the attitude of self-supremacy, man's contact with the world will not affect him contrary to the way he desires to be affected; because he controls the impressions that come from without, and can completely change their natures before they are accepted in consciousness. Or, he may refuse to accept them entirely.

In the midst of adversity he does not permit the adverseness of the circumstances to impress his mind, but opens his mind to be impressed by the great power that is back of the adversity. His mind is not impressed by the misdirection of power, but by the power itself. Therefore, instead of being disturbed, he is made stronger.

There is something of value to be gained from every disagreeable condition, because within every condition there is power, and there are always greater possibilities latent than the surface indicates.

Through original thinking these greater possibilities are discerned; and when mind is in the attitude of self-supremacy, it may choose to be impressed by the greater possibilities only, thus providing more material for the reconstruction of man, and his destiny, on a larger and superior scale.

It is therefore evident that self-supremacy is indispensable; and it is attained by placing all life, all thought and all action upon the principle that man is inherently master over everything in his life; and by refusing absolutely to believe that we can be controlled by environment under any condition whatsoever.

Chapter 6 of Christian Larson's 'Your Forces and How to Use Them'

The Power of Subjective Thought, The Path To Greater Things

The first important factor to consider in connection with the study of thought is that every thought does not possess power. In modern times, when thinking has been studied so closely, a great many have come to the conclusion that every thought is itself a force and that it invariably produces certain definite results; but this is not true, and it is well, for if every thought had power we could not last very long as the larger part of ordinary human thinking is chaotic and destructive.

When we proceed to determine what kinds of thought have power and what kinds have not, we find two distinct forms. The one we call objective, the other subjective. Objective thought is the result of general thinking, such as reasoning, intellectual research, analysis, study, the process of recollection, mind-picturing where there is no feeling, and the usual activities of the intellect. In brief, any mental process that calls forth only the activities of the intellect is objective, and such thinking does not affect the conditions of mind and body to any extent; that is, it does not produce direct results corresponding to its own nature upon the system. It does not immediately affect your health, your happiness, your physical condition nor your mental condition. It may, however, affect these things in the long run, and for that reason must not be ignored.

Subjective thinking is any form of thinking or mind-picturing that has depth of feeling, that goes beneath the surface in its action, that moves through the undercurrents, that acts in and through the psychological field. Subjective thought is synonymous with the thought of the heart, and it is subjective thought that is referred to in the statement, "As a man thinketh in his heart so is he."

Subjective thought proceeds from the very heart of mental existence; that is, it is always in contact with everything that is vital in life. It is always alive with feeling, and originates, so to speak, in the heart of the mind. The term "heart" in this connection has nothing to do with the physical organ by that name. The term "heart" is here used in its metaphysical sense. We speak of the heart of a great city, meaning thereby, the principal part of the city, or that part of the city where its most vital activities are taking place; likewise, the heart of the mind is the most vital realm of the mind, or the center of the mind, or the deeper activities of the mind as distinguished from the surface of the mind.

Subjective thinking being in the heart of the mind is therefore necessarily the product of the deepest mental life, and for this reason every subjective thought is a force. It will either work for you or against you, and has the power to produce direct effects upon mind or body, corresponding exactly with its own nature. But all thinking is liable to become subjective at times. All thoughts may sink into the deeper or vital realms of mind and thus become direct forces for good or ill. Therefore, all thinking should be scientific; that is, designed or produced with a definite object in view. All thought should be produced according to the laws of right thinking or constructive thinking. Though objective thinking usually produces no results whatever, nevertheless there are many objective thoughts that become subjective and it is the objective mind that invariably determines the nature of subjective thinking.

Every thought therefore should have the right tendency, so that it may produce desirable results in case it becomes subjective, or may act in harmony with the objective mind whenever it is being employed in giving directions to the subjective. In this connection, it is well to remember that subjective thinking invariably takes place in the subconscious mind, as the terms subjective and subconscious mean practically the same; though in speaking of thought, the term subjective is more appropriate in defining that form of thought that is deep, vital and alive, or that acts through the mental undercurrents.

To define scientific thinking, it may be stated that your thinking is scientific when your thought has a direct tendency to produce what you want, or when all the forces of your mind are working together for the purpose you desire to fulfill. Your thinking is unscientific when your thought has a tendency to produce what is detrimental, or when your mental forces are working against you. To think scientifically, the first essential is to think only such thoughts and permit only such mental attitudes as you know to be in your favor; and the second essential is to make only such thoughts subjective. In other words, every thought should be right and every thought should be a force. When every thought is scientific, it will be right, and when every thought is subjective it will be a force.

Positively refuse to think of what you do not wish to retain or experience. Think only of what you desire, and expect only what you desire, even when the very contrary seems to be coming into your life. Make it a point to have definite results in mind at all times. Permit no thinking to be aimless. Every aimless thought is time and energy wasted, while every thought that is inspired with a definite aim will help to realize that aim, and if all your thoughts are inspired with a definite aim, the whole power of your mind will be for you and will work with you in realizing what you have in view. That you should succeed is therefore assured, because there is enough power in your mind to realize your ambitions, provided all of that power is used in working for your ambitions. And in scientific thinking all the power of mind and thought is being caused to work directly and constantly for what you wish to attain and achieve.

To explain further the nature of scientific thinking, as well as unscientific thinking, it is well to take several well-known illustrations from real life. When things go wrong, people usually say, "That's always the way"; and though this may seem to be a harmless expression, nevertheless, the more you use that expression the more deeply you convince your mind that things naturally go wrong most of the time. When you train your mind to think that it is usual for things to go wrong, the forces of your mind will follow that trend of thinking, and will also go wrong; and for that reason it is perfectly natural that things in your life should go wrong more and more, because as the forces of your mind are going wrong, you will go wrong, and when you go wrong, those things that pertain to your life cannot possibly go right.

A great many people are constantly looking for the worst. They usually expect the worst to happen; though they may be cheerful on the surface, deep down in their heart they are constantly looking for trouble. The result is that their deeper mental currents will tend to produce trouble. If you are always looking for the worst, the forces of your mind will be turned in that direction, and therefore will become destructive. Those forces will tend to produce the very thing that you expect. At first they will simply confuse your mind and produce troubled conditions in your mental world; but this will in turn confuse your faculties, your reason and your judgment, so that you will make many mistakes; and he who is constantly making mistakes will certainly find the worst on many or all occasions.

When things go wrong, do not expect the wrong to appear again. Look upon it as an exception. Call it past and forget it. To be scientific under these circumstances, always look for the best. By constantly expecting the best, you will turn the different forces of your mind and thought to work for the best. Every power that is in you will have a higher and finer ideal upon which to turn its attention, and accordingly, results will be better, which is perfectly natural when your whole system is moving towards the better.

A number of people have a habit of saying, "Something is always wrong"; but why should we not say instead, "Something is always right"? We would thereby express more of the truth and give our minds a more wholesome tendency. It is not true that something is always wrong. When we compare the wrong with the right, the wrong is always in the minority. However, it is the effect of such thinking upon the mind that we wish to avoid, whether the wrong be in our midst or not. When you think that there is always something wrong, your mind is more or less concentrated on the wrong, and will therefore create the wrong in your own mentality; but when you train yourself to think there is always something right, your mind will concentrate upon the right, and accordingly will create the right. And when the mind is trained to create the right it will not only produce right conditions within itself, but all thinking will tend to become right; and right thinking invariably leads to health, happiness, power and plenty.

The average person is in the habit of saying, "The older I get"; and they thereby call the attention of the mind to the idea that they are getting older. In brief, they compel their mind to believe that they are getting older and older, and thereby direct the mind to produce more and more age. The true expression in this connection is, "The longer I live." This expression calls the mind's attention to the length of life, which will, in turn, tend to increase the power of that process in you that can prolong life. When people reach the age of sixty or seventy, they usually speak of "the rest of my days," thus implying the idea that there are only a few more days remaining. The mind is thereby directed to finish life in a short period of time, and accordingly, all the forces of the mind will proceed to work for the speedy termination of personal existence. The correct expression is "from now on," as that leads thought into the future indefinitely without impressing the mind with any end whatever.

We frequently hear the expression, "I can never do anything right," and it is quite simple to understand that such a mode of thought would train the mind to act below its true ability and capacity. If you are fully convinced that you can never do anything right, it will become practically impossible for you to do anything right at any time, but on the other hand, if you continue to think, "I am going to do everything better and better," it is quite natural that your entire mental system should be inspired and trained to do things better and better.

Hundreds of similar expressions could be mentioned, but we are all familiar with them, and from the comments made above, anyone will realize that such expressions are obstacles in our way, no matter what we may do. In right thinking the purpose should be never to use any expression that conveys to your mind what you do not want, or what is detrimental or unwholesome in any manner whatever. Think only what you wish to produce or realize. If trouble is brewing, think about the greater success that you have in mind. If anything adverse is about to take place, do not think of what that adversity may bring, but think of the greater good that you are determined to realize in your life.

When trouble is brewing, the average person usually thinks of nothing else. Their mind is filled with fear, and not a single faculty in their possession can do justice to itself. And as trouble is usually brewing in most places, more or less, people have what may be called a chronic expectation for trouble; and as they usually get more or less of what they expect, they imagine they are fully justified in entertaining such expectations. But here it is absolutely necessary to change the mind completely. Whatever our present circumstances may be, we should refuse absolutely to expect anything but the best that we can think of. The whole mind, with all its powers and faculties, should be thrown, so to speak, into line with the optimistic tendency, and whatever comes or not, we should think only of the greater things that we expect to realize. In brief, we should concentrate the mind absolutely upon whatever goal we may have in view, and I should look neither to the left nor to the right.

When we concentrate absolutely upon the greater things we expect to attain or achieve, we gradually train all the forces of the mind and all the powers of thought to work for those greater things. We shall thereby begin in earnest to build for ourselves a greater destiny; and sooner or later we shall find ourselves gaining ground in many directions. Later on, if we proceed, we shall begin to move more rapidly, and if we pay no attention to the various troubles that may be brewing in our environment, those troubles will never affect us nor disturb us in the least.

The mental law involved in the process of scientific thinking may be stated as follows: The more you think of what is right, the more you tend to make every action in your mind right. The more you think of the goal you have in view, the more life and power you will call into action in working for that goal. The more you think of your ambition, the more power you will give to those faculties that can make your ambitions come true. The more you think of harmony, of health, of success, of happiness, of things that are desirable, of things that are beautiful, of things that have true worth, the more the mind will tend to build all those things in yourself, provided, of course, that all such thinking is subjective.

To think scientifically, therefore, is to train your every thought and your every mental action to focus the whole of attention upon that which you wish to realize, to gain, to achieve or attain in your life. In training the mind along the lines of scientific thinking begin by trying to hold the mind upon the right, regardless of the presence of the wrong, and here we should remember that the term "right" does not simply refer to moral actions, but to all actions. When the wrong is coming your way, persist in thinking of the right; persist in expecting only the right. And there is a scientific reason for this attitude, besides what has been mentioned above. We know that the most important of all is to keep the mind right or moving along right lines, and if we persistently expect the right, regardless of circumstances, the mind will be kept in the lines of right action. But there is another result that frequently comes from this same practice. It sometimes happens that the wrong which is brewing in your environment, has such a weak foundation that only a slight increase in the force of the right would be necessary to overthrow that wrong completely; in fact, we shall find that most wrongs that threaten can be overcome in a very short time, if we continue to work for the right in a positive, constructive, determined manner.

It is when the individual goes all to pieces, so to speak, that adversity gets the best of them; but no individual will go to pieces unless their thinking is chaotic, destructive, scattered, confused and detrimental. Continue to possess your whole mind and you will master the situation, no matter what it may be, and it is scientific thinking that will enable you to perform this great feat. To make thinking scientific, there are three leading essentials to be observed. The first is to cultivate constructive mental attitudes, and all mental attitudes are constructive when mind, thought, feeling, desire and will constantly face the greater and the better.

A positive and determined optimism has the same effect, and the same is true of the practice of keeping the mental eye single on the highest goal in view. To make every mental attitude constructive the mind must never look down, and mental depression must be avoided completely. Every thought and every feeling must have an upward look, and every desire must desire to inspire the same rising tendency in every action of mind.

The second essential is constructive mental imagery. Use the imagination to picture only what is good, what is beautiful, what is beneficial, what is ideal, and what you wish to realize. Mentally see yourself receiving what you deeply desire to receive. What you imagine, you will think, and what you think, you will become. Therefore, if you imagine only those things that are in harmony with what you wish to obtain or achieve, all your thinking will soon tend to produce what you want to attain or achieve.

The third essential is constructive mental action. Every action of the mind should have something desirable in view and should have a definite, positive aim. Train yourself to face the sunshine of life regardless of circumstances. When you face the sunshine, everything looks right, and when everything looks right, you will think right. It matters not whether there is any sunshine in life just now or not. We must think of sunshine just the same. If we do not see any silver lining, we must create one in our own mental vision.

However dark the dark side may seem to be, we cannot afford to see anything but the bright side, and no matter how small or insignificant the bright side may be, we must continue to focus attention on that side alone.

Be optimistic, not in the usual sense of that term, but in the real sense of that term. The true optimist not only expects the best to happen, but goes to work to make the best happen. The true optimist not only looks upon the bright side, but trains every force that is in them to produce more and more brightness in their life, and therefore complies with the three essentials just mentioned. Their mental attitudes are constructive because they are always facing greater things. Their imagination is constructive because it is always picturing the better and the ideal, and their mental actions are constructive because they are training the whole of their life to produce those greater and better things that their optimism has inspired them to desire and expect.

In this connection, we must remember that there is a group of mental forces at work in every mental attitude, and therefore if that attitude is downcast, those forces will become detrimental; that is, they will work for the lesser and the inferior. On the other hand, if every mental attitude is lifted up or directed towards the heights of the great and the true and the ideal, those forces will become constructive, and will work for the greater things in view.

In the perusal of this study, we shall find it profitable to examine our mental attitudes closely, so as to determine what our minds are actually facing the greater part of the time. If we find that we are mentally facing things and conditions that are beneath our expectations, or find that our imaginations are concerned too much about possible failure, possible mistakes, possible trouble, possible adversity, etc., our thinking is unscientific, and no time should be lost in making amends. When you are looking into the future, do not worry about troubles that might come to pass. Do not mentally see yourself as having a hard time of it. Do not imagine yourself in this hostile condition or that adverse circumstance. Do not wonder what you would do if you should lose everything, or if this or that calamity should befall. Such thinking is decidedly unscientific and most detrimental. If you entertain such thoughts you are causing the ship of your life to move directly towards the worst precipice that may exist in your vicinity. Besides, you are so weakening this ship through wrong treatment, that it will someday spring a leak and go down.

Think of the future whenever it is unnecessary for you to give your attention to the present, but let your thought of the future be wholesome, constructive, optimistic and ideal. Mentally see yourself gaining the best that life has to give, and you will meet more and more of the best. Think of yourself as gaining ground along all lines, as finding better and better circumstances, as increasing in power and ability, and as becoming more healthful in body, more vigorous and brilliant in mind, more perfect in character, and more powerful in soul. In brief, associate your future with the best that you can think of along all lines. Fear nothing for the days that are to be, but expect everything that is good, desirable, enjoyable and ideal. This practice will not only make your present happier, but it will tend to strengthen your mind and your life along wholesome constructive lines to such a degree that you will actually gain the power to realize, in a large measure, those beautiful and greater things that you have constantly expected in your optimistic dreams.

In living and building for a larger future, we should remember that our mind and thoughts invariably follow the leadership of the most prominent mental picture. The man or woman who clearly and distinctly pictures for themselves a brilliant future will inspire the powers of their entire mental world to work for such a future; in fact, all the forces of thought, mind, life, personality, character and soul will move in that direction. They may not realize as brilliant a future as they have pictured, but their future is certainly going to be brilliant, and it is quite possible, as is frequently the case, that it may become even more brilliant than they dreamed of in the beginning.

When the average mind thinks of the future, they usually picture a variety of conflicting events and conditions. They have nothing definite in mind. There is no actual leadership therefore in their mind, and nothing of great worth can be accomplished.

When we look into the lives of men and women who have reached high places, we always find that they were inspired with some great idea. That idea was pictured again and again in their mental vision, and they refused to let it go. They clung tenaciously to that idea, and thereby actually compelled every force and element within them to enlist in the working out of that idea. It is therefore simple enough that they should realize every aim and reach the highest places that achievement has in store. Such men and women possibly did not understand the science or the process, but they were nevertheless thinking scientifically to a most perfect degree. Their ambition pictured only that lofty goal which they wanted to reach. All their mental attitudes were constantly facing that lofty goal, and thereby became constructive; and all the actions of mind were directed toward the same goal. Accordingly, everything within them was trained to work for the realization of their dream, and that is what we mean by scientific thinking; that is what we mean by thinking for results. And anyone who will train themselves to think for results in this manner, will positively secure results; though in this connection it is well to remember that persistence and determination are indispensable every step of the way.

When we do not secure results at once, we sometimes become discouraged, and conclude that it is no use to try. At such times, friends will usually tell us that we are simply dreaming, and they will advise us to go to work at something practical, something that we really can accomplish; but if we ignore the advice of our friends, and continue to be true to the great idea that we have resolved to work out, we shall finally reach our goal, and when we do, those very same friends will tell us that we took the proper course. So long as the man with ambition is a failure, the world will tell him to let go of his ideal; but when his ambition is realized, the world will praise him for the persistence and the determination that he manifested during his dark hours, and everybody will point to his life as an example for coming generations. This is invariably the rule. Therefore pay no attention to what the world says when you are down. Be determined to get up, to reach the highest goal you have in view, and you will.

There are a great many ambitious men and women, who imagine that they will succeed provided their determination is strong and their persistence continuous, regardless of the fact that their thinking may be unscientific; but the sooner we dispel this illusion, the better. Unscientific thinking, even in minor matters, weakens the will. It turns valuable thought power astray, and we need the full power of thought, positively directed along the line of our work if we are going to achieve, and achieve greatly. The majority of the mental forces in the average person are working against them, because they are constantly entertaining depressed mental states or detrimental habits of thought; and even though they may be ambitious, that ambition has not sufficient power to work itself out, because most of the forces of their mind are thrown away.

We therefore see the necessity of becoming scientific in all thinking, and in making every mental habit wholesome and beneficial in the largest sense of those terms. But scientific thinking not only tends to turn the power of thought in the right direction; it also tends to increase mental power, to promote efficiency and to build up every faculty that we may employ. To illustrate the effect of right thinking upon the faculties, we will suppose that you have musical talent, and are trying to perfect that talent. Then, we will suppose that you are constantly expressing dissatisfaction with the power of that talent. What will be the result? Your mental action upon that faculty will tend to lower its efficiency, because you are depressing its action instead of inspiring those actions. On the other hand, if you encourage this talent, you will tend to expand its life, and thereby increase its capacity for results.

In this respect, talents are similar to people. Take two people of equal ability and place them in circumstances that are direct opposites. We will suppose that the one is mistreated every day by those with whom he is associated. He is constantly being criticized and constantly being told that he will never amount to anything; he is blamed for everything that is wrong, and is in every manner discouraged and kept down.

What would happen to the ability and efficiency of that man if he continued under such treatment year after year? He simply could not advance unless he should happen to be a mental giant, and even then, his advancement would be very slow; but if he was not a mental giant, just an average man, he would steadily lose ambition, self-confidence, initiative, judgment, reasoning power, and in fact, everything that goes to make up ability and capacity.

We will suppose the other man is encouraged continually. He is praised for everything, he is given every possible opportunity to show and apply what ability he may possess; he is surrounded by an optimistic atmosphere, and is expected by everybody to advance and improve continually. What will happen to this man? The best will be brought out in his power and ability. He will be pushed to the fore constantly and he will climb steadily and surely until he reaches the top.

Treat your talents in the same way, and you have the same results in every case. To state it briefly, make it a point to encourage your talents, your faculties and your powers. Give every element and force within you encouragement and inspiration. Expect them all to do their best, and train yourself to think and feel that they positively will. Train yourself to think of your whole system as all right. Deal with your mental faculties in this manner, under all circumstances, and deal with your physical organs in the same way.

Most people among those who do not have perfect health, have a habit of speaking of their stomachs as bad, their livers as always out of order, their eyes as weak, their nerves as all upset, and the different parts of their systems as generally wrong. But what are they doing to their physical organs through this practice? The very same as was done to the unfortunate man just mentioned, and we shall find, in this connection, one reason why so many people continue to be sick. They are keeping their physical organs down, so to speak, by depressing the entire system with unwholesome thinking; but if they would change their tactics and begin to encourage their physical organs, praise them and expect them to do better, and to treat them right from the mental as well as a physical standpoint, they would soon be restored to perfect health.

In training the mind in scientific thinking, the larger part of attention should be given to that of controlling our feelings. It is not difficult to think scientifically along intellectual lines, but to make our feelings move along wholesome, constructive, optimistic lines requires persistent training. Intellectual thought can be changed almost at anytime with little effort, but feeling usually becomes stronger and stronger the longer it moves along a certain line, and thus becomes more difficult to change.

When we feel discouraged, it is so easy to feel more discouraged; when we feel dissatisfied, it is only a step to that condition that is practically intolerable. It is therefore necessary to stop all detrimental feeling in the beginning. Do not permit a single adverse feeling to continue for a second. Change the mind at once by turning your attention upon something that will make you feel better. Resolve to feel the way you want to feel under all circumstances, and you will gradually develop the power to do so. Depressed mental feelings are burdens, and we waste a great deal of energy by carrying them around on our mental shoulders. Besides, such feelings tend to direct the power of thought towards the lower and the inferior.

Whenever you permit yourself to feel bad, you will cause the power of mind and thought to go wrong. Therefore, persist in feeling right and good. Persist in feeling joyous. Persist in feeling cheerful, hopeful, optimistic and strong. Place yourself on the bright side and the strong side of everything that transpires in your life, and you will constantly gain power, power that will invariably be in your favor.

Edward Walkers 'Thoughts are Things'

Your Latent Powers

Another of the several important revelations attending the truth that "Thoughts are Things," is the startling fact that the average individual is merely "scratching the surface" of his thought-power in his everyday thinking. It is now accepted as an established scientific fact that the creative faculty of thought may be operated not only in the direction of outward materialization, but also in the direction of developing the powers of the self . . the faculties of one's own mind . . in brain building, in short. It appears that the human race has been merely picking up the nuggets of thought from the surface of the mind, and allowing the rich deposits lying beneath to remain undisturbed. As Professor William James says, we have not used our "second wind" of thought. In this connection we think that the following quotation from a recent magazine article of Professor James will be of interest to you. Here it is:

"Everyone knows what it is to start a piece of work, either intellectual or muscular, feeling stale or cold, as an Adirondack guide once put it to me. And everybody knows what it is to 'warm up' to his job. The process of warming up gets particularly striking in the phenomenon known as 'second wind.' On usual occasions we make a practice of stopping an occupation as soon as we meet the first effective layer (so to call it) of fatigue. We have then walked, played or worked 'enough,' so we desist. That amount of fatigue is an efficacious obstruction, on this side of which our usual life is cast. But if an unusual necessity forces us to press onward, a surprising thing occurs. The fatigue gets worse up to a certain critical point, when gradually or suddenly it passes away, and we are fresher than before.

We have evidently tapped a level of new energy, masked until then by the fatigue-obstacle usually obeyed. There may be layer after layer of this experience. A third and fourth 'wind' may supervene. Mental activity shows the phenomenon as well as physical, and in exceptional cases we may find, beyond the very extremity of fatigue distress, amounts of ease and power that we never dreamed ourselves to own, sources of strength habitually not taxed at all, because habitually we never push through the obstruction, never pass those early critical points."

Thus we see, on the evidence of one of the world's greatest authorities on psychology, the fact that there are great "layers" of thought-power in the mind of man, which are seldom used. It is true that Professor James speaks of this "second wind" of thought as reached only by great effort, and under exceptional circumstances . . but one may go still further in this matter. Not only may these hidden powers of mind be reached by great effort, and under exceptional circumstances, as stated, but they may be uncovered by simple methods of gradual development by the use of desire, will and imagination. One may develop any mental quality to a remarkable degree by means of the simple methods to be described in this chapter. One may suppress the activities of undesirable faculties in the same way. And one may actually create a new character for himself by the same procedure.

This method of self development, unfoldment of the latent powers of mind, reconstruction of character, brain building, or whatever we may prefer to call it, depends upon the operation of thought in the two directions mentioned in preceding chapters of this book, namely (1) the law of materialization, under the operations of which thought tends to materialize itself into objective reality; and (2) the law of attraction, under the operations of which thought tends to draw to itself the particular materials conducive to its materialization and expression. In the preceding chapters we have shown you how thought acts in accordance with these two laws in the direction of outward manifestation. We now invite you to consider thought employing the same laws in the direction of inward manifestation . . in manifestation in the brain which it uses. Without entering into theory, we may say that we hold that the brain is merely the organ of the mind . . the thinking machine which mind uses to produce thoughts.

But, note this important fact . . it is a machine also capable of being used to build up, enlarge, add to, and change itself. Mind not only uses the brain to produce thoughts, but it also uses thoughts to build up brain. By turning thought back upon the brain, it causes brain to develop in order that better and stronger thoughts may be produced, and so on . . action and reaction, ever. A strange procedure, but strictly in line with nature's evolutionary processes. And now let us plunge at once into the heart of the method that may be used in this brain-building, self-development, character creation, etc.

This inner building work of thought is accomplished by the employment of desire, will, and the imagination, operating under what in scientific parlance is termed the Law of Use. By the latter is meant that principle of nature which causes a part, muscle, organ, or mental faculty (as well as many other things) to develop by active employment and use. You know how a muscle develops by use, and how a part tends to flabbiness, and even atrophy, by disuse. The same rule applies to the mental faculties or brain centers. The fire of desire generates an energy which demands expression and materialization; the imagination supplies the mental picture of the quality or power desired, which serves as a pattern or mould for the thing itself; the will holds the attention firmly upon the desire, mental image, and activity; and the active employment, by use, of the rudimentary faculty or brain centre tends to build up a stronger and more active centre or faculty. The law of attraction, and the law of materialization, respectively, aid in the building up process. And thus is the latent power developed.

You find yourself deficient in certain qualities. Then begin to realize just what these qualities are, in detail, and form a mental picture of yourself "as you will be" when you develop these faculties or qualities. Make the mental picture as deep and clear as possible . . strive to imagine yourself as acting by reason of these qualities. See yourself as already in possession of them. Give the imagination a loose rein in this matter, so far as the forming of mental pictures is concerned, although do not give yourself over to day dreaming at the expense of action. Then cultivate the strongest kind of desire for the materialization of the said qualities or faculties. Want them "hard." Hunger and thirst after their attainment. Fill yourself with ambition and aspiration in that particular direction. Use your will in giving your strongest attention to the matter at frequent intervals, and in preventing anything else to "sidetrack" you.

Also use the will in the direction of preventing you from acting along lines calculated to interfere with the cultivation of the ideal. Then endeavor to exercise, employ and use whatever faculties or qualities you may already possess along the lines of the ideal. No matter how little of the desired quality you may possess, use it to the utmost . . employ it actively upon all occasions . . exercise it freely and frequently . . for by so doing you set the laws into operation, that will make it grow and develop. You will notice that this method consists of the seeing, desiring, willing and acting along the direct lines of the object to be attained. These four phases are necessary . . you cannot omit any of them without weakening the method. Many fail in similar practices because they content themselves with mere thinking and desiring, and omitting the willing and acting, particularly the acting. Every time you act out some little detail of your ideal, you strengthen yourself ten-fold in that detail. The manifestation of a thought strengthens the brain centre controlling that thought, and adds to its dynamic power. If you will keep before your mind the idea of strengthening of a muscle, you will be able to see more plainly the process whereby you may strengthen your mental muscles, or brain centers.

Take the instance of a baby learning to walk. It sees others walking, and forms the mental picture of the act . . if it were brought up in the company of crawling creatures, alone, it probably would never think of walking but would crawl about on all fours. Seeing others walk, it forms the "idea" or mental picture of walking, and then wants to walk itself . . it forms the "ideal." Then finding it difficult to walk, but still wanting to do so, its desire is set on fire and it begins to manifest a burning desire to stand erect and step out. It uses its will to that purpose, and it develops not only the leg muscles, but also the coordinate brain centers governing walking, and strengthens both by use. And in the end it does walk . . why? Because it knew what it wanted; wanted it hard enough; used will in the process; kept its attention and imagination busily on the task; and finally, used every opportunity to manifest the mental state into action. It saw itself walking before it could manifest the act; it wanted and desired to walk before the desire could be materialized; it tried hard to walk before it succeeded. And in doing these things it unconsciously brought into operation the various mental laws of thought materialization and expression.

And these are just the stages of the process of brain building, character development, self creation. This is the way you may mine the deeper strata of thought expression . . this is how you may catch your "second wind," or third, fourth, or fifth wind, in fact. The method is scientific and simple . . but it requires patient and persistent practice. The thinking must be supplemented by acting. Acts and thoughts react upon each other, each action and reaction tending to strengthen and develop. Thoughts along a given line made it easier for you to act along those lines. Acts along those lines render it easier for you to think along them. "To him who hath, shall be given."

In conclusion, we think it well to say that in this process of development and brain building, the rule already stated that "to restrain a mental quality or faculty, develop its opposite," is in full operation. If your self building requires the restraint of some faculty or quality of thought, the best and simplest plan is to develop the opposite quality or faculty. The average person considers that his "character" or "nature" has been given to him once and for all, and is as unchangeable as the motion of the earth around the sun. And it is unchangeable, unless he proceeds to turn back upon his brain the power of the thought evolved therefrom.

That which enables the man to build up outside things by reason of his creative thought; that enables him to materialize his thought-forms; may also be used by him in the direction of the addition to, alteration, development and unfoldment of his own thought-machine. By means of thought-power he may explore the deep recesses of his mind, or dig down into its depths, bringing forth to the light of consciousness many rare and beautiful things. A man's mind is like a great unexplored forest, in the majority of cases. Only by exploration along scientific lines may he discover what he has in it. By intelligent application of these principles he may rid that forest of the noxious and dangerous creatures lurking in its depths, and at the same time bring forth many things that will well serve him in his life work.

Why spend our days in striving for help from outside . . why pay great prices to others . . when within ourselves are to be found the most valuable of qualities and possessions, awaiting the hour of discovery and development? For, after all, all this development, creation and building is in the nature of "unfoldment" of things that are wrapped up, or enfolded in our mental being. They are there, else they could never be unfolded. They are latent within our mentality, awaiting the time of expression and manifestation. They are there as seeds, awaiting the water and sun and chance to grow, blossom, and bear fruit. They are there in static form, awaiting the process whereby they are transformed into dynamic forces. They are there in possibilities, awaiting transmutation into actualities. They are there as ideals, awaiting the call to reality.

Verily a great day is before us, when our ideals become real, our dreams come true.

Edward Walkers 'Thoughts Are Things'

Creative Thought

We explained to you the operations of the law of attraction, under which thoughts tend to attract or draw to themselves the things in harmony with themselves, and which are conducive to the outward expression of the thought. In connection therewith we called your attention to the fact that there is an universal tendency toward expression and manifestation. All things have the inward urge prompting the fullest expression and manifestation, and the law of attraction serves to draw the materials for the same. Accompanying this active principle of nature, there is another law operative on both the mental and physical planes, and this law we now ask you to consider. We refer to the law of materialization, or objective creative effort.

The law of materialization is universal . . it is found on all planes and manifests in various ways. Its underlying principle is its inward tendency to create forms, and outward manifestation. In the mineral world we find a constant state of motion, change and building up of form. The electrons group themselves into atoms; the atoms into molecules; and the molecules into various shapes and forms and varieties. Underlying it all, science perceives the constant effort of the inner to express itself in the outer . . the invisible striving to become visible . . the unmanifest striving to become manifest.

We shall not dwell on this side of the subject . . we mention it merely to illustrate the universality of the law. And not only do physical things possess this inward urge toward outward materialization, but thoughts, being "things," also possess and manifest it to a great degree. Thoughts strive to take form in action. Thoughts strive ever to materialize themselves in objective material form. A strong mental state produces mental unrest in its efforts to materialize itself. In its striving for birth on the material plane it sets into operation both the law of attraction, before mentioned, and also starts into operation the subconscious activities of the mind in the direction of thinking out plans and means wherewith the materialization may be effected.

Before considering further the operation of this law in the thought world, let us pause a moment and consider how perfectly natural and common a thing is the materialization of thought. At first mention it seems unusual to say the least. But when we begin to consider that the entire creative and inventive work of man is simply the result of the materialization of his imaginings, the matter takes on another aspect.

Every material thing that man has created, built, erected or constructed has first existed as a thought in the imagination of the inventor, maker or builder. Every house that has been built has had its preceding thought-form in the imagination of the architect or designer. This is true of every bridge that ever has been constructed, and of every piece of machinery. The locomotive, the steamboat, the telegraph, the telephone, the electric light, the telescope, the microscope, the printing press . . every invention, in fact . . has had its mental image preceding its material construction. It existed first as a thought-thing, and then as a material-thing. And yet some people doubt the "thingness" of thought, and regard the imagination as mere "fancy."

There is, it is true, a negative form of imagination that is but little more than mere fancy, but in its positive phase, the imagination is the great creative workshop of the world. And those who understand its mighty power no longer allow it to "run away with them," but, instead, set it to work, well harnessed, and then reap the result that comes to those who understand and apply the great laws of nature. Some of the statements that will follow may seem strange to you, but if you have firmly grasped the idea of the "thingness" of thoughts, you will see in the phenomena simply the transformation of the subtle form of things into a visible and material form.

Just as Morse's telegraph was but the materialization of his thought-form of it; just as Edison's electric light was but the materialization of his thought-image of it; just as the Brooklyn bridge was but the materialization of its designer's imaginative-forms . . so are the great business enterprises, the great telegraph lines, the great railroad routes, the great trusts, the great financial houses, just the result of the thoughts of those who created them. Think of this for a moment until the truth of the statement sinks into your mind. Then listen to this further statement: Just as these things are objectified forms of subjective ideas . . materialized forms of immaterial thoughts . . so the ideas, mental images, ideals, hopes, and aspirations of all of us, are the molds, patterns, or dies of the material things of our future.

We are making patterns today that will be materialized tomorrow. We are making today the molds from which the materialized things of the future will emerge.

But, it may be urged, all ideals do not become real, all hopes are not realized, all aspirations are not possible of expression and attainment . . why? The answer lies in the fact that the majority of people do not know how to desire . . do not know what they want. So far as desire is concerned, they content themselves with mere "wishing," or "wanting" or fretting because they haven't the thing . . real, active, burning, creative desire is foreign to their natures. They say they want things . . but they "don't want them hard enough."

The men who attain are those who are filled with the burning thirst of desire which leaves nothing undone to satisfy itself. The desire hardens into will, and bends and draws everything toward its manifestation and accomplishment. Desire is the motive power that is behind all attainment, achievement and action. Unless one possesses it he does not act and move.

And as to the matter of getting things, very few people really know just what they do want . . they lack clear mental images of the desired thing. The same people who know exactly what they want so far as a small thing is concerned . . and accordingly get it if their desire is strong enough, and the will is firm . . are at sea when it comes to imaging great things. They content themselves with merely vaguely wanting something different from what they have . . and the result is that they wander around from one thing to another, like a ship that has lost its rudder.

The strongest desire . . the most rigid will . . will fail to accomplish anything for the person who has not formed a clear mental picture or idea of exactly what he does want. Therefore, in the materialization of thought, one should first take mental stock of himself, then pick out the things that he really wants to accomplish or to acquire and then proceed to build up the strongest kind of desire for those things. In this way he sets into operation the law of thought materialization, and incidentally the law of attraction, and the preliminary operations whereby the ideal becomes real are started in motion.

A clear-cut mental picture, or idea, of the things that one wishes to accomplish, serves as a nucleus around which the creative forces of thought center, and which they use as a basis of creative materialization. There must always be this creative center around which thought may build. This center must be formed in that wonderful creative region of thought . . the imagination. In the imagination you must form the clear mental picture or ideal that you wish to make real. At first you will be able to see it but dimly, but repetition will deepen the lines, and broaden the form, until the ideal will be seen in the actual process of realization and materialization. You will find that the ideal will develop and grow under the attention that you are giving to it. New details will work into the picture, and the fainter portions will come into plainer view, while the important details will stand out in still bolder relief.

Very often you may not be able to form the complete mental image at the start, in which case do not be discouraged but try to see the first step, or the first detail of the thing, as clearly as possible. This will serve as the "seed-image" from which the complete picture will develop. Until you are able to form the ideal of what you want, in your imagination, you do not really know just what you do want. Train the imagination to show you the picture of the thing you want . . this is the first important step in thought creative effort.

Then bestow upon your mental picture, or ideal, a constant supply of desire. Look at your picture, and then long for it, crave it, hunger and thirst for it . . and by so doing you will set into motion the natural laws of the thought world, which will tend to make real your ideal. You will find new plans, methods, and means flashing into your mind from the great subconscious regions . . and the law of attraction will bring to your aid the persons, things and environments conducive to the materialization of your thought; or else will lead you to them. You and the means will be brought together somehow, someway, sometime. It will not all be done at once. Just as the crystal slowly forms around its center, so will your materialized thought form around the ideal that serves as its center. Just as the tree grows from the seed, so will the tree of objective form and shape and condition grow from your seed ideal, if it be kept watered with care, attention and persistency, and warmed by the sun of desire. Thus shall our dreams come true . . our ideals become realities . . our subjective thoughts become objective things.

And so we see that the generally reviled imagination is really the mystic creative workshop of the mind, in which are first created the patterns, molds, and designs of all that shall afterward become the material realities of life. Consequently we should exercise care in the selection of the subject and objects of our imagination.

Drive out the negative pictures which tend to materialize their corresponding realities. Keep the attention and the imagination firmly fixed on the positives. Practice will enable you to do this. Hang bright pictures in the gallery of the mind.

Frank L. Hammer's 'Life and its Mysteries'

THOUGHT

The mystery of thought! In infancy our bodies awaken to enjoy the world into which we are born. Then our minds awaken to curious questioning and restless desire for knowledge. Then our souls awaken to conscious search for life's spiritual meaning and purpose.

What is thought? Thought is a product of mind . . not the brain. The material scientist says: "A certain formation of brain cells creates a certain kind of thought." Whereas certain thoughts produce a certain brain cell formation.

Thought has the same relation to the mind as the wind has to the atmosphere, for thought is the mind's vibration, and thinking is the process of setting the mind into motion.

Where do thoughts come from? There are three primary sources.

Firstly: It is possible, through deep, spiritual contemplation, to receive thoughts directly from Universal Mind. Every human being can contact his Heavenly Father without the aid of any intermediaries, either spiritual or physical. "To be pure in heart" is the only stipulated requirement.

Secondly: Many thoughts emanate from the subconscious mind. Deep within this mind there takes place an involuntary accumulation of impressions and suggestions which come to the surface after a more or less prolonged gestation. Indeed, this storehouse of memory, this record of life, is a prolific source of thoughts and many people are entirely too much under its influence.

Thirdly: The principal fountain of thought is the mental atmosphere which is permeated with the thoughts of other people, both embodied and disembodied. We have all had the experience of wondering where some thought came from; it was probably in the "air," and our brains, being sensitive receiving sets, "picked" it up.

There is no such thing as original or isolated thoughts; what is new is their manner of expression or restatement. We cannot conceive of anything which is not; the ideas are somewhere existent and have always been in the mind substance. Our task is to give new shape and semblance to the thought elements which otherwise remain undifferentiated and formless. And those whose patterns are the most unlike the whole mass or group thought are considered the most original.

Thoughts resemble the temperament of the person in whom they appear. Consequently, no one's thoughts should constitute another's authority any more than every head should be forced into a hat of fixed pattern or unalterable dimensions.

Many people are totally unaware of the power of thought and the effect it has upon their lives. These people invariably consider failure, misfortune, unhappiness and numerous other undesirable conditions as things that just accidentally happen, whereas they are created by the individual's wrong habits of thinking.

Similarly, liberation from these conditions is achieved through right thinking. In order to change the outer environment, it is necessary first to change the inner. If you do not want an undesirable fate or future, do not contemplate an undesirable one. Think about what you do want . . not about what you do not want.

Right thinking is the key to health, happiness, prosperity and success. The power of thought can either fill our lives with good or leave them utterly empty. Everything one needs for his well-being exists in the universal mind. It is ours for the taking, for we are heirs to the kingdom of God, co-sharers with His opulence, wisdom and love.

Plato said: "All reality exists in the mind. The outer phenomenon, that which appears, is only its outer expression. The visible universe is the reflection of the invisible."

Everything in the universe had its origin in thought, wrought out and preserved in stone, iron and wood, which upholds all structures from a toy to a battleship. All art, literature, music, law and religion existed first in the mind. Burn all books, destroy all churches, demolish all art and they would all be embodied again and again through thought . . the creative force, for it is impossible to destroy mind wherein exists their eternal pattern or idea.

Thought is the power that heals. Disease, like all else, has its origin in mind; therefore, the mind must be healed first. The mind must become harmonious before the body can be, because mind through thought is the power that rules and governs the body.

People have been killed by thought. Fear and worry have buried many of their victims. Hatred, envy and jealousy have wrecked countless lives. Poisonous thoughts affect the body like poisonous drugs. Persons in public life have been made deathly ill and often their lives shortened by the volume of destructive thoughts sent them on the ebb tide of popularity. This has happened to practically all reformers, leaders, religious and moral teachers who labored for the welfare and upliftment of humanity.

Men, animals and plants all grow from within. Life is sustained by the drawing in of congenial matter and by the expulsion of foreign matter. The law of attraction is found throughout all life. Our mind always attracts thoughts which are akin to our own and resists those opposed to our mental constitution. The mental atmosphere is filled with thought forces from which we attract only those which are like our own. If you are gloomy, sad, full of worry and vexation, you are certain to attract similar thoughts, which will make you sadder and more gloomy. On the contrary, if you are confident, hopeful and cheerful, you will attract that kind of thoughts to you.

Mind, like the body, grows on the food which nourishes it, and takes on the nature of the thing it dwells upon. And the food of the mind is thought. Therefore, the mind either becomes refined, sensitive, spiritual; or gross, material and dull; determined by the nature of thoughts which constantly occupy its attention. Thoughts are reproduced on the countenance. Sensual thoughts create a sensual face; spiritual thoughts create a beautiful, spiritual expression. Not only does our youth leave us, but our face tells how it has left us. Faces are open books wherein is written the history of our thinking.

How you have thought is revealed by the lines indelibly engraved in the palms of your hands, by the shape of your head and how you walk. An index to the thoughts of another is to imitate his posture and walk, then observe the effect it has on your thinking. Involuntarily, you will feel and think as the person you are imitating. There are no "secret" vices or habits. They are loudly proclaimed on the countenance. Emerson truly said: "What you are speaks so loudly no one can hear what you are saying."

Thoughts are the essence of heaven and hell. People say there is no hell, yet have one in their hearts and carry one around in their minds. For heaven and hell are not localities, but states of consciousness. "And what matter where I be, if I be still the same?" Persecuting memories, or a condemning conscience, put a man in Hades whether he lives upon this earth or elsewhere. Peace of mind and serenity of spirit are bliss. And the heaven we will find on passing over is one we have prepared by our thinking and by the service rendered to our fellow men.

Few pleasures are comparable to a trained and cultivated mind. The mind is developed by thinking and not by cramming it with other people's thoughts and opinions. It is not a bucket to be filled, but a dynamo to be set into motion.

There are no limits to its accomplishments, for the soul already knows all things; we only need to develop our instrument so that it can draw upon this inexhaustible storehouse of knowledge. A mind which has been strengthened by discipline can meet vicissitude and disaster with greater fortitude and courage. And it is never too late to undertake its cultivation, for, unlike the body which attains its zenith early in life, the best years for mental productivity come in the latter years after the body has lost its prime. It is impossible to learn anything which will not be of use to us sometime.

There is a true story of a professor at Cambridge who, at the age of eighty, began the study of Latin. When asked by curious observers of what use Latin would be at his age, he replied: "I intend to use it in my next life."

As today our powers are not of heritage only, but acquirements from previous lives before coming to earth, so studies today undertaken, no matter how near to the evening of our days, will surely bear fruit, not alone in our present life, but in the future.

"Guard well thy thoughts, for thoughts are heard in heaven," is a literal truth and explains the efficacy of prayer. For thoughts are the links between invisible substance and the visible form. Thought is a tangible substance and, united with will, is a projectile.

Mrs. C. L. Baum's 'Studies in Divine Science'

Spiritual Guidance

Perhaps it has occurred to you many times to ask: What shall be the true and infallible guide of life? You have learned that true guidance must be spiritual and come from within, but perhaps you have wondered how you were to recognize the promptings of that invisible spirit, that still small voice, so that you might follow it confidently, knowing that it would lead you only into Truth. Let us consider the various guides that might be followed, and by eliminating the false, see more clearly wherein we may safely place our reliance.

The voice of the external is not a safe guide. It recognizes the negative as well as the positive and labels its life of personality with disease, lack, sorrow and death. It produces shadow conditions that darken the years of the soul while on the earth plane, and speaks of unreality as though it had power to affect the true life. Taken all in all, the voice of the external world and its activities is designed to lead us only into a belief of confusion and mixed thought from which it will be very difficult to extricate ourselves. It is best to abandon it completely and cease from following after it.

As you give the subject a little thought you will experience a growing distrust of the generally accepted means of ordering your life. The preachers cease to interest you and the physicians fail to heal you. Having experienced everything which the external has to offer, you are forced to the conclusion that you must look elsewhere for true guidance.

You turn to the mental realm. You begin to think and reason. You find someone whom you conceive to be a great soul and who seems to have found the Truth. You temporarily establish yourself in his doctrine. You think his thoughts and order your life accordingly. But even this proves unsatisfactory to your soul's desire and you begin to wonder where this great soul got his knowledge of Truth. You argue that there must be some original source of all knowledge, and you determine to get your own ideas at the fountain head.

You have heard and read much concerning the silence and the voice of the silence, and you seek the invisible guiding power through this medium. Here again you may be temporarily unsuccessful. We regard the whole invisible plane as the silence simply because we are more or less in ignorance of what the invisible holds. There are thousands of voices and countless thoughts in the mental atmosphere, and it is as unlikely that one should learn truth from that atmosphere as from the confusion of tongues in the external. All of the thoughts that come for admission to your consciousness, do not carry the truth you are seeking. The mere fact that a thought comes to you from the invisible is no test of its infallibility, and thus we see that a false guidance may be encountered in the silence as well as in the outer.

The mental confusion that this gives rise to is well illustrated in anyone who desires spiritual help, but who is aware of two voices within . . one urging reliance on Divine Science and the other arguing that no help can come from such a source. Each of these silent voices comes in turn to control such an individual, and unless discrimination is made between the true and false voice, the right step will not be taken.

Impulse may be mistaken for the still, small voice that you are listening for. But impulse is only a shadow brother of intuition, and will often lead you astray. It is the experience of many who first come into this thought, that they may listen in the silence for many months and sometimes years before they experience the voice of the Spirit as the guiding force in their lives. They listen apparently in vain, waiting intently, but hearing nothing until some day they suddenly hear the true voice of spiritual guidance. There is no confusion in thought at such a time and the experience is one never to be forgotten. The life is changed, the shadows flee and the individual becomes conscious of the divine self within.

Now you may rightfully question: Whence comes this voice and to whom does it belong? It is the voice of your real self and comes wholly from within you. It is of the divine indwelling Presence, holy and pure, knowing and expressing only the truth which is suitable for your state of unfoldment. It speaks with few words, gives no long intellectual discourses. It speaks simply and does not argue. All argument is caused by disagreement among the thought children of your own mentality and has no connection with the voice of Truth. To abide by the result of argument in your mentality is not to be compared with following the voice of the intuition; the one leads to confusion, the other to clear vision and action.

You will get no false guidance from the voice of your inner true self. It stands back of all the unreality that your mentality brings to you, and is always ready, to help when recognized and appealed to. But even though you hear this voice, you may not choose to follow, for the voice calls not to ease, comfort and material joys. It counsels you to follow and uphold whatsoever things are true; and in the conventional standards of the world today this Is not always easy or pleasant. To be true to self is sometimes the hardest task we can take up, for we have been following untrue paths for so long that the old habits are hard to break.

You will not always have to go into the silence in order to hear the voice of your inner self. It always speaks and tells you what is right. You need ask no outer teacher, no book, no invisible friend for the Truth; for the Presence that is within you is greater than all that is without. Listen and obey the voice. Speak the Truth. Act without hesitation or argument.

If at any stage in your unfoldment you feel that you are not ready for the highest statement made by those whose consciousness is more expanded than your own, do not strive to force yourself to believe simply because someone else whom you respect makes the statement. Lean only on your own perception, rejoicing in the measure of truth that you do perceive and you will And that you will be guided into greater comprehension of truth. The whole race is growing into a higher consciousness and the Presence within is pressing forward for greater expression. This is an evidence of confidence in the divine promptings from within, of true self-confidence, which is the beginning of spiritual growth.

At first It Is not your part to lead, but to follow. You are not expected to blaze the new trail, but to rely on the leading of the Spirit within, keeping the thought receptive and willing to listen to the voice of Truth. Until you learn to have faith in your own divine promptings you are a follower and not a leader. As you progress and are lifted up, as your convictions grow In strength and your consciousness of truth increases, your light will illumine the way for others. Every great religious or philosophical movement has had a leader to whom the Truth was revealed In the highest degree. If all the followers of such movements had received the name revelation, the progress of the Truth would have been wonderful.

Do not make laborious efforts at spiritual insight. Let your silent periods be short and many rather than long and few. Neither should you hasten to convert the world to something which you may, as yet, only believe without having a firm conviction and knowledge of its truth. You are in no danger of losing the respect of others if you quietly stand fast in your faith, bearing witness to the Truth as you know it. You may be sure that if your light Is always shining, you will be sought out by such as wish to have the dark places of their lives illumined. The voice from within will guide you in these matters as in all else.

The Presence whose guidance we seek is everywhere. It is the same Spirit which was in Jesus and which is now in you and in us all. To know its voice and live in harmony with it, is peace and joy and life eternal.

C. W. Kyle's

The Eternal Surprise

There is a power latent in every man which, when aroused, changes him at once into another being. It thrills, awakens and transforms him into a new man, making of him a veritable dynamo of tremendous energy. His conscious identity with this newly awakened power is amazing, and the use he makes of it astonishes all who have previously known him.

From a man of inaction he becomes a leader. He seeks advice from no one, but realizing his awakened powers he relies upon himself, and goes forward sustained with a confidence and enthusiasm, nothing doubting, to the accomplishment of his own desires.

He has become an awakened soul, knowing and fearlessly exercising his newly realized powers of dominion. He knows just what he wants; he is determined to get it and he goes out and gets it. He has come to know himself. The supreme lesson of life is that of self-realization.

You are living in a world of magic. You have more power within you than that ever recorded of any genii of whom you have ever read or dreamed. Wake up! Learn who you are before you condemn yourself to a further life of inaction and inefficiency.

To come to recognize yourself is the best elixir of life you will ever know. It will take a psychological operation to rid you of your self-imposed limitations. Well, here it is. Words have a magic power. The greatest event in all the record that infinite intelligence has made, was manifest by the power of the Word. "In the beginning was the Word and the Word was with God and the Word was God." What is the meaning of that? It means that God pictured in Mind all that is, and then spoke it into actuality, creating man in His own image, an individualized center of His every attribute . . consciousness, creative power and love.

Did you never pause to think that man is the only instrument God has fashioned through which His word may be most fitly spoken? The man who has not come to realize this truth is apt to find that most of the paths of life lead down to the bottom of the hill, where those who have taken them lie bound by their own thoughts of limitation, which are more powerful to imprison than though made of steel. If you are there, awake and burst your bonds! Stand forth free and rejoice in your strength, for you are the ruling Prince in the House of the King of Kings.

To come to recognize yourself is to experience the greatest event you will ever know. Though you may be presented at court and dine with the king, that event will be as nothing of importance to you beside it; though the king should bestow all honors upon you within his power, they will prove inconsequential, compared to the wonderful honors you will find awaiting you, when you come to know yourself.

You are a king and a creator in your own right. You have made yourself just what you are, and you have the power to change yourself into a being greater and more powerful than it is possible for you to conceive. You are possessed of unlimited powers, and if limited you now are, you, yourself, have raised the walls of limitation, and you have power to remove them or you may let them stand. You are ruler of your own kingdom.

When you come to know yourself as you are, the very splendid powers which are yours will awaken in you such respect for them that you will feel called upon to live at your very best, at all times, in order to be worthy of the high dignity of your position in life. This knowledge will put new blood in your veins and a song of joy in your heart. Your whole being will be filled and thrilled with a sense of being so much greater than that you have ever felt before, that no thought of fear or failure will ever again find lodgment in your mind.

Love and faith and Courage will shine out in your every word and act, and dignity will mantle you as one to the purple born; the light of kindly determination will fill your eyes and you will be fired with an enthusiasm that will render you invincible, where before you have been faltering and filled with indecision.

I wish above all else to introduce you to yourself . . the real man that you are, and have you see yourself as you were made in the image of God, endowed with His every attribute, and in actual possession of all the tools wherewith to make yourself greater than any conception of greatness that has ever entered into the heart of man.

Don't refuse the offer of this acquaintanceship, for the one great lack of man upon this planet, the one thing in which he stands in direst need, is nothing more or less than a more intimate and thorough acquaintanceship with himself.

If I may, even in a small way, be instrumental in furthering your acquaintanceship with yourself, I feel assured that I shall ever stand high on the list of your cherished friends.

I am aware that it may appear presumptuous on my part to assume the role of one intimate enough with your life to make bold to introduce you to any person, to say nothing of the implied knowledge on my part and the lack of it on yours, to undertake to introduce you to yourself. It may be, however, that the awakened curiosity in your minds as to how I have acquired sufficient knowledge of you to assume to introduce you to yourself, will cause you to refrain from taking offense.

Again, it is generally assumed that one who introduces one person to another stands as sponsor for the one introduced, a responsibility, I have no doubt that each one of you have, at one time or another, found to be more or less embarrassing. In this case, I hasten to assure you, that I cheerfully assume full responsibility, for the personage I would introduce to you is worthy of the highest honors you may bestow, and one whom you will feel highly honored to know. If you will cultivate his acquaintanceship, and be guided by his advice, whatsoever of good you may desire will come to you.

Concentration will enable you to further this acquaintanceship as nothing else can. The young man who had fallen to the level of the swine, "came to himself, " and felt no need of asking the advice of any one, and if you are, living a life short of the realization of your best desires you should come to yourself, and know that "the kingdom of God is within you, ' ' and that if you will only concentrate upon it earnestly enough, and long enough, that you shall here and now come into possession of and enjoy every good your heart may desire. Health, wealth, honor, power, station, peace and love are awaiting the exercise of the powers that you possess, in order to be and abide with you, just so long as you may will them to remain.

When man comes to know that he is the being of power, intelligence and love that he truly is; that he is master of his own thoughts, and that he has access to the Source of Infinite Life, his thoughts take on a splendor and beauty which finds their expression in living every moment of his life at its best.

He finds that all intelligent choice and necessity of action, to be one and the same; that the right way of thinking is the only way open to the man of the enlightened mind; that all growth is, in its final expression, upwards, and that consciousness is ever passing from a lower to a higher plane and in so doing that a sane, sensible and normal life is assured by maintaining a state of equilibrium between his inner sense and his environment.

We are free to select the thoughts with which we feed our minds, more free than we are in selecting the foods with which we feed our bodies. This is well, for the character of our thoughts is far more important to our health and happiness than the nature of the foods we eat.

Clean thoughts not only make clean minds but they also make clean, healthy bodies. A body ruled by a strong, clean mind is best fortified against all of the current ills of life. Your thoughts build into your body the very substance of which it is composed. Thoughts of envy, malice, hatred and all thoughts that lead to despondency, devitalize the blood and affect the body ruinously. Anger is a positive poison to the blood, while thoughts of kindness, cheerfulness and good-will are powerful tonics, stimulating digestion, and contribute, in the most wonderful way, to the harmonious working of all the vital organs of our bodies.

When man comes to realize the power of mastership which he wields over his body he will become more cautious in his thinking than in his handling of sharpened tools. He will send out only thoughts of strength, of health, of harmony and love. When he learns to do this he will find that his bodily intelligence will respond promptly and eagerly, every cell in his whole system taking in the full force and character of his thought and, if he has thought wisely and constructively, he will find his body to be a radiant expression of all that he has commanded it to be.

Extreme as these statements may at first glance appear, they will be found upon examination to be the most practical and useful truths of life.

Thought wedded to purpose is the only way by which our plans may be carried out. It is impossible for us to set too high a standard for our thoughts. Man finds himself a weak, vacillating creature, without purpose because he has been taught that he is a weak, negative creature. It is high time that his attention be called to the possibilities of his being, when his latent powers are aroused and placed in action.

Wherein lie the powers of dominion said to have been given man, unless by the power of the awakened spirit within him, he may make all conditions to serve him? We know that success comes only to the man who has a definite object, who thinks strongly and who strives earnestly and fearlessly in the battle of life.

The man who marks a straight line from his desire to its realization and who permits no allurements to draw him aside, is the man who wins. No man who has not done so may or should succeed.

To permit a doubt to enter the mind as to the essential unity of the human soul with the source of all power, all intelligence and all love, is to render every effort ineffectual;

to cloud the mind and to paralyze the arm and, in a word, to invite inevitable disaster and defeat.

Why, then, should the intelligent investigator stop short of accepting and announcing the inevitable conclusion to which he is driven? Doubt, fear and prejudice and all products of negative thought, when allowed to enter the mind, drive out constructive thinking by devitalizing the mind of its power and energy. A knowledge of what we can do must precede the effort to do.

Henry Thomas Hamblin's 'Dynamic Thought'

Success and Character Building

The Will and the Conscious Mind stand as sentinels at the door of the subconscious mind. To them is given the important task of deciding what shall, or what shall not, enter. Every kind of thought and suggestion, inimical to our welfare, meet us and strike us on every hand. Harmful thoughts seek to enter our minds at every turn. Books, magazines, race thought, the mental outlook of friends and acquaintances are all against our mental development. The attitude of mind of the average person, of the common ruck, is not inspiring. It does not suggest "success," it expresses at best, only a passive acceptance of life. It takes like as it is, things as they come. It is not often that you meet a man who is conscious that he is "Master of his fate, the Captain of his soul."

How then can you escape all this deadening, destroying mental atmosphere?

FIRST. You must, in habit of thought, separate yourself from "the crowd." You must shut out their pessimistic-belief-in-circumstances . . weak-failure-low-lewd type of thoughts altogether, and live in an entirely different world . . the inner world of your own creative thought. If you meet a noble or inspiring thought . . and later you will be the recipient of a continuous stream of the finest thoughts the world has ever known . . let it in.

I do not mean that you are to look down upon your fellows, for nothing is more destructive or contemptible. You must mix with your fellows, and while holding yourself proof against low and weak types of thought, seek to raise their minds by your own hopeful suggestions. When a friend talks as though failure were a possibility in his life, suggest instead that success is hastening his way. When people are sad, try to cheer them by hopeful suggestions. When they look on the dark side of life, show them the bright side. When they rail and rave, pour oil on the troubled waters. Seek to cheer people up and resolutely refuse to accept the suggestions of their minds.

The greatest antidote to this deadening atmosphere of doubt and helplessness, of ignorance and materialism, of fear and failure, due to the world's wrong habit of thought is the use of that mind cleansing denial "There is no evil." It goes right to the root of all trouble and failure, all that is undesirable in our lives, and destroys it.

The word "evil" embraces everything in life that is not of the highest good; failure, poverty, fear, sickness, disease, pain, ill-health, unhappiness; all that limits, confines, cramps and fetters one's life, all these and much more are included in this one word. By this denial, all this evil atmosphere is neutralized, and the mind is cleansed, ready for the affirmation

"Only Infinite Good" and these two words "Infinite Good" cover everything that we can possibly desire. Peace, Power, Plenty, Health, Happiness and Joy; Success, Achievement, Love, Service to all mankind, what more can one desire?

Therefore mix with your fellows, they are your brothers and sisters; seek to do all the good that you can, but continually cleanse your mind and thought by the use of the denial of evil, and build up your character and life and circumstances by affirmations of Infinite Good.

Thus while you are still mixing with the ordinary everyday type of men . . and they have much that is lovable and noble in their characters . . yet you will be as the poles apart.

SECOND. Everything that you read must be examined and criticized. You must remember that books, papers, magazines, letters, unless you consciously prevent them, will convey suggestions to your subconscious mind and in course of time become translated into action. Therefore if you read books of passion your life will be unbalanced and perhaps wrecked by gusts of violent desire, which call loudly to be satisfied. On the other hand, if you will read books written by lofty minds, you will receive thoughts which inspire and strengthen you.

You should therefore choose your reading wisely. Read the best literature, and do not then accept as Truth all that you read. Refuse resolutely to accept any idea that is not in agreement with your new conception of life. All ideas of man being the puppet of powers outside himself, of being the sport of fate and the victim of circumstances must be rigorously rejected.

All that tends to strengthen your new conception of life, which is, that all things are delivered into your hands, and that you have the power to conquer both yourself and all difficulty and thus make your life sublime . . all that tends to strengthen this mental attitude should be accepted.

The Will and the Conscious Mind stand at the gate; by them you must examine every thought, every suggestion. Hold everything up and examine it in the light of your newly found knowledge, and if it cannot stand this searching test, cast it from you.

You can never be successful if you allow thoughts of weakness or failure or fear to enter your subconscious mind. The one great outstanding characteristic that distinguishes successful men from the unsuccessful, is their absolute belief and faith in their own ability to succeed. Thoughts of failure, or fear, never enter the mind of the truly successful man.

If you examine the character of any great and truly successful man, you will find this dominating characteristic . . absolute faith in his own success, and with it an entire absence of fear or weakness.

Therefore it is certain that you can never be successful if you allow doubt and fear to enter your mind; it is only when by mind control you have cast out fear and doubt that you can enter the path that leads to success.

Some men are successful and are not conscious of the laws which govern success, They unconsciously work according to law . . by instinct rather than knowledge. It is because they are naturally men of LARGE FAITH and UNFAILING COURAGE that they have become successful. Therefore you, too, in order to succeed, must have a large faith and unfailing courage. Faith in the power within you and a courage that is born of knowledge.

Thus can you be placed on the same footing as that of any other successful man, in fact you will be better equipped than the naturally successful man, for possessing knowledge will enable you to avoid many errors, into which he, through ignorance of the law, might fall.

Therefore in your reading you must close your eyes to all suggestions which are antagonistic to your newly found knowledge.

THIRD. By denial and affirmation you create a new mental outlook.

By denial we obtain immediate relief from our troubles. For instance, if, when you are in pain you will deny that there is pain in your perfect mental World and raise yourself above the ordinary life of the senses, and realize that you, your higher mental self, are a perfect mind, or mental creature, incapable of being attacked by pain, then the pain will quickly go. In the same way whatever trouble may confront you, by denial you obtain immediate relief.

Denial kills the evil thought which is the cause of all the trouble, and cleanses and purifies the mind, making it ready for the affirmation.

Always precede an affirmation by the necessary denial. If you are going to affirm health, then first deny ill-health, sickness and disease. If you are going to affirm success, first deny failure, if you wish for prosperity and plenty, then first deny poverty and want, so as to get the mind ready for the affirmation "I AM success; prosperity and plenty are already mine."

But, you exclaim, how can I truthfully affirm that I am that which I know myself not to be? The answer is: There are two YOUS. There is the finite, outside, surface, material YOU, and there is the great and glorious inner spiritual and mental being which is the real YOU. The former is a weak and coarse reflection of the latter. This glorious and real YOU is perfect and lives in a perfect mental world. When you affirm in your perfect Mental World, that you are perfect you mean the real and sublime YOU, and you are telling the truth.

Whatever good quality you affirm is quite true, because you (yourself, the real YOU) are perfect. By denial of evil and imperfection and by the affirming of infinite perfection you destroy evil in your material life and bring it more into harmony with the perfect life. Therefore what you affirm in your perfect mental world, is later, and sometimes instantaneously, manifested in your material world.

An affirmation has been described by one writer as "a statement of Truth consciously used so as to become the directing power of Life's expression." This is a good and true definition. Scientists will tell you that the submerged mind of man acts only upon suggestion. So powerful is the hidden mind and so subject is it to suggestion that we have in affirmations a weapon of extraordinary power for good, and in negative suggestion a terrible power for evil.

When we use an affirmation we make a statement of Truth which, if repeated often enough, will sink down into the recesses of our mind and become part of our very life. It will galvanize the hidden forces of our mind into activity and guide them into the path of achievement.

If in the past you have been a failure, then by constantly affirming "I AM Success," you will gradually eradicate the weak-fearing-give-up-too-soon attitude of your material mind, and build up in its place the mental outlook of courage, cheerfulness, optimism and belief in your ability to succeed.

Failure or lack of success in life is not, as I have already pointed out, due to outward circumstances, but is simply a weakness of character. By affirmations you can build up your character and make its former weak points strongest in your armor.

It is by affirmations, then, that man can control himself, build up his character and shape his own destiny.

It was for this reason that I gave you in your first lesson the affirmation, which is a denial and affirmation combiner, "The old life is dead, I have entered the new life of Success and Power." In that affirmation if consciously applied and persevered with, you kill the old life of failure and partial success, and step out definitely into a new life of power and accomplishment.

As a consequence, you will look upon life in a different way, you will act in a different manner, you will attract a different kind of people.

Soon you begin to see evidences of the truth of these teachings manifested in your life and circumstances.

Therefore you can by affirmations make yourself proof against the harmful suggestions that meet you on every hand.. By affirmations you build up the courageous, confident, hopeful, cheerful, absolutely certain attitude of mind, which is the only type of mind that can readily succeed.

As you begin to see evidences of the working of your newly found power, you feel lifted up in a strange and wonderful way. You feel as if you are being carried forward, by invisible powers, to success; it is as though some impelling force were pushing you in the back and urging you forward to the goal of your endeavor.

Therefore, persist and persevere with your affirmations. Continue to look for difficult tasks, and unpleasant, but very necessary duties, and aided by the power of affirmations. DO THEM.

Make affirmations to suit your own peculiar needs. If you are too energetic and inclined to run yourself to pieces, and rush and tear about and get your own nerves and everybody's else, on edge, affirm as follows: "I AM perfectly calm, cool and collected. I refuse to get excited or flustered. I work quietly and methodically."

Then mentally picture yourself at work in a very calm, cool and collected way, without hurry, fluster or excitement. You will find your work go much better in consequence, and certainly not less quickly.

If, on the other hand, you are inclined to be lazy or lethargic, affirm as follows: "I AM the personification of industry and energy. I AM busy from morning until night." Then picture yourself hard at work, doing good work and plenty of it. This you will find will help you vastly in enabling you to "stick" to your task, and to keep sticking to it day after day.

Thus you have within your grasp the power by which you can overcome every weakness of character; a key which will unlock every door; an art which is the open sesame to the unlimited treasure house of the Universal Mind.

By the use of this wonderful power you can turn failure into success, sorrow into joy, sickness into health, mediocrity into genius.

To you all things are possible . . strength of purpose, the joy of achievement, all the glories of a life of self-mastery.

Unto you it is given to taste of the delights of heaven while yet upon earth . . for heaven and hell are within you, they are but mental states.

Unto him who attains to the dazzling height of self-mastery, unto him who can stand erect, and unafraid, and untroubled by the things that vex and rend the hearts of men; unto him who is master of his passions, his emotions, his circumstances and his life; unto such a one has come that for which the world has longed and strived in vain, about which philosophers, poets and seers have, for centuries, spoken and written, and yet never have been able to grasp or to hold.

He who overcomes himself, overcomes the world; all its treasures are poured at his feet; "all the Divine Forces hasten to minister to his eternal joy."

My Favorite Pages